THE HOUSING CRISIS IN
CALIFORNIA
AND BEYOND

An Insider's Expose

SINGCHOU WU

authorHOUSE®

AuthorHouse™
1663 Liberty Drive
Bloomington, IN 47403
www.authorhouse.com
Phone: 833-262-8899

Published by AuthorHouse 01/13/2021

ISBN: 978-1-6655-0417-1 (sc)
ISBN: 978-1-6655-0416-4 (hc)
ISBN: 978-1-6655-0447-8 (e)

Library of Congress Control Number: 2020920323

CONTENTS

—

FIGURE INDEX

—

TABLE INDEX

PREFACE

I came to the US in 1962 from Taiwan. To me, America was the land of opportunity. I started working the next day, and got paid $1 an hour. Nobody told me that federal minimum wage was $1.15 an hour. It didn't matter to me, because after just over a year, I had saved enough to go to graduate school. After five years, I got a Master of Science Degree and a Ph.D. in Statistics and a teaching job at California Polytechnic State University. I bought my first house in October 1972 in the town of San Luis Obispo. To an immigrant like me, this was an important milestone: I realized my American Dream. I was about the last one among my friends to become a homeowner. One of my friends started a minimum wage job in LA about the same as I did. He saved a few hundred dollars after a year, and he was qualified to buy a house under construction in Orange County. A year later, he was the proud owner of a brand-new house.

But in the last few decades, America has changed, most of the changes are for the better. I am an ethnic minority; I am sensitive to racial relations. After the Civil Rights Movement and Federal legislatures, racial relations have vastly improved. Improvements are normal and expected in every country and society. But unfortunately, not everything has changed for the better. Can a minimum wage worker afford to live in San Francisco? Can a minimum wage worker in California qualify to buy a house with two years' saving? Could I repeat the feat if I start my new life in California today? It appears that America is no longer the land of opportunity that I used to know! So, what has happened? Why don't we see anyone protesting against the missing "land of opportunity"? Why don't we hear discussions about the missing "land of opportunity"? Don't we miss it? I do! I like to see people living close to their jobs. I like to see every native-born American having the same opportunities that an immigrant had about 50 years ago—a minimum wage worker could be the proud owner of a brand-new house in two years.

The high cost of housing problem is a local issue, so it hasn't had the attention it deserves. There has been little discussion of the cause, the consequences or the solutions for the crisis. This book calls for more focus at the state or national level on the problem of high housing costs in California and beyond. This book also explains the cause of the problem, shows the consequences of the problem and presents solutions to the problem.

I dedicate this book to two excellent public servants in the City of San Luis Obispo, Mr. Nick Nicolas, a career building inspector, and Dr. Allen Settle, ex-Mayor of San Luis Obispo. Without Mr. Nicolas' guidance and help, I could never have learned much about nuts and bolts of housing construction. He demonstrated what it meant to be a superb public servant and he put some of his colleagues to shame. Dr. and Mayor Settle educated me about the essence of local control of land-use and he went out of his way to help me, an ethnic minority, against institutionalized discrimination and prejudice at the expense of his own political career.

I also like to thank my good friend Dr. George Tao for his encouragement. He and I attended the same high school and university in Taipei. We didn't know each other back then, because George is a few years of my senior. We meet on an internet forum and we are at the different ends of polarized thoughts about politics and current issues. But we agree on at least one issue. When he asked why the housing costs in some places in the US were so ridiculously high and why there were so many homeless people, I offered a few answers to his questions. He congratulated me for a rather thorough and in-depth understanding of the problem. His compliment propelled me to write this book.

I would also like to thank my long-time friend, Dr. George Hsi, an excellent engineer. During the process of learning about the housing construction, I encountered numerous questions about various building codes. He answered some of the questions right away, any questions that he couldn't answer, he always got the right answers for me soon. I would like to thank Mayor Lynn Cooper, Councilman Munger and Councilman Bond for their understanding and support in 1981. They voted to reverse the Architectural Review Commission 0-7 vote against the approval of one of my building projects. They made me a lifetime believer of Conservatism.

I would like to thank Mr. Vincent Bugni for his excellent work proofreading my manuscript.

CHAPTER 1

—

Housing Conspiracy - High Housing Costs

Introduction

In the US, a worker needs to work only a few hours a month to buy a month's supply of food. Yet, in some places in the US, a full-time workers' monthly paycheck is not even enough to pay for the monthly rent of a one-bedroom apartment where he or she works. So, it is not surprising that a worker with a full-time job may be homeless. Could this be the land of opportunity? Why are there so many homeless people in the US? Why are housing costs so expensive in many places in the US? Who is responsible for the high housing costs in those places? What are the impacts of high housing costs? Is there a solution to this problem? This book will answer these questions for you!

It is surprising that there is a crisis of high housing costs in the US today. Building a house is not a big deal. The greatest president in US history, Abraham Lincoln, built his own log cabin. As a statesman, he was second to none, but he was not known as a great do-it-yourselfer. If he can do it, any average able-bodied person can do it.

We can all agree that Abe Lincoln's log cabin differed greatly from a modern dwelling that we might have today. These days, there are many new materials, machinery, and equipment that Abe Lincoln didn't have when he built his log cabin. We can count a few dozen different trades in housing construction. Each one of these trades would want you to believe that it is impossible for an amateur to build a modern house nowadays. But don't let that fool you. Housing construction requires very little skill, just a lot of know-how. In this Internet age, know-how is easy to come by. With a cell phone in hand and an Internet connection, one can easily get any information online.

Building a house today is not much harder than building a log cabin 200 to 300 years ago. When we look at an expensive house, most likely, the expensive part is not actually the house, but the land the house sits on. In 2018, realtor Coldwell Banker's Website showed that Saratoga, California had the most expensive median price for a 4-bedroom, 2-bath house. This house sounds like a rather modest middle-class dwelling. But in Saratoga, the median price was about $2.5 million. According to the assessor's record, the land value was about $2 million and the improvement (the house) was about $500,000. The piece of land may be only 100' x 100' or 10,000 square feet, less than 1/4 of an acre.

If a person has a 10 acre piece of land in the vicinity, does that mean the land, big enough for 40 houses, is worth about $80 million? Not necessarily. The value of the land depends on what one can use the land for. If one can put 40 houses on the land, then the land is worth about $80 million. If the land is reserved for open space, it may not be even worth $2 million. If one can put 500 units of high-rise condominiums on it, it may be worth more than $250 million. If the land value can vary so much depending on what we may use the land for, then who controls the land-use?

Land-use is a local issue, so local politicians have full control. The United States of America is a democratic country, where voters control all levels of government. Local politicians are elected too, so in theory, voters control local land use. However, once we elect politicians, they have minds of their own. They are not robots programmed to follow voters' wishes. They are the pillars of society. They are the leaders who guide us. Also, we live in a capitalistic society, and one of the basic rules of Capitalism is that selfishness is not completely harmful.

Under a set of ground rules, everyone takes part in the economic endeavor to enhance one's own welfare. Yet, together, we benefit from each other and enable the economy to move forward smoothly. So, for politicians, like everyone else, their first and primary concern is how to survive. Everything else is secondary.

What is a politician's priority? Winning elections! But campaigns need money. The US has a rather clean and uncorrupted government at almost all levels. Voters and various organizations contribute generously to national and state candidates. Some local candidates may have trouble, especially local candidates for small cities and rural counties. A clean government does not allow any illegal campaign contributions. However, every two to four years, local politicians need donations for reelections. It doesn't take long for them to realize they have absolute power on land-use decisions. It doesn't take long for them to figure out how to get the most contributions. Imagine that a small city has plenty of affordable housing. There is no need for any new units. The city planning and building department have practically nothing to do at all. Now, imagine the opposite. There is a severe shortage of housing. Housing prices soar. Everyone with a piece of land near the city wants to have the land annexed into the city and wants it to be zoned for housing development. Landowners and developers are dying to win favors from local politicians. This explains the major reason why Silicon Valley has such outrageously high housing prices. There are many little cities and many elected politicians. They all need campaign contributions every two or four years.

How do they make sure that there is not enough supply? The answer is: "Allow mostly single-family detached houses, no high or median rise apartments or condominiums." It doesn't take long for politicians to learn that it is not enough just to limit the supply of housing. To make sure there is a severe shortage of housing, they need to make sure there is a steady demand for housing. But high housing costs discourage people from moving in and encourage people to sell and move out. How can local politicians increase demand? If there is no real demand because of high costs, politicians and bureaucrats can create an arbitrary demand by limiting occupancy with zoning regulations. About 40 years ago, almost all cities in California had an ordinance to limit the occupation of single-family detached houses to a maximum of 3 unrelated individuals. A family of 8 may live in a 4-bedroom house, yet 4 coworkers, otherwise unrelated, could not live in a similar house. For example, many cities in California try to limit boarding houses. These cities require a full bathroom for every three occupants. How considerate are the local politicians and bureaucrats? They really care about the welfare of the folks living in a boarding house! When I arrived in Los Angeles in 1962, I lived in a boarding house that had two toilets, two showers, and two lavatories for 24 bedrooms. It should be detrimental for me to live in such substandard housing! It had to be my pure luck that I escaped such poor living conditions without any ill effect. In the morning, there was never any trouble for me to get ready to work. When I needed to take a shower, I did not have to wait. This was how it worked; the toilet, shower and lavatory were not in the same room but separate compartments. So, six residents could use these six plumbing fixtures at the same time. I was very impressed and said to myself: "Wow! This is how rich Americans are!" I noticed that none of the rooms had more than one occupant. This could happen only in America! Anywhere else, some of the rooms would have more than one occupant. Yet, according to today's zoning requirements, the boarding house needs 6 more full bathrooms. Without the additional bathrooms, the boarding house would be shut down. If these 24 occupants cannot afford today's housing cost, Los Angeles would have 24 more homeless people and I would be one of them. Every time I think about these senseless zoning requirements, they make me shiver. When I look at a homeless person, I always feel that it could be me! If this zoning requirement makes sense, we need to ask those who put this requirement on the books a simple question: "HOW many restrooms do we need for a jetliner with 150 passengers and crews?" Do we need 50 restrooms? Yes! Why not? If three occupants need a full bathroom, then three passengers on a commercial airplane need a restroom. If the local government really cares about their residents' welfare, ask them why they don't put a restroom on every city bus. Let us give a little credit to ourselves: we are the only mammal that can thrive within the arctic circle and any tropical jungle, we can survive in deserts and wetlands and live by the beach or on the Himalayas mountain range.

Politicians and bureaucrats, please just leave us alone! We are very adaptive, and we can get by just fine. We can overcome any natural obstacles, but we are helpless in the face of your senseless rules. Please don't kick me out on the street!

There is a high housing price problem, but we must know that it is not necessarily the high cost of housing construction. The US is a free country and has a well-established modern transportation system; labor and materials can move freely. The cost of construction is about the same everywhere except perhaps in Hawaii and Alaska. The high cost of housing is high land cost for housing construction. But if we let the free market or the supply and demand to decide the land value, the US should not have a problem with high housing costs at all. There is plenty of land available for housing construction just about everywhere in the US except perhaps in Oahu (Hawaii), Manhattan, San Francisco, and a few similar exceptions. Even in Silicon Valley, if you drive along Interstate 280 from Los Altos towards San Francisco, you see more open rolling hills than developed suburbs until South San Francisco. With an abundance of land, should Silicon Valley have such a crisis of high housing prices?

It is reasonable and understandable that Manhattan has high housing costs. Similarly, we understand why Oahu, an island, and San Francisco, a narrow peninsula, have high housing costs. Therefore, it is hard to see why anywhere else would have outrageously high housing values in the US.

1.1 The Food Industry Makes Food Inexpensive and Enjoyable

Ever since the dawn of human history, human beings have spent the majority of their time looking for or producing food. To survive, man needs three necessities: food, clothing and shelter.

Out of the three necessities, the importance of food far outweighs the other two. To determine the importance of food, we don't have to look far. As recently as 1980, China had over 80% of its population living in rural areas, most of them producing food. Today, about 35% of China's labor force is still in agriculture (in the U.S., this is less than 2%). There are 425 million agricultural workers (200 million farming households) in China. A little over a decade ago, China was home to 700 million farmers. They made up about 60 percent of the population. Yet, during the time of the Great Leap Forward (1958 to 1962), 18 to 55 million people perished depending on which estimate you believe. Out of the total, about 10% of them were summarily executed or tortured to death. The great majority of the rest died from hunger. Authors Joe Hasell and Max Roser in their essay, Famines, 2013, revised 2017, put the number of deaths around 25 million. They also assembled a global dataset on famine from 1860 until 2016. They estimated that in total 128 million people died in famine over this period. [Source; Our World in Data]

If one doesn't want to look half a globe away to see the importance of food for human survival, we don't have to. We can look right here at home. Just go back a few hundred years in history. After the pilgrims on the Mayflower landed in Plymouth, close to half of them did not survive the first winter. Poor and inadequate food made the settlers susceptible to disease. They had to work hard and adapt to the changing weather. Lack of shelter was also probably responsible for their hardship. But once a sturdy shelter was built, it lasted at least a couple of years. Even a makeshift shelter would last a few days or more. Food would be their major requirement for survival. Even in today's world, 800 million people do not have enough food to lead a healthy and active life. That's about one in nine people on earth. The vast majority of the world's starving people live in developing countries, where 13 percent of the population is undernourished. Of the three necessities for survival of human beings, food is the most pivotal one. There are crucial differences between the three necessities. If a person has a piece of clothing for protection from bugs, cold or sunburn, that clothing will last for years. Regarding shelter, nobody needs to build a shelter every day. However, food is a daily necessity.

A person can gorge on too much food at a time but still get hungry the next day. A person may amass a large quantity of food, but fresh food only lasts a day or two. Dry food may last much longer, but it is constantly under attack from all sides: from thieves, birds, and animals to invisible bugs, bacteria, and fungi. We cannot over-emphasize the importance of food for human survival. Throughout human history, securing enough food has been a constant effort for people everywhere. No wonder early civilizations all started from river valleys where agriculture flourished and yielded vast amounts of food. Because of the abundance of food in these river valleys, they could release a large portion of the population from food production to engage in other endeavors. The Egyptians in the Nile Valley built pyramids and temples. The Sumerians of the ancient Fertile Crescent of Tigris and

Euphrates River Valleys developed the earliest human civilizations. They invented plows, wheels, and writing. The Indians in the Indus River Valley (now northwest of India and Pakistan) developed cotton cultivation to meet man's clothing needs. They also invented the modern numeral system that was erroneously credited to the Arabs. The Chinese in the Yellow River Valley invented silk, the compass, and printing.

Now let's look at what science and technology did to help humans survive. The US, with less than 2% of her population engaging in agricultural activities, can not only feed the entire US population but also help feed the rest of the world. Today, the US Federal minimum hourly wage is $7.25 (Year 2020). In some grocery stores, one can find a one-pound loaf of fresh bread for a buck. A worker earning only a minimum wage in the US can earn enough to buy a loaf of bread in 8.5 minutes. This is an amazing accomplishment. This represents tremendous efficiency in the US food production and delivery system. Imagine how long it takes to grow and harvest wheat, transport that wheat to the flour mill, deliver the flour to the bakery, prepare the dough, and bake and deliver the bread to the grocery store. The whole process may take several months and span over a distance of over a thousand miles. Man does not live on bread alone. But if a person can manage his food budget properly and eat only self-prepared meals, he can easily live healthily on about $100 worth of food a month. For an average worker in the US, this is the earning of a few hours' work per month. We need to take our hats off and salute everyone in the food production and delivery industries, including scientists, farmers, ranchers, bakers, truck drivers, grocery store workers, managers, entrepreneurs, etc. Their efficiency makes inexpensive food available to all of us, so we don't have to work ourselves to exhaustion just to buy enough food to stay alive and healthy. In America, food is no longer just a critical need for survival. Most people in the US use food for enjoyment or as an expression of our lifestyle. We can afford to be choosy or even picky. In most grocery stores, we can find a wide variety of food ingredients for any taste and budget. You will never find another country anywhere in the world that has such a broad selection of food available as inexpensive as we do here in America. For most people in the US, going to a restaurant to have a meal is just as common as going to a store to buy a bag of groceries. Here, many people do not like to cook. Some people eat in restaurants as often or more often than they cook for themselves. In the 2004 movie, "Super Size Me", Director Morgan Spurlock's social experiment in fast-food gastronomy, we see him attempting to subsist solely on food from the McDonald's menu for an entire month. His weight balloons, his energy level plummets, and he experiences many unexpected — and terrifying — side effects. Most of us do not have any objections to fast food. We decide what we want to eat. Every kind of food is available. If a person overeats, that person will gain weight. If the person has no self-control, they may become obese. If we want freedom of choice, we cannot ignore the responsibility that comes with it.

A lot of people are glad to have so many choices. A meal may cost several hundred dollars per person at a fancy restaurant, but nobody forces anyone to eat there. Luckily, most sit-down restaurants cost only about one-tenth of that amount. Most meals from fast-food restaurants cost only a few dollars or just 1% of a meal at a fancy restaurant. It is great that we have this freedom of choice. Not only we have solved the most crucial part of the problem of survival, but we also have many options for enjoying a meal. For this luxury, we can thank American ingenuity, science and technology, hardworking American farmers, and other workers in food industries and the free market system in the US. Last but not least, we are glad that the government doesn't get too involved in food production and distribution. The federal government's food safety inspection program is necessary, and so are our local governments' health inspection programs for restaurants. It is great that the US Dept. of Agriculture doesn't go beyond their Diet Pyramid to educate us about our diet. The local politicians in New York City and San Francisco just tax sugary drinks and ban plastic straws in restaurants. I am sure a lot of them would like to go much further because there is a lot to criticize the fast food industry. If we allowed politicians to regulate the food industry as they regulated the housing industry, food prices would have gone through the stratosphere. In the early 1970s, the cost of a typical family house was in the vicinity of $20,000 to $30,000, and a typical family car cost about one-tenth of a family house. A study showed that if a family car was built like the way a house was, the price of the car would have been around 2 million dollars!

Let us take a look at another necessity for human survival, clothing.

Thanks to science and technology, the clothing industry, like the food industry, is efficient. Cotton and synthetic fibers are abundant and readily available at a very affordable price. Clothing is inexpensive, functional, and comfortable.

A specially designed dress may cost thousands of dollars, but mass-produced clothing for a man or a woman costs only about two hundred dollars (less than one-tenth of the cost of the expensive ones). If a person's clothing budget is tight and he cannot afford two hundred dollars to buy a dress or a suit, he can easily buy new clothing for under a hundred dollars. What if a family with children cannot even afford $20 to buy a new jacket for a kid? No problem at all! Just visit yard sales during the weekends! We can find clean and usable clothing for almost nothing or a few dollars at most.

As far as human survival is concerned, finding proper clothing was never as serious a problem as finding food. If it was cold and one didn't have the proper clothing to stay warm, one could always build a fire to stay warm or migrate to a warmer place. That was when there were no borders or passports and humans were free to wander around. Nowadays, although science and technology have reduced the clothing problem for humans to an insignificant level, millions of people still die of hunger or suffer from malnutrition.

1.2. Shelter is Necessary, but is not as Crucial as Food for Human Survival

Next, let us look at the need for shelter for human survival. Shelter is the third most vital need for human survival. If science and technology can solve the problem of providing food and clothing for human survival, can't they also solve the problem of providing shelter for human beings? We would think so.

The need for food for human survival is far more crucial than the need for clothing or shelter. If we have any doubt, we do not have to look very far for answers, we just ask ourselves. Given the choice between sleeping in a car for two days with enough food to eat or staying in a 5-star hotel with no food for two days, which one would most of us choose? I don't need to ponder. I would choose to sleep in a car every time. Farmers, scientists, and entrepreneurs have solved the problem of providing food for human survival so beautifully and efficiently. It seems like builders and developers ought to be able to solve the lesser problem of providing shelter for the US population. We should not ignore the contributions of the free market and the democratic political system. China, during the Great Leap Forward, had neither a free market nor a democratic government. The result of this horrible policy was a famine that killed more than a few millions of Chinese, this number could even be ten times higher. Also, look at today's Venezuela. Thanks to the socialist authoritarian government, millions of its population are on the verge of starvation.

Unfortunately, the US has a problem providing affordable shelter for her population, especially in California. Why is this? The US has a system of democratically elected government with checks and balance. The media is free and not controlled by any one person or group.

The free market system is viable and functional. Workers in the US put in longer hours than workers in other rich countries. Although the US is the leader in science and technology, some of the hard-working people here have trouble making ends meet. They barely get by and sometimes cannot make it regardless of how hard they work. Why does this happen here? It is not because food is expensive. A worker never needs to work more than 15 hours per month to buy enough food to stay healthy. However, high housing costs can be crippling.

For example, in San Francisco, a person would be lucky to find a one-bedroom apartment for $3000. The city's minimum wage was $15.59 (July 1, 2020) per hour, more than twice the federal standard. If a person is working for minimum wage, then they need to work overtime or 50 hours per week, just to pay the rent. Even if the person shares an apartment with a roommate, they must spend more than 50% of their take-home pay for rent alone. Something must be terribly wrong in the US, especially in San Francisco!

Throughout most of the history of mankind, people have always needed to spend up to half of their working hours producing food for survival. This began to change after the Industrial Revolution. Still, famine killed a lot more people than lack of shelter did. In the US, we need less than 2% of the workforce to produce food, yet we force lower-wage earners to spend 1/3rd to 1/2 of their take-home pay just for housing. In human history, housing problems or lack of housing rarely killed large numbers of people. The Eskimos can build igloos with readily available materials. The Mongolian nomads can carry their woolen tents with them during a long drive. They can set up their tents in a few hours. Those who live near hilly regions can find or dig caves for shelters. Those who live in areas with warm to hot climates may not need a shelter to survive, though they may want one for privacy.

In the US, science and technology can reduce the costs of food and clothing for human survival to a trivial amount. It seems unreasonable for the cost of shelter to balloon up to half of a person's income. It has never happened in human history before and it is a shame that it is happening in the US today!

Food and clothing are no longer major obstacles for people's survival in the US, simply because there are abundant supplies as well as a wide range of choices. A meal at a three-star Michelin restaurant may cost as much as a thousand dollars. Yet, most people can stay alive and healthy with one hundred dollars worth of food a month. A fancy designer's dress may cost a few thousand dollars, but a lot of people in the US don't even spend a tenth of that a year for clothing. However, for housing, we don't have as nearly as wide a range of choices as we do with food or clothing.

In Silicon Valley, the most expensive house may be twenty million dollars. Of course, there are many houses available for one-tenth of that or around two million. But most people with fairly high-paying jobs in Silicon Valley still cannot afford a two-million-dollar house. For those who make only a median or low income, what choices do they have? They cannot afford a two-million-dollar house. Maybe they can afford a place for one-tenth of that, but there is absolutely nothing available at $200,000 a unit. Not even a studio apartment is available in Silicon Valley, at that price.

In some places in California, houses that cost two million dollars per unit may be the most expensive ones. For example, this author lives in San Luis Obispo. Within the city limits, a two-million-dollar house is about the most expensive one. However, one cannot find anything at one-tenth of the cost. No housing units are available at $200,000 a unit. So, it is clear from the history of mankind that the most essential necessity for human survival is food. But the cost of food is no longer a threat to the survival of the majority of the world's population, at least for those living in rich countries. Not only there is an abundance of supply of food, but there is also a wide range of choices to satisfy the taste of the filthy rich and the needs of the poor. There is an even wider range of choices for clothing.

Yet, when it comes to the choices of shelter, another necessity for human survival, the choice is very limited in the US. Since a shelter costs a lot more than a meal or a dress, the range of choices should be wider and not narrower. This is historically true. A royal palace costs a million times more than the cost of a peasant's hut. Luckily, we don't have powerful emperors anymore, and hence we do not need these kinds of choices. The limited choices for shelter in California or the US may not be entirely bad. Everyone either gets the best or nothing. Isn't it great? If everyone can afford it, it is great! If one forces the best on someone who cannot afford it, the person is worse than a murderer! As a person is almost starved to death, we insist that the person either to have a meal at a Michelin three-star restaurant or to have nothing at all. If a large portion of the population cannot afford expensive housing prices, then the arbitrarily narrow choices of housing are not only unreasonable but also unsustainable. We need to identify the culprits who take our choices away from us and force some of us to spend more than one half of our income on keeping a roof over our heads.

1.3 Limited Choices of Housing: Who is Responsible?

A modern house is quite different from a house built 1000 years ago. A modern house has a lot of frills and amenities that a house built 100 years ago didn't have. A modern house has double glazed windows to soundproof the building as well as for insulation, fire sprinkler systems, a gas line and outlets, electrical lights and outlets, indoor plumbing with cold and hot potable water, gas or electrical range outlet, washing machine hookups, an exhaust vent for a stove, garage for automobiles, etc. These are the visible parts.

There are also some hidden features: insulation for the living space, fire-resistant and long-lasting roofing materials, earthquake and wind-resistant structure, a sturdy foundation, etc. But don't let these frills and amenities intimidate or fool you. If you pay a high price for a housing unit, these frills and amenities contribute very little to the total price.

In contrast, a meal we eat today may not be very different from a meal our ancestors ate a hundred years ago or even a thousand years ago. Maybe we eat a little bit less now because our daily routine is not as physically strenuous and demanding as it was before. Admittedly, a modern house has numerous features to make the occupants' lives easy, comfortable, safe, and healthy. But the cost of these features is minimal compared to other costs. For example, in 2018, a brand new 4-bedroom, 2-bathroom, single-family house, with a double garage and 2500 square feet of living space was for sale for $250,000 in Waco, Texas.

If this house is located in Silicon Valley, the price will be almost 10 times higher. Just as any realtor will tell you, the value of a house depends on location, location and location! So, if you are wondering who is responsible for high housing costs, the answer is "local politicians, local politicians, and local politicians!" Of course, in Silicon Valley, without including the land, nobody can build a house like that for $250,000, because everything is expensive there. When the housing prices are several times higher in an area, obviously, just about everything else costs more in the area too. Even nationally advertised fast food restaurants are no exceptions. A McDonald's in the Bay Area where I buy coffees frequently doesn't sell "senior coffee" as it advertises.

A reasonable estimate of the construction costs in Silicon Valley is probably twice as much as that in Waco, Texas. So, construction costs can justify only a small part of the high housing cost in Silicon Valley or in California. Silicon Valley has a lot of high paying jobs, so there is a high demand for housing and buyers who can afford to pay a high price. Even this may still be only partially correct. In Seattle, there are also a lot of high paying jobs, and thus, there is a high demand for housing and many buyers can afford to pay high prices. But housing prices are far more reasonable in the Seattle area than in Silicon Valley.

One may argue that California's or even Silicon Valley's housing prices are far from the most expensive ones in the world. That is certainly true.

TIME magazine dated February 6, 2017, had a short note on DATA (Page 11):

"EXPENSIVE HOMES, LOW WAGES

These are some of the world's most expensive cities to live according to the 2017

Demographia International survey, which ranks 406 metropolitan housing markets in nine countries using a ratio of median house price to median income:

Table 1: Median House Price to Median Income

City	Median House Price	Median Income
Hong Kong	$5,422,000	$300,000
Sydney	$1,077,000	$88,000
Vancouver, BC	$830,100	$70,500
San Jose, California	$1,000,000	$104,000
Bournemouth and Dorset, UK	$330,900	$37,300

The ratio of "Housing price" to "Median income" was more than 18 in Hong Kong. In San Jose, California, it was less than 10. But the median "Housing Price" and "Median Income" in Hong Kong were not $5,422,000 and $300,000 respectively. TIME magazine obviously forgot to convert Hong Kong dollars to US dollars. The exchange rate at the time was HK$7.8 to US$1. So, the median housing price in Hong Kong was HK$5,422,000/7.8 = US$695,128, which is actually cheaper than the median price in San Jose, Sydney, and Vancouver.

Thus, the TIME article talked about the affordability of median-priced housing units in different cities. A median-priced housing unit in Hong Kong and a median-priced house in San Jose, California were not the same at all. In San Jose, a million US dollars could buy, in 2017, a 4-bedroom 2-bathroom single-family house with a double garage and a spacious fenced yard. In Hong Kong, the land value was extremely high because of the high-density of the population. There were none or few of these kinds of houses. If there was one, it was located on a remote island and cost millions of US dollars.

Most high-price housings are located in cities with high population density, like Tokyo, Manhattan, Monaco, London, etc. But there are exceptions. Sydney, Australia has the second-highest median housing price compared to median income. Australia, with a population of 24 million, is less populated than Texas, but the area of Australia is more than ten times the size of Texas. Granted, Sydney is a bustling metropolis with a population of five million, which is more than 20% of the population of Australia. I talked to a few realtors and homeowners in Sydney about the high housing prices in the city. They said that many of the new riches in China didn't trust the Communist regime and wanted to put their money in real estate in foreign countries. Sydney appeared to be a popular city for Chinese to buy houses. This was almost the same story I heard in Vancouver in the late 80s and early 90s before Hong Kong was turned over to China when many Hong Kongers bought houses in the Vancouver area and pushed up housing prices.

Texas' largest city Houston with 2.3 million people is not too far behind Sydney in size. Yet, the median house-value is only about a fifth of that in Sydney.

A report in July 2018, showed that the average price for a condo in Vancouver was $657,000 and the price for a detached home is $1.58 million. The population of Vancouver is only about 600,000. So, it is obvious that the housing price is not decided by the free market and is highly manipulated. Vancouver, Sydney, and Houston are all located on open plains unlike Hong Kong, which is mainly an island and a peninsula, or San Francisco, which is at the tip of a peninsula. So, the three cities, Vancouver, Sydney, and Houston have plenty of room to grow and, thus, ought to have low median-house prices. It is extremely unusual when one is priced five times higher than the other. By 2019, Sydney's housing prices came down a little and so did the prices in San Francisco. In other words, as there is a limit on manipulated housing prices inflation, it is not likely to sustain for long. Actually, it is far more than just unusual. It is unreasonable. High housing prices are worse than theft or robbery. Theft and robbery do not happen to victims every day. If it happens once, the victims can try to find a way to prevent it from happening again and again. However, when workers spend 1/3rd or 1/2 of their income on rent alone, it is like theft or robbery every month, year after year. The victims may not even know who is responsible for it. Of course, the culprit of this scandal is not a single person or even a single group of individuals.

Millions of people in California are paying or have paid for the high cost of housing. The overpaid amount is huge – trillions of dollars. This huge amount of money is shared by quite a few people. We would like to know who they are.

First, California's housing prices were not always this high. Right after WW II, when GIs returned home, they could choose to settle down just about anywhere. US Census data shows that, in 1950, the median value of a single-family house was $9223 in Ohio and $9564 in California. There was a difference of less than 5%. But from 2013 – 2017, the median-priced and owner-occupied house was $135,100 in Ohio and $443,400 in California. The difference was more than 300%. Second, rapid population growth in California may account for a small part of the difference. If the free market can satisfy the increased demand in California, then the price difference should be negligible like in 1950.

By the early 70s, I finished a doctoral degree in statistics, got a teaching job and paid off the loan I incurred when I was a graduate student. In 1972, I bought my first house for $23,000. That was 1.5 times my annual salary as an associate professor (beginning level) – not a very high-paying job – at a California State University. In October 1972, the median house sales price in the US was $27, 572, [https://dqydj.com/historical-home-prices, 9/16/2020] much higher than what I paid for my first house!

The house was a single-family dwelling with 4 bedrooms and 2 bathrooms and a two-car garage. Until the early 70s, California's housing was still fairly affordable. In 2019, a beginning level associate professor's annual salary was about $90,000 and a house similar to the one I bought for $23000 in 1972, was about $650,000. So, while an associate professor's pay increased about 5.6 times in 45 years, housing prices increased about 28 times during the same period.

Luckily, it is still relatively affordable compared to Silicon Valley. Unfortunately, San Luis Obispo does not have high-paying jobs like in Silicon Valley. Seattle, Washington has plenty of high paying jobs, but its housing prices are not nearly as high as in Silicon Valley. San Luis Obispo is a small town in a rural area, with an abundance of open fields for housing development, yet San Luis Obispo's housing prices are comparable to those of Seattle.

San Luis Obispo's housing prices should be somewhere between that of Waco, Texas and that of Seattle, Washington. Yet, prices are about three times higher in San Luis Obispo than in Waco.

By any standard, San Luis Obispo is a very pleasant place to live. In some reports, it is rated as one of the best little cities to raise a family in the US. So, let us not compare San Luis Obispo to Waco, Texas. Instead, let us compare San Luis Obispo to Santa Maria, a city about 30 miles away in Santa Barbara County.

About half a century ago, San Luis Obispo and Santa Maria had about the same housing prices and population. Half a century later, Santa Maria has tripled the population and one half the housing price as San Luis Obispo. This demonstrates the fact that housing prices and population growth can be manipulated.

Who controls population growth in the US? Legally, no one is in control. The US is a free country, and everyone is free to move around. But practically, local politicians have a lot of control over population growth. They have the final say about any real estate developments.

The high cost of housing in California forced residents to pay trillions of extra dollars. It continues to force residents to pay and it will make residents pay in the future as well for the privilege to live in California. This extra cost is huge. There are a lot of people to blame in the housing establishment in California.

1.4 The Housing Market is not a Free-Market

The housing industry is highly regulated everywhere in the world. The US is no exception, some regulations are absolutely necessary. But every regulation pushes up the housing cost for consumers. Normally, available land and population density are the dominating factors for housing prices. According to these two factors, California, even Silicon Valley, should NOT have high housing costs at all. We need to examine how regulation can push housing prices sky-high and who is responsible.

Because of the high housing costs in California, there are a large number of people who spend more half their take-home income just for housing needs. Are they just low-income workers? Not necessarily.

About 20 years ago, my family doctor had just finished his internship and chose to practice in San Luis Obispo. He complained, causally, that he could not afford to buy a house in the city. If he bought the house he liked, he would need to spend about half of his after-tax income for mortgage payments. He said that he might move out of the state.

A year later, I was due for another annual checkup, and, sure thing, he had left.

If a physician can not afford the high housing costs in San Luis Obispo, there must be a lot of others who are even less able to afford to buy a house. If they spend more than half of their take-home pay for rent, what are their prospects for the future? Bleak at best. If they cannot build up savings to protect them from rainy days, they are only a couple of paychecks away from homelessness.

When a group of people are willing to work hard and contribute to the community, the community has an obligation to allow them to have comfortable and satisfying lives. It is unfair to require anyone to spend half of their take-home pay just for a roof over their heads. It is not good for the community either.

A good community cannot have a group of hard-working people feeling desperate and unhappy, even if they are only a minority of the community. In fact, because they are a minority, they feel that their pleas fall on deaf ears and that their grievances are ignored.

This kind of community is not a stable community.

Many think that if there are people spending half of their take-home income for housing needs or if there are homeless people anywhere in the US, it is a failure of the free-market system in this country. It is obviously a failure of the housing market that there is a great demand for housing and that the housing market is unable to provide an affordable supply of houses to satisfy the demand. The US is a free country with a free-market economy. If a free market economy fails to satisfy the crucial demand for housing, isn't it a failure of capitalism in the US? Generally speaking, the US economy is a free-market economy and, of course, the free-market economy is based on capitalism. The housing market has failed not only the young people but also a lot of others who cannot afford to live where they like to live or near where they work. In 2019, Donald Trump proclaimed in several rallies: "America will never be a Socialist country!" In 2019, surveys showed that the majority of young people preferred Socialism over Capitalism in the US. When we have young physicians, who cannot afford to live where they practice, it is safe to say that housing expenses are a major burden for most young people in the US today. Can anyone blame young people for turning to Socialism for relief? If another generation of young people feel the same way in the near future, can anyone guarantee that "America will never be a Socialist country"?

1.5 Young People Turn to Socialism

Young people are the future of a country. If the majority of today's young people in the US favor Socialism over Capitalism, it is very likely, in a generation or two, that the US will become a Socialist country. This leaves two questions to be answered: What was the cause of the rise of socialism in the US? What can we do to remove the cause?

What makes people, especially young people, turn to socialism? In the last few decades in the US, regarding income, the rich are getting richer and the poor are getting poorer.

This fact alone will force some poor people to turn to Socialism for help. But the rich getting richer is nothing new in the US, throughout US history, the rich have always gotten richer. During the industrial revolution, those who were in the forefront of the revolutions in new materials, (iron & steel), in new energy, (coal and petroleum), new machines, (steam and intern combustion engines), new production methods, (interchangeable parts and assembly line), new transportation, (rail road and automobile) and in new communication methods, (telegram and radio), all became super rich. Many view the super rich, like John Rockefeller, Cornelius Vanderbilt, Andrew Mellon, Henry Ford, etc. as captains of industry helping the US to be the dominating superpower. More Americans consider them heroes rather than villains. Most Americans don't hate the rich just because they are rich. So, the rich captains of the industry didn't contribute to the growth of Socialism in the US then. Now, the new super rich in the current information revolution doesn't contribute to the growth of Socialism either. The fact the rich are becoming richer demonstrates that the US is a fertile breeding ground allowing pioneers and innovators to flourish. This represents the strength of the US economy and not a short-coming of capitalism in the US. It has to be something else for the rise of socialism in the US today.

However, one of the major causes of the stagnation of the real wage of unskilled workers in the last 20–30 years in the US is a large number of undocumented workers in the country. By one estimate, there are about 26 million undocumented aliens in the US. Most of them are unskilled workers from Latin America. This group, of course, puts downward pressure on the wages of the unskilled labor force in the US. This is a problem for the US, but it is not within the scope of this book to discuss or to solve the problem.

Next, let us look at the expenditures of low-income individuals. The housing cost must be the largest expenditure for most of them. A lot of them spend half of their take-home income or more for housing needs. A medical bill for a sudden illness or an accident may be extremely high or even far more than the person's annual housing expense. Thankfully, most of us will not face this type of cost. College tuition can also be very expensive. Luckily, it is not for the rest of one's life. For most, nothing else will cost them more than the expense of housing month after month, year after year.

When people spend half their income on housing needs, they feel desperate. Who do they turn to? They don't turn to Republicans for help. Republicans preach small government and self-reliance. We are not talking about freeloaders here. These are full-time workers and may even work overtime. They are just forced to spend too much on housing.

In San Francisco, a lot of city government employees cannot afford to live in the city. The lowest paid custodian reported on the Official City Website on July 25, 2020 was $12.90 per hour between June 2017 to June 2020. Of course, a lot of workers in California are in a big jam, "just about making it". They will try to get help in any way they can. And who are the ones offering help? Answer: Socialists.

Did it surprise anyone that a great number of young voters enthusiastically supported Bernie Sanders? It should not. When young workers need to spend half of their take-home pay for housing needs, they have little left for anything else. They are desperate and need help. If young physicians cannot afford to live where they practice, the problem is not limited only to low-skilled young workers.

Did Bernie Sanders offer free housing for all? No! He was smarter than that. Even though high-housing costs put a lot of young people in a big jam, Bernie Sanders rarely talked about any housing problem in the primaries. He wanted to offer universal health care and free college education for all. So young people joined and cheered him on in droves.

Bernie Sanders was very smart to avoid discussing the housing problem in the campaigns because it was a national campaign and housing was supposed to be a local issue.

He started his political career in local politics, like most politicians. He was the mayor of Burlington, Vermont, the state's largest city from 1981 to 1989. He understood very well that housing was highly regulated and controlled by local politicians. He avoided the issue of housing, mainly because he didn't want to blame any of them for the problem. If he won the Democratic Party's presidential nomination, he needed all local democratic politicians' support in the general election. He was smart but not very honest because the housing problem could not stay as a local issue forever and we needed a national solution for the problem. If we want to solve the housing problem, or to be more precise, the problem of HIGH housing prices, can we look for solutions from the socialists? The answer is a big "NO!"

High housing prices are not uniform in this country. If housing prices are extremely high at a particular place, we just blame the those who control the local land use. However, there may be exceptions. Local politicians cannot be blamed for Manhattan's high housing costs. There is very little land available for new housing development. Also, a lot of people like to live in The Big Apple, especially, in Manhattan. Everywhere else in the US, we can blame local politicians for their arbitrary decisions to limit the supply of affordable housing.

So, on the supply side, it is definitely not a FREE market. We cannot blame the lack of entrepreneurship in the housing market for the failure to provide affordable supply. Politicians rarely make decisions based on housing demands.

1.6 Two-Pronged Strategy

Usually, when the price of anything goes up, in a free-market, consumers can always consume less to force the price down. Yet, in housing, this kind of freedom of choice is not allowed. Many cities in California used to have ordinances prohibiting more than three unrelated individuals from occupying any detached house.

This demand is unnatural almost like forced feeding, except it is worse. If housing price is high, can two or three individual share a room so they can live close to their jobs? No! local zoning ordinance doesn't allow that. The Supreme Court of California declared this kind of ordinance unconstitutional. In the case, 'The City of Santa Barbara v Adamson [(1980) 27 Ca.3d 123 California Supreme Court]", the city didn't even allow one person in each bedroom. The house in the lawsuit had 25 rooms including 10 bedrooms and 5 bathrooms. A family of 20 individuals and 4 generations might live in the house. But for unrelated adults, the limit was 5. If three persons want to share a room, there are many possible reasons to prohibit such an arrangement. Over-crowding is unhealthy and unsafe, especially during the Covid-19 pandemic. But the City of Santa Barbara had trouble to justify why one person couldn't occupy one room, so the city lost the case. This, unfortunately, is not the only way to create arbitrary demand. There are many other ways for those in control of land use to create demand.

If housing costs are too high, many working poor become homeless, and become a burden to the community. Local politicians don't care at all! Of course, they always pay lip service to prove that they are not totally heartless. But they don't really to want solve the problem! In this sense, these elected public servants are worse than the worst tyranny in history. Tyrannies always want their subjects to be productive and useful. Just as slave masters always want slaves to be productive. A tyranny would try to keep subjects healthy and working. Therefore, a tyranny would never kick a productive worker to live on the street and becomes a burden to the community. But these elected local politicians give American democracy a bad name!

Why do they act in such unreasonable ways? They are reasonable alright! They want to push the housing prices up so that only the rich can afford to live there. The most important part is that as housing prices soar, homeowners get a big windfall. Homeowners are usually voters too. When they get a windfall, they are happy and they vote for the slow-growth incumbents.

When the local government caters to the rich, there are other advantages too. The rich don't need much social service, so the local government can fund other things like making downtown beautiful, closing a street to build a Mission Plaza, building trails in park and things like that.

Let us consider another situation. If five college students live in a house with three bedrooms and one bathroom in a college town, do you see anything wrong with this arrangement? It may be a little inconvenient in the morning when all five of them are in a hurry to get ready for 8 o'clock classes. But nothing is terribly wrong except they violate the municipal codes. If all five of them are A+ students and they don't mind the inconvenience to save a few bucks, why can't the city officials leave them alone? Who are the municipal codes designed to protect? The five students? Why do we need to turn five good students into criminals? But who are the victims? We don't see anyone claiming to be the victim. But there are victims! They are the ones who establish the law and enforce the laws. If they let college kids circumvent the codes and alleviate the problem of housing shortage, then who needs the bureaucrats in Planning and Building departments. In Asia, many college students are living in much worse housing than five in a three-bedroom house with only one bath. There it is more like eight students in a housing unit with 2 bedrooms and 1 bath. We are not talking about student housing in third world countries. We are talking about Japan, South Korea, Taiwan, Hong Kong, or Singapore, every one of these countries had a median household income higher than that of the United Kingdom between 2006 and 2012. Again, I have firsthand experience in four students sharing a 2-bedroom apartment with only one bathroom. This was exactly the arrangement I had on campus when I studied for my master's degree in the US. My roommate and I got along fine. The "crowded" living quarter did not turn the two of us against each other or anyone else. Now, more than 50 years later, we still get together occasionally to meet with each other's families, children, and grandchildren. My roommate and I can proudly proclaim that we have realized our American Dream and reached middle-class status rather easily. We are just glad that the university we attended didn't have the senseless rule of limiting only 3 students to one bathroom. The crowded living quarter we "endured" didn't seem to have any devastating effects on us.

Now there are still rules in the book, they just changed from three to five. So, local politicians control land use to limit the housing supply. They also use zoning regulations to limit the number of occupants in housing units to create an artificial demand for housing. These two-pronged strategies complement each other to create a housing shortage and to guarantee that local politicians totally control the housing market and easy for them to manipulate.

Is this a free housing market? Hardly, but a person still has some choices. In Silicon Valley, the person may have free choices to a buy house in Palo Alto or in Los Altos, where the prices are about the same. Really, it is not much of a choice. When the price is 3 or 4 million dollars for a house, the choice is available to a very small group of people who can afford to buy. But don't blame the free market for the lack of choices. What should we call this system of highly regulated housing market? If the housing market is not a free market, then what is it? The opposite of a free market is the Socialistic central planning. In the US, it is planning, but it is just not centralized.

In California, all of the local governments have planning departments and planning commissions to regulate land-use and housing development. Land-use is a local issue, federal and state governments usually let local regulators do whatever they want.

State governments may set a few guidelines and then let local governments handle the rest. Because it is a local issue, local governments don't draw a lot of national attention or scrutiny. That suits local regulators just fine. They can get away with a lot of senseless decisions and rules.

For example, suppose a person purchased a piece of land that was zoned for high-density housing development. If this buyer did not contribute to the campaign of local politicians, they could just rezone the piece of land to agricultural use. Meanwhile, a neighboring parcel may be rezoned from agricultural to high-density housing. Later in the book I will present the proof of what happened to me in the County of San Diego. Some may think what happened to me is only racism against a first-generation immigrant of ethnic minority. But we should never forget a historical lesson. Hitler was democratically elected too, did he hurt only Jewish people?

Some voters were surprised to learn that they voted for politicians who would prohibit four unrelated individuals from occupying a 4-bedroom house. Almost all voters are surprised to learn that local governments can even dictate the color of paint for a building. The housing market in the US is not controlled by a "central" planner, it is planned by a whole army of local politicians and bureaucrats. Hence in its planning, it is very similar to the economy of a socialist country. Instead of individuals being free to decide for themselves, the government wants to make housing decisions for everyone else.

First, politicians and bureaucrats prefer single-family-detached houses over multi-family housing. Of course, single-family detached houses provide a much better quality of life for occupants than high rise dwellings can. There is a lot of open space, so single-family houses provide better air quality and generate less noise and traffic than high-density dwellings do. They don't want too many unmarried adults to occupy single-detached houses. Single-detached houses are mainly designed for families; too many unmarried adults may destroy the harmony of the neighborhood. Too many unmarried adults may party a lot, get intoxicated often, and set bad examples for kids in the neighborhood. Local politicians just don't believe that most residents are capable of making housing decisions for themselves, so they, the smart politicians want to make the important decisions on housing for the rest of us. Isn't this socialism?

Socialists want to dictate what to produce, how to distribute products, how to pay individuals, etc. These are very important. Socialists do not trust the invisible forces of the free market to decide for us. They want every economic function to be carefully planned. Housing is now a dominating part of the US economy. If the US becomes a socialist country, then those who are in power will decide where housing units are to be built, what kind of housing units are to be built, when housing units are to be built, how many unmarried adults may occupy a house, and who will get which unit. Right now, local politicians do not make decisions about "who will get which unit", but they already make every other decision about housing development as if the US were a Socialist country. So, it is fair to conclude that the US housing market is not a free market. It is not 100% socialist yet, but very close. Please let us not blame capitalism for the high housing cost in California or in the US.

So, why do we have such high housing prices in many places in the US? It is not the failure of the free market, but the lack of it. It is not the free market that pushes up housing prices. High housing costs are the result of socialistic planning. So, no wonder, socialists do not talk about housing problems or high housing costs. They do what they do best, hand out free goodies. The trouble is that there are too many handouts but not enough incentives for hard work. We can look at the Soviet Union or China under Mao's rule, or closer to home, we can observe this economic stagnation in Cuba and Venezuela. During the mid-term elections in 2018, it was clear that socialism had continued to grow. A socialist upset the democratic incumbent in a leadership position in a Congressional District, the State of New York, and she easily won a seat in the US House of Representatives. The rise of socialism in America is mainly the result of high housing costs that destroy the social mobility of a large portion of the population. Yet the Socialists never even talk about high housing prices.

It is very smart of them not to talk about the housing problem. If they want to talk about the issue of housing shortages or high housing costs, they have to explain the cause of the problem. If we focus any attention on the problem, it will be clear to everyone that the problem is the result of the socialistic manipulation of the housing market.

On the supply side, local politicians want to decide what, where, and how to build housing units. On the demand side, they use arbitrary limitations to restrict the number of occupants in a housing unit. In case of boarding houses, some cities require one bathroom for every three occupants. In California, some small two-bedroom apartments in an independent and assisted living facility for seniors require an entrance fee of two million dollars for a couple. So, obviously, we need a variety of choices. For retired seniors, they don't need to rush at all, so why can't four people share one bathroom? Why do local politicians impose these kinds of restrictions? Socialism creates housing problems in the US. Can we expect Socialism to help us to solve the problem?

Socialists take advantage of the high housing costs in the US. They ride on the wave of discontent that results from housing shortages. They don't want to talk about, much less solve, the problem. They cannot thank local politicians enough for creating a housing shortage.

1.7 High Housing Costs Changed California's Political Landscape

For now, Socialists are only a minority within the Democratic Party. But each poll shows that a majority of young people in the US prefers Socialism over Capitalism. After a generation, Socialists may just take over the Democratic Party and win national elections.

High housing costs may push the US to become a Socialist country. At the very least, it has changed the political landscape in this country. For example, California used to have a healthy two-party political system. Richard Nixon and Ronald Reagan both started out in California and became presidents of the US. California today has about the highest housing costs in the country. In recent general elections, Republicans cannot even come up with candidates for some statewide offices. Many of us don't seem to understand the relationship between the decline of the Republican Party and the explosive housing costs in California. A healthy two-party system requires a delicate balance. Anything that can tip the balance can also destroy the political system.

Orange County, California, used to be a solid Republican territory. As housing prices rose, the county turned blue. When rising housing costs get out of hand, those who could not afford the high housing cost needed help. They turned to the Democrats. You don't need a lot of voters to switch sides to tip the balance. When the majority of young people prefer socialism to capitalism, it is more than enough to tip the balance in the Democrats' favor. Of course, demographic change also played a role here, we cannot attribute the change to housing price alone. In this sense, Republicans in California cannot blame their demise on housing prices alone. They still do not pay enough attention to the demographic change in the state. In 2019, My wife and I attended a Republican fundraising event for a local candidate and two of us were only two ethnic minorities of any kind in the gathering.

If we look at the seven states in the US with the highest median house prices, it is no surprise that all seven of them were blue states in the 2016 presidential election:

> Hawaii,
> California,
> Massachusetts,
> Colorado,
> Washington,
> New York,
> Oregon.

Washington DC has the highest housing prices next to Hawaii. This is no surprise, it has been a blue district for a long time. When high housing costs can turn a state from a contested state to a solid blue state, we don't expect Democrats to solve the problem.

Surprisingly, the Governor of California, Gavin C. Newsom, actually made an effort to increase the supply of new housing. The state government filed a lawsuit against the City of Huntington Beach for failing to comply with state mandates on affordable housing in 2019. It is fairly obvious to Democrats in California that they don't need to worry about any challenge from Republicans in the state, as California is a solid blue state now. Yet, they do need to guard against the radical wing of the Democratic Party, namely, the Socialists. The worse the housing problem is in California, the better it is for the Socialists.

So, it is no surprise that Socialists don't talk about housing problems. If they won't address the most pressing problem of high housing costs in the US, what else do they offer? They cannot just offer freebies. Now socialists have come up with the "Green New Deal". It is laughable that anyone wants to go green but refuses to even address high housing costs. High housing costs are completely the opposite of going "green".

The major reason that California has high housing prices is that there are too many single-family houses on spacious lots, and not enough affordable apartments or condominiums. Too many single-family houses on spacious lots contribute to environmental disasters and energy waste. They also make public transportation inefficient and driving private automobiles a necessity.

In Silicon Valley, can any gardener or hotel clerk afford to live there? Probably not. Perhaps a gardener can afford to live 30 minutes or maybe an hour away. This is not a healthy community.

We need workers in a community, yet we don't allow them to live there. It is literally quite unhealthy, because of all the air pollution caused by the long commutes required of many of the workers. Even some of the workers in high tech-firms in Silicon Valley don't live in Silicon Valley. Either they cannot afford to live there, or they prefer not to pay the outrageously high housing costs to live there. Instead, some of them live in other communities, some as far away as Paso Robles, which is about 200 miles south. Housing prices in Paso Robles are about one-fifth of those in Silicon Valley. Also, the town is the center of the new wine country of California.

How does it work? They work four days a week in Silicon Valley and ten hours per day. Most of them drive to work on Monday morning and return home on Thursday evening. During the workweek, they may pay for a bed to sleep in somewhere near their work place, perhaps in a dormitory-like or boarding-house setting. News reports show that some of them sleep in their cars overnight and use the company's gym facilities to take showers. In 2020, during the pandemic of Covid-19, the San Francisco Bay Area was a hot spot of infestations. If some of the workers in Silicon Valley chose to live in Paso Robles, we expect the city to be a hot spot in San Luis Obispo County. Sure thing! As the county cumulated 277 positive cases on June 5, 2020, 122 cases were in Paso Robles. The City of Paso Robles has about 11% of the population in the County, it had about 44% of the Coronavirus infestations at early stage of the pandemic. Yet a week earlier, the headline on the local paper declared that nobody seemed to know why the city had the most cases.

The long weekly drive seems like a senseless waste of fossil fuel. It seems even crazier to waste our precious and limited time in a long commute. Socialists want universal health care and free college education, but they don't think that high housing costs are a problem at all.

Socialists promote "Green New Deals" and set a goal to eliminate fossil fuels by 2050.

These are noble goals. Yet they don't see the enormous waste of energy due to unnecessarily long commutes as a problem at all. If they don't even talk about high housing costs, there are only two possibilities. If Socialists don't understand that high housing costs are an environmental problem, this means that they are not very smart.

Or, if they know it is a problem and yet refuse to address it, they are not very honest.

Senator Elizabeth Warren did talk about high rents and her solution was a typical Socialistic one – rent control. Like most far-left politicians, she did not even want to have an honest discussion or debate to understand the causes or solutions for the most serious problem faced by the country. They just wanted to win elections, so that they would be in power. They believed that a government decree for free universal health care, free college education for all, and rent control for the needy could solve all the serious problems we have today.

The evils of high housing costs are numerous. If the waste of energy associated with high housing prices is a big iceberg, waste due to long commutes is only the tip of the iceberg.

Any comprehensive solution for environmental change cannot ignore the problem of high housing costs in the US. Yet Bernie Sanders, the Socialist Candidate for the 2020

Democratic Presidential nomination for president, chooses to not talk about housing problems in the US. Instead, he wants to break up big US agricultural conglomerates. I like to repeat two sentences at the beginning of this chapter:

"In the US, any worker needs to work only a few hours a month to buy a month's supply of food. Yet in some places in the US, a full-time worker's monthly paycheck is not even enough to pay for the monthly rent of a one-bedroom apartment where he works."

Agriculture is a bright spot in the US economy, by any standard. The regulation of the housing industry is the most corrupt part of the US political system. Bernie Sanders chooses to ignore this and attack the most efficient sector of the US economy. He appears to be a dog barking at the wrong tree.

In summary, why does California have run-away housing prices? The simple answer is too many single-family houses and not enough multi-story-high-density dwellings. Since housing is a local issue and local politicians have total control over all housing developments, so we need to hold them responsible for the high cost. Why do they promote single-family housing? Because they want provide some housing units but they don't want solve the problem of the housing shortage. Not only they don't want solve the problem of housing shortage, they want to create artificial demand to create a housing shortage. Why do local politicians create housing shortage? Severe shortage pushes housing prices sky-high, so only the rich can afford to live there and the poor stay out. When housing prices go up, homeowners, most of them are voters, get a windfall. They want more and vote for the incumbents. This is the best way for local politicians to get re-elected. When housing prices go to the stratosphere, housing developments become a lucrative business. Anyone who can profit in the business will be eager to make campaign contributions to all incumbents in the local government. So local politicians have over-flowing campaign war chest and the votes, if they push housing prices up and up. To them, this is heaven on earth!

As local communities cater to the rich, there are other benefits too. The rich pay a lot of taxes but requires very little social services. So, the local communities can do things to please the rich, for example, make downtown beautiful. So local politicians get the credit. Should we blame them for the homelessness? You be the judge! Obviously, they don't care if many hard-working folks live a life in hell!

CHAPTER 2

—

Who is Responsible for the High Housing Costs in California?

There are three levels of government in the US: local, state, and federal. Local politicians in California are county supervisors, mayors, and city council members. The US is a mature democracy and all levels of the government are rather clean. Clean government means no widespread corruption. A well-developed democracy has rule-based operations with checks and balance. It is obvious that we prefer a clean government to a dirty one. A democratic government requires regular elections, elections require campaigns, and campaigns require money. At the local level, few voters pay close attention to all the issues. Politicians, those in a small town or rural counties, cannot draw enough contributions through their charisma alone.

The situation in a major metropolitan is different. Take Los Angeles County, for example: its GDP (Gross Domestic Product, the monetary value of all the finished goods and services produced within a country's or a region) is larger than that of many small countries. The five county supervisors are powerful politicians. A lot of donors are eager to make campaign contributions to them. They have no trouble raising contribution for their campaigns. But housing development is a fertile ground to harvest campaign contributions. Hence, they take advantage of it too.

2.1 Local Politicians Control Local Land-Use

If we look at a small city, the mayor and city council members have rather limited power, except on land-use. School Boards run schools. We earmark a part of local property tax for schools. The mayor and the city council members have little or no control over school curriculum, hiring, or operation. Law and order are always important in local politics. In a city, the mayor and city council members control the budget of the police department. But day-to-day management, hiring and promotion have clear rules and are left to the chief. City procurements must follow very specific processes and are closely scrutinized.

Except for their power over land-use, in a small city, the mayor and city council members have little or no significant authority over anything else. With land use, they are remarkably powerful. They can act like Gods. God gives and God takes away. A city council's decision may make a difference of millions of dollars to a landowner or a developer.

Landowners, developers, contractors, architects, etc. know the importance of city councils' decisions. If anyone has a project up for approval, it would be silly for the person not to make campaign contributions in advance. If the person has made enough contributions and has a good project, it will sail through. Otherwise, it may be delayed or rejected. Not a word is said, and everything is legal. Everyone is happy. Projects get approved and politicians get their campaign contributions.

Suppose there is a piece of land next to a city. The owner would like to have the land annexed to the city and zoned for housing development. If it is outside the city limit and zoned for agricultural use, the land may be worth $20000 dollars an acre. If it is within the city limit and zoned for a low-density housing development, say, four houses per acre, it may be worth about $1 million an acre. If it is zoned for high-density housing, one may build twenty-unit condominiums or apartments per acre and it may be worth $2 million an acre.

Suppose the city needs 100 new housing units a year. A six-acre piece of land zoned for a high-density housing development will add 120 new housing units to the city. It will more than satisfy one year's new housing needs for the small city. If the six acres are zoned for 4 housing units per acre, then it satisfies only 1/4 of the annual new-housing needs and the city may allow a few more similar projects to satisfy its housing demand.

From the local politicians' position, it is much better to zone the piece of land for low-density housing development. If one project with 120 new housing units can satisfy a whole year's housing needs for the city, no one else can propose any other housing developments in the city. City bureaucrats will be doing nothing for most of the year and landowners will not need any favors from them.

If 120 units are approved in a single project, who will be the winners and who will be the losers? The winners are those buying these new units. The 120 units exceed the annual housing demands of the city. If the supply exceeds demand, prices go down. The buyers of these new units can buy nice dwelling units at reasonable prices. The renters in the city are also winners. When there are empty housing units in the city, the owners of these units would like people to live in these units both for financial reasons and safety concerns. A housing unit incurs expenses such as mortgage payments, utility bills, insurance premiums, maintenance costs, etc. Rental income will help to cover these costs.

One-month vacancy of a rental unit is one-month rent lost, the owner can never recover it and still has to pay all expenses. If there are a lot of empty units in town, then the rent will go down a great deal. The rental market is highly competitive, no one can save a vacancy for future use. Unlike other commodities, if the price of a commodity drops a lot, the seller may withdraw the commodity from the market and hope the price will bounce back. When rental supply exceeds demand, the rent drops a lot to induce more demand for the extra units. Rental units' owners may cut rent so much that they may lose money.

But losing less is better than losing more. Besides, an empty housing unit attracts vandalism, and in the worst-case scenario, it may even be burned down. The owner of an empty rental unit will reduce rent as much as necessary to get the unit rented. Who are the losers? There are many more losers than there are winners. In addition to landlords, bureaucrats and local politicians are big losers, local voters may not be thrilled either.

There is an over-supply of housing units, so housing prices are sluggish, which means that they are not rising and maybe even lowering a little. Everyone who owns a house or condominium in the city is unhappy and homeowners and voters are almost the same groups. Unlike renters, usually they do not vote.

There are other losers. During the construction, a lot of heavy machines and equipment are needed. They make a lot of noise, generate dust, and cause damage to the streets. When a high-density housing project is completed, there is suddenly more traffic in the neighborhood. More occupants make more noise and produce more pollution. Obviously, the neighbors around this new housing development are not happy. If the housing prices go down because of over-supply, then all homeowners suffer. So, not only will the local government resist these 120 units being built, but local voters will also fight against this kind of project tooth and nail.

What would be the likely development? Let us look at a few possibilities. If the owner of the six acres has good connections to the local politicians, the city might allow 24 units on the parcel or four units per acre. Another possibility is that the city may require the owner to donate two acres for open-space or a park reserve. Usually, the landowner will take whatever is offered. It is pretty much a "take it or leave it" situation. There are almost no rules at all. Local bureaucrats and politicians can do whatever they want. Where is the separation of power or checks and balance in the local government? There is none!

In the beginning, in the US, except for a few big cities, there were mostly small counties and towns with populations from a few hundreds to a few thousands. A local politician who wanted to get elected probably had to shake every voter's hand. So, the voters had rather free access to every elected official at the local level, elected officials dared not act against the wish of the majority of voters. Hence, checks and balance were not essential or critical at the time. But now, there are few small towns with populations in the hundreds or small counties with a population of few thousands. Yet the local political systems have not caught up with the new reality. In theory, there are still checks and balance, since there are district attorney, grand jury, the judicial branch, etc. Besides, local politicians usually do not control news media. But as these powerful people often socialize and mingle together, how effective are these checks and balance? Usually, these powerful ones develop a strong fellowship and they often cover-up for each other. Their first priority is 'Don't rock the boat'! Please don't think these are just groundless accusations. I will describe my firsthand experience later on. Because we have a housing crisis on hand, we know these checks and balance for local governments don't always function as they should.

2.2 How Can Local Officials Limit Housing Supply?

Housing is a local issue. There are few checks and balance locally. Local bureaucrats and politicians are very smart and learn quickly. As long as they come up with good excuses for their decisions and pay lip service to affordable-housing, they can keep the housing supply tight to force housing prices to go up. Once the majority of homeowners have had a taste of the windfall of house-value appreciation, they will tolerate or even encourage the limited housing supply.

For the six-acre parcel of land that we mentioned in the last section, why do they allow 24 units? Why not require the owner to donate 2 acres for open space and the other four acres to be divided into eight parcels of one-half acre each? Only a total of eight houses can be built. Then, very soon, the city will have a housing shortage and housing prices will soar.

What is keeping us from ending our California housing crisis? The answer is the local government employees who enjoy the crisis. It is only a problem for those who cannot afford the high cost of housing. To the local bureaucrats and politicians, the worse the housing shortage is, the better. Housing developments are a lucrative business. Politicians enjoy the attention and campaign contributions from the landowners, developers, architects, and builders who compete to win favors from them to get their projects approved.

Yes, elected officials and career bureaucrats work closely together as a team. But what is the goal?

If the housing shortage benefits them, and it does, they will work to enhance their own welfare. They will do things that worsen the housing shortage. This does not help the public.

As an example, politicians often increase the lot size for a single-family house, which limits supply. They often reduce the number of units allowed on parcels for multi-family housing. Again, this reduces the housing supply. So, they make sure that housing is always in short supply. As housing prices increase, politicians' power increases, and bureaucrats have full employment.

Another thing bureaucrats do is to make the approval process for housing development more complicated and time-consuming. What does this do? It slows down the housing supply. It also forces developers to compete to buy access to politicians for help. The two groups work closely and flawlessly. The result is that housing prices soar sky-high.

Why should any of them care? Local bureaucrats, politicians, and everyone else in the housing business profit from high prices. Even most of the local voters profit from high housing prices too. Those who are profiting from high housing costs form a powerful coalition of the housing establishment! Or, more appropriately, the housing Mafia!

But they need the public's approval, you might say. Who are the victims? There are many! But they are no matches against the housing establishment. The victims include those who buy houses at ridiculously high prices. But they may not even consider themselves victims. If the housing price continues to rise, they can enjoy a windfall and become winners. This is, cannot beat them, join them!

Other victims are the ones who work but cannot afford to live in the city. Too bad, poor losers. The local politicians pay little attention to them at all as they cannot vote. Last, but not least, renters are a sizeable group of victims of high-housing costs. Renters may vote, so local and even state politicians pay attention to them. Yet, renters are a small group compared to homeowners. Even if renters may out number homeowners in a city, renters are less likely to register to vote. Some landlords may not be very knowledgeable about rental market, thus, occasionally, there are units priced below going rate. Experienced renters are always on the lookout for good deals. Renters usually don't stay put for long and often don't bother to register to vote after each relocation.

Since the victims are not very important to the politicians, they only pay lip-service to affordable housing. They only do enough to satisfy California's State requirements. The result is that California has a lot of single-family houses on spacious lots. But it does not have enough multi-story housing developments. This is a serious problem for the state of California. Housing prices are sky high.

The high price of housing has an adverse economic, political, social, and environmental effect on the state, the entire country and beyond.

Before a project reaches the city council, it may require a city staff and planning commission review. Usually, the mayor and each council member appoint a commissioner. The planning commission is important to the housing development. Many local politicians start their political careers from planning commissions. It is an important step in their own development.

The mayor and the council members always appoint their closest friends or allies to the planning commission. Campaign donations are public records. It should surprise no one to expect city employees and planning commissioners monitoring the records and taking action accordingly.

Like the public, local politicians and city employees come in various shades and shapes.

Some are perfectly straight, and some are very crooked. In the last half-century, while the US population increased only 65%, California's population has more than doubled. We would think in California, there would have been changes implemented to meet the rising housing demands. We would imagine that acres of land zoned for agricultural have rezoned for housing development and acres of land that zoned for low-density housing have rezoned for high-density housing to accommodate population growth, not the other way around.

Every county in California is divided into five districts. Voters in each district elect a supervisor. Many good supervisors try to serve all the constituents in their districts. However, there are just as many who may not be so honest.

A supervisor has absolute power over land use in the district. There is an unwritten rule among supervisors regarding any decision about land use. Only the supervisor from the district may make a motion to bring an issue to a vote. If the motion is not outrageous, other supervisors will not kill the motion out of respect for a fellow supervisor. This is an "If you scratch my back, I will scratch yours." situation.

Suppose a supervisor wants to approve a huge high-density housing development in the district. Because this project can satisfy a large demand for housing in the county, other supervisors may think this hinders housing development in their own districts. The motion may not get a second or may not get approval, because it infringes upon other supervisors' fair share. Thus, any low- density development that does not interrupt housing development in other districts will easily get through.

When it comes to down-zoning a piece of land, it almost always benefits other supervisors. However unfair or illegal the action may be, do not expect any supervisor to stick his or her neck out for justice. Voters are smart, so most politicians are fair and square. But the fundamental fraud of the system and lack of checks and balance cannot guarantee the system to be free of corruption.

A crooked supervisor may look at the district as his or her own private domain. This kind of supervisor considers every vacant lot to be his or her own piggy bank. Worse yet, some supervisors may demand to be a silent partner in every lucrative housing development. Since millions of home buyers and renters pay for the high cost, there is enough profit to go around. Just about everyone in the housing establishment can cut a piece of the pie and eat it too. You almost never hear an outcry from the insiders. Suppose a person bought a piece of land for high-density housing development. If the person failed to make regular campaign contributions to local politicians, the politician might down-zone the land back to agricultural use. Millions of dollars of the person's investments might be wiped out by a single vote. So, campaign contributions are not just needed to facilitate housing development. They are also needed to preserve the value of land for housing development. No wonder housing prices in California have skyrocketed. If you think I am making a lot of serious and groundless accusations against the integrity of the local politicians, I do not blame you. Can I present any facts to back up my claims? Yes! I will now share with you what I experienced firsthand.

In the early 80s, the Diablo Nuclear power plant was under construction. It was only several miles from my house and about ten miles from most of my real estate holdings. The Three Mile Island nuclear power plant accident had just happened in 1979, so I tried to diversify my holdings. I picked San Diego County to hedge my bets. In case there was any mishap at the Diablo nuclear power plant, and I lost all of my real estate in San Luis Obispo, I wanted to have something to give me a fresh start. I invested in two motels in the east of San Diego with a relative and a friend and bought a three-acre commercial lot in the northern part of San Diego County. The location appeared to be fairly good: It was a corner lot at the intersection of two major roads and one road had access to a freeway, Highway 78. I picked San Diego County for two reasons: it was a low earthquake risk area and a Republican stronghold.

Since I became a US citizen, I usually voted for Republican tickets in national elections. At local level, Republicans were more likely to respect property rights and the free-market function in housing development, thus less likely to manipulate the housing market.

After about 10 years, suddenly I received a notice that San Diego County was updating its General Plan and my parcel was to be re-zoned to agricultural use. Under the commercial zoning, the parcel would allow 100 units of two-bedroom housing units. My land was in District 5 and I tried to contact the supervisor's office to find out the justification of the proposed zoning change. I met Supervisor John McDonald's assistant. He told me there was no justification necessary for any zoning change. I tried to understand why as the population increased in the north San Diego County a parcel of land zoned for 100 two-bedroom housing units was down-zoned to one dwelling only. He answered: "God gives and God can take it away!" If supervisors were truly Gods, I could pray for mercy! But I knew about this fake god. Prayer would be useless, but offering might work. It was against my principle not to fight for justice. I fought tooth and nail against the change. I never imagined a landowner needed to bribe local politicians to maintain the zoning of a piece of land. It was probably not too late for me to make a campaign donation to Supervisor McDonald to save the Commercial Zoning. But I decided to fight instead of giving in. To me, everything is a learning process. Here, I just wanted to learn how corrupt the local politicians could be. If I could learn some truth, it was fine to lose the value of the land. To me, knowledge is power. To learn is far more important than to save the value of a piece of land. The recorded deed of the piece of land had a clause that no Chinese may own the title of the land. I heard about such discriminatory clauses before, but I had never seen it in writing on an official document until I bought the piece of land. I also heard that the Supreme Court ruled this discriminatory clause unconstitutional during World War II. I argued that the local politicians and bureaucrats in San Diego tried to make a mockery out of the Supreme Court's ruling. If they changed the zoning of my land from commercial to agricultural, then I would wish the Supreme Court didn't make the ruling. I would not have owned the land and I would not have lost a significant part of my life savings. I asserted that even in the 20th Century, a Chinaman still couldn't get Chinaman's luck in San Diego. Local newspapers in Northern San Diego even reported my clash with the Chairman of the Planning Commission. During the final hearing prior to the vote to adopt the revised General Plan, the Planning Commission limited every registered speaker to 3 minutes. I thought 3 minutes was not enough for me, so I asked my wife and my older son to register to speak. My son was a student at UC Santa Barbara. When my wife and I drove down from San Luis Obispo to San Diego, we picked him up. All three of us registered to speak at the hearing. After I spoke, I tried to let my son and wife each to yield 3 minutes to me. The Chairman denied my request. I turned the microphone to my son to continue my argument, the Chairman denied my son's right to speak. He said he understood my point completely and my son and my wife did not need to speak. I refused to accept his decision and told my son to continue unless someone physically and forcefully took the microphone away from him. My son tried to use his 3 minutes to argue for my case. But before he finished his presentation, the chairman claimed his time was up and ordered security to take the microphone from him to deny my wife's right to speak.

Usually, politicians always like to get their way, but they do not like any bad publicity, especially if a citizen exposes their unlawful or unethical practices regardless of the consequences. In the face of strong resistance, they are often willing to compromise. The chairman simply violated my son and my wife's right to speak. He thought he was so powerful that he forgot who he was. He was used to seeing every landowner and developer at Planning Commission's hearing to be humble and submissive. He probably expected me, an ethnic minority, to be more submissive than anyone else. He was upset and lost his control when I dared to refuse to listen to him. When Commissioners and Supervisors vote on anything, it is difficult to prove their unlawful motivation or intention. But when they disregarded the due process, like denying my wife's right to speak, it was fairly obvious. I filed a complaint to the Grand Jury of San Diego about his misconduct. As I expected, they took no action against the Chairman of the Planning

Commission. I wrote to the Grand Jury foreman that they should be renamed to "Grand Joke". I tried to provoke them to file charge against me, so I would have a chance to expose their unlawful actions against me. I was disappointed.

I attended the Supervisors meeting that would decide the fate of the General Plan Update. Four supervisors were present:

District 1: Supervisor Brian Bilbray;
District 2: Supervisor George Baily;
District 3: Supervisor: Susan Golding;
District 5: Supervisor: John McDonald;

The District 4 Supervisor Leon Williams was absent. Both supervisors Golding and Bilbray were in favor of maintaining the existing Commercial Zoning for my land. They urged Supervisor McDonald to move to reverse the Planning Commission's decision. Supervisor Baily didn't speak strongly but didn't object to maintaining the existing Commercial Zoning. It was an embarrassing moment for Supervisor McDonald. His colleagues expected him to make a motion, but he refused. Apparently, because the piece of land was in his district, only he could make a motion about its use. The Planning Commission's recommendation was adopted without amendment.

I suffered a disastrous financial loss. I would do my best to expose this kind of corruption. I received a call from Supervisor McDonald's aide informing me that the Chairman of the Planning Commission just lost his job. Supervisor McDonald wanted the Chairman of the Planning Commission to be the scapegoat for the fiasco. His aide seemed to encourage me to stay in good terms with his boss. He also hinted that it was possible to reverse the zoning change at the next update of the General Plan.

In my effort to keep the Commercial Zoning for my land, I argued that it would be a shame to down-zone my commercial land to agricultural use as my land was located at a busy intersection of two major roads. A ministorage would be a better use of the land than any agricultural operations. Supervisor McDonald's aide specifically mentioned that If I wanted to build mini-storage facility on my land, all I needed to do was to apply for a Variance. A Variance is a rule that allow local politicians and bureaucrats to ignore all zoning regulations.

Usually it is reserved in favor of the best-connected landowners and developers. I told him that I could not even keep the value of my land that I paid for, how could I expect any special favor from his boss? I knew perfectly well what he wanted me to do. I was not naïve enough to take the bait.

Usually, the Chairman of the Planning Commission is the most powerful person except for the five supervisors in a county. Many politicians started their careers from the position. Even though the supervisors adopted the Planning Commission's recommendation without amendment, the supervisors seemed to blame the chairman for the mishandling of my case. The first thing that I did afterwards was an application to the Assessor's Office for a reduction of the assessed value of the land. Everyone I contacted in the Assessor's office told me it was illegal to rezone a piece of land from commercial down to agricultural because none of them had heard about it before. I talked to a few insiders knowledgeable about land use regulation. They informed me that it was not illegal to down zone a commercial parcel to agriculture, and it was extremely rare. Usually an R4 (High-density housing) may be down-zoned to R3 (median-density housing), but not all the way down to agriculture. One possibility was that the population increase was not fast enough in District 5 of San Diego County.

While the general plan changed my land from commercial to agricultural, it also changed another parcel about the same size from agricultural to commercial in the same district. This kind of arbitrary change is a common form of corruption statewide. Apparently, it was common enough, in 2019, California AB (Assembly Bill) 330 temporarily suspended the practice of down-zoning of any parcel in the state. Both chambers of the Legislators passed the bill overwhelmingly, and Governor Newsom quickly signed it into law.

Unfortunately, it was twenty years too late for my land in San Diego. But AB330 represented a great hope for the State of California. This bill was the first of its kind that the state put a specific restraint on the land-use authority of local governments.

San Diego County is one of the richest counties in California, and supervisors are powerful politicians. They receive plenty of contributions for their political campaigns and need not rely on their authority on land-use for a campaign fund. However, local politicians always know what the easiest way is to get a campaign contribution. Once they get addicted to it, it will be hard for them to quit.

I became a US Citizen in 1980. I immediately started to make campaign contributions to Republican candidates. Once anyone made a few contributions, additional requests from various candidates and organizations almost would never stop. But after the disaster in San Diego, for about 10 years, I refused to make any donations to Republican candidates or organizations in California. If any callers cared to listen, I would explain how much I had suffered from the down-zoning and I emphasized that I picked San Diego because it was a Republican stronghold. I wondered if my bad-mouthing about Supervisor McDonald affected his political career. He seemed to have ended his career rather fast. After serving two terms as Supervisor, he disappeared from the San Diego political scene. Supervisor Golding was elected to two terms as the Mayor of the City of San Diego and Supervisor Bilbray was elected to the US House of Representatives from two different Congressional Districts in San Diego. Perhaps San Diego voters were just smart, they knew good public servants from mediocre ones.

2.3 Bigger Houses on Bigger Lots

California has too many single-family houses. It is the major cause of high housing costs in California, but it is not the only one. California's population has more than doubled in 50 years. Despite this, local governments still encourage single-family developments. Perhaps, at least, the lot sizes for single-family dwellings have gotten a little smaller to accommodate population growth. In reality, as population increases, the average lot size for new single-family house also increases, and the house gets bigger too.

In Morro Bay, a little beach town on the Central Coast, there were some small lots, 25'x50' approved in the 50s for single-family houses. Later on, if any of these lots were still vacant, the city required two or four neighboring lots to be combined to get a building permit for a single house. How did the City do it? Here is a classical example, from time to time California may experience a few years of below average rainfall. This is a common phenomenon that surprises no one and every city or county should expect it. In Morro Bay, the city declared emergency because of water shortage, then it declared a moratorium on new housing construction. Moratorium is a temporary prohibition of an activity. What would be a free-market approach to solve the problem? The first step of the solution would raise the price of water. The price increase would encourage consumers to conserve, meanwhile, it would induce additional supply. Like most cities in California, the city supplied water. If the city could raise water rate, city could increase investment in water supply. But Morro Bay city officials didn't believe in Capitalism or they were afraid of voters' backlash, so they did not raise water rate. They believed they had a better way to solve the problem. Anyone thinks there is a better way than the free-market approach, the person almost always uses socialistic manipulation. If they raised water rate, Socialists believe the poor bear the most of the burden. Because water is a necessity for everyone, so everyone needs a minimum amount of water to survive. The poor pay a bigger percent out of their income for water than the rich do. It is equivalent to regressive taxation; it hurts the poor more than the rich. Morro Bay city officials wanted to protect the poor. It was a noble cause, like almost all the Socialist's causes, no one could argue against it.

Suppose an owner wanted to build a house. If the water usage for the new house is estimated at, say, 300 gallons per day. Then the owner had to create a saving of 300 gallons per day in the City of Morro Bay, before the building permit was issued. One way to save water was to distribute water saving plumbing parts. Like an aerator for a kitchen faucet might count as 5 gallons saving, a low flow shower head as 7-gallon saving, etc. Just about every city in California had this kind of program. Because I own rental housing; I collected quite a few of these plumbing parts. I always kept those aerators. They did reduce water usage and spatters. But I always threw those showerheads into recycle cans. At first, I gave it a try, but didn't like it. I never found a single individual who would like to use it. Like most social engineering schemes, this one failed too. If the maker of this showerheads could only sell it in hardware stores, the maker would be out of business fast. They could never fool consumers.

The Morro Bay City Officials soon came with a new approach. If anyone still had 25'x50' lot, city required two or four neighboring lots combined to get a building permit for a single house. The city used water shortage as an excuse to increase lot size of single-family detached houses. It sounded reasonable, but it contradicted their noble goal to protect the poor. Morro Bay needs a lot of low-wage workers for its hotels, restaurants, and assisted living facilities. I wonder how could these workers afford the high housing costs in Morro Bay.

This author has moved into three new houses in the last 50 years. These three houses are within one mile of each other. They are in three different housing developments next to each other. The first one was approved in the late 60s and the lot size was 50'x100' or about 1/8 of an acre. The second one, approved in the mid 70s, was 1/3 of an acre and the 3rd one, in the 90s, about an acre. This is a typical example in California, and it matches the national trend in size of dwellings. The average number of people living in a household has been decreasing, yet the median housing size has been increasing. In 1960, the average household size was 3.33 and in 2010 it was 2.58. Yet, during the time, the median size of a house has increased (derived US Census data):

Table 2: Median House Size from 1940-2014

Year	Median House Size (ft2)
1940	1,177
1950	983
1960	1,289
1970	1,500
1980	1,740
1990	2,080
2000	2,266
2010	2,392
2014	2,657

The trend is clear except the years around 1950 when there was a sudden surge in the housing demand for returning GIs after WWII.

This is a national trend, not just in California. California just didn't buck the trend, even with its rapid population growth.

We have seen how local governments restrict high-density housing developments and increase the lot size for single-family houses. These policies contribute to high housing costs in California. But this is not the end. Local governments add a lot of unnecessary regulations and red tape on housing developments. The housing industry is a highly regulated industry to begin with, and some regulations are definitely needed for city planning. Also, some regulations are necessary for safety, energy efficiency and health. But some regulations appear to be not only unnecessary but also absurd.

2.4 California, the Birth Place of Red Tape on Land Use

The expansion of the US started from the thirteen states in the North-East part of the county, but the beginning of the zoning law did not start from the East. Instead, it started from the West. Los Angeles City Council established the earliest zoning ordinance on September 24, 1908. The ordinance created three large residential districts, and they all prohibited business such as laundries, lumberyards, and in general, any industry using equipment driven by motors. Some restrictions made sense and others didn't. Lumberyard created a large amount of noise that was a form of pollution. Lumberyard also generated a lot of traffic of heavy loads. The heavy traffic caused damages to the roads around it, as well as odor from animal pulled carts or exhaustive emission from motor vehicles. The prohibition against laundries had a racial component since Chinese owned most of the businesses. The zoning ordinance didn't start from a noble mission and the result of the law is plainly visible in California; high housing cost, wasteful water and energy usage in housing and destructions to the environment.

Whenever landowners or developers have trouble navigating through the bureaucrats, they need to get accesses to elected officials. Making a campaign donation is the easiest way to buy access to local politicians. If this becomes clear to bureaucrats, everyone tries to make lives hard for landowners and developers. The best way to fit in is probably to invent new rule and red tape to slow down the process. Before long, regulations on housing grow almost like a living organism, with cells dividing and multiplying. These regulations become more and more complicated and spread like a raging wildfire.

In California, there is a group of professionals who make a living by helping landowners or developers cut through local red tapes for housing development. You will not hear them complaining about any red tape. Without it, they would have to find other lines of work.

You don't hear landowners or developers complaining either. First, they don't dare to. If they don't want to jeopardize their project, they better shut up and be submissive. Second, any red tape costs them a little, but the business is lucrative. The cost is just a cost of doing business. They probably don't want the process to be too easy either. If it was easy, then everyone could do it. As it is now, they are the only ones who have the know-how and the inside track. If anyone dares to complain, that person would probably better of finding another city or county to do business, or maybe even another state.

The trouble is, a landowner cannot take a piece of land to another place. You don't hear national news media investigating the high cost of housing much. In Silicon Valley, Palo Alto has high housing costs, yet, next door, in East Palo Alto, it is much lower. Just like Manhattan has very high housing costs, yet Harlem has abandoned buildings. So, housing cost is a local problem.

Suppose that the profession of economists cannot help the government lessen the impact of business cycles. Every business cycle swings back and forth to the extreme of boom and bust, destroying many lives every once a while. What would the rest of the public think of the profession? We know there is a profession of city and regional planning. The US is lucky to have rather mild weather. Americans are a bunch of hard-working people and blessed with a vast amount of natural resources including land, stable and clean government. Under these premises, Americans should enjoy the highest standard of living. Every able-body with a full-time job should enjoy a comfortable life. The profession of city and regional planning in California should have an easy job to provide affordable housing. They have a vast amount of resources including land to do it, unlike planners in Hong Kong or Monaco who have very limited land to work with. Planners in the Netherlands have to provide housing where the land is under water. There is a term: "War with the seas" in Dutch. The sea is rising, so the Dutch have very limited land for housing developments; they build houses on floating platforms. Luckily, Californians have plenty of land for housing developments, we don't need to build houses on water as a necessary part of our housing supply. In San Francisco, one can find houses on floating platforms. That is great! San Franciscans have the capacity to learn. We don't need houses on floating platform to solve the problem of housing shortage in the US. But every little bit of supply of housing helps. We need to learn from others more, so, let us learn from everyone else around the world, don't just learn from Dutch. Let us not to be so arrogant that we refuse to learn, then we shall solve the problem of housing shortage.

Unfortunately, we don't war with the sea like Dutch, we war with bureaucrats instead. I learned to build houses before the Internet Age and there was no DIY channel on TV. When I faced with any obstacles, I didn't know anyone who would share trade secrets with me. How did I overcome all the problems? Most of the time, I simply tried to think what might work. I tried one way. If it didn't work, I tried another. I went to various construction sites at different stages of the building, pretending as a casual observer to learn the ways professionals worked. I was able to solve almost all problems I encountered. But when I was faced with obstacles that bureaucrats threw at me, I was totally helpless.

Comparing planners elsewhere, planners in California have failed us. But don't blame them, blame their bosses, the local elected officials. Never in the history of mankind, any able-body individual needs to spend one half of the person's life to erect a shelter until now in the US. When a legitimate worker in the US needs to spend one half or more of the wage for housing cost, it is equivalent to force the person to spend one half of the persons work life for a roof overhead. Not that a person cannot erect a shelter in reasonable time, in fact, any able-body individuals can. It is the local government's regulations prohibit individuals from building shelters for themselves. Even within the Arctic Circle, an Eskimo can build an igloo in a few hours.

Figure 1: Floating house in the Netherlands

Figure 2: Floating house in Mission District, San Francisco

Did the zoning regulations serve their purposes? Probably not. The reason Chinese operated most laundry business resulted from racism. Chinese labor came to the US to build railroads. It was hard and dangerous work. After the construction boom of railroad ended, local communities didn't let Chinese workers enter other professions.

During gold rush, Chinese rarely had "Chinaman's Chance" to keep registered claims or to prospect at choice spots. That was how the term "Chinaman's Chance" started. How could Chinese labor survive? Because most decent women didn't come to the Wild West. So Chinese labor ended up doing what normally considered women's work. Cleaning dirty laundry, sewing and cooking were the kinds of work that Chinese labor were allowed to do. Not because Chinese labor was not manly enough to do the work, but because Chinese could only do what other men didn't want to do. But local communities still didn't leave Chinese alone. This was one of the reasons that zoning ordinance started in California. But if we look at those communities with the most restrictive zoning ordinances, usually Chinese communities are thriving. San Francisco has one of the highest housing prices. San Francisco County data showed that in 2010, 33.3% of the residents were Asians and 18.6% of residents spoke Chinese at home. It is safe to say that at least 20% of San Franciscans were Chinese in 2010. I assume those who spoke Chinese at home were Chinese, and at least another 1.4% of the population in SF were Chinese who didn't speak Chinese at home. One of my sons was in the group. In Silicon Valley, there were even more Asians and Chinese. If the purpose of zoning ordinances is to exclude Asian or Chinese, the ordinances fail miserably. But the collateral casualties are significant; including but not limited to creating homelessness, destroying lives, contributing to global warming etc.

To prove that building a house is not a big deal, my experience is an excellent example. My construction experience started in 1975. My family adopted a dog for our two boys, we needed a dog-house. I designed it and built it in a couple days with two sheets of plywood. Before the dog-house, my only experience with construction tool was nailing a cross stand to a Christmas tree. In 1962, I was working for a grocery store making about $1.50 an hour. The owner also sold a bunch of Christmas trees. When he got the shipment, he showed me how to nail two pieces of wood to the bottom of the tree to let it stand vertically. After the dog-house, I felt confident enough to move up a notch. The next summer my wife and I added a room about 400 square feet to our house. We even added a fireplace in the room. However, the room addition didn't have any plumbing which was considered the most difficult part of residential buildings. The most challenging part of the construction in this project was to connect the new roof to the existing one. Adding a room was rather simple, my wife and I did it in one summer. During the summer, it rarely rains in this part of California. But I had a dream, while I removed the shingle to connect the new roof to the existing one, suddenly it was pouring down hard! Should I take it as a warning or just ignore it? I would rather be wrong for over cautious. I planned carefully. We got up early in the morning to remove shingles around 6 AM, working cautiously not to bother our neighbors. Except for a circular saw, I had only simple hand tools. We finished around 10 PM, but the roof was all done and water tight. I was exhausted and ready for bed. In no time, I fell into sound sleep. Then suddenly, wind was howling, and a thunderstorm hit the area hard. It didn't bother me; I fell into sleep again. I felt the warning was God-sent. It was true that God help those who help themselves. This incident gave me extra confidence. My wife and I were ready for a bigger project.

In 1978, we built a duplex of two 3-bedroom and 2 and half bathroom townhouses. We were never very strong and had little experience, but we complete the duplex without too much trouble. We didn't even hire a plumber or an electrician for the building. However, we had to hire a plumber to connect the sewer line to the main line under the street. When I start my duplex project, the building inspector, Mr. Nick Nicolas, in charge of the construction was the same inspector who guided me through my room addition two years earlier. He made many inspections and didn't remember the details of every inspection. I reminded him about my room addition; he complimented my work and said it was a nice one. I complained about his boss, the director of the Building Department, Jack Kellerman, giving me a hard time. He did not like the director either. He said that his boss should not worry about any owner/builder. He asked: "You will not mess it up for yourself, will you?" I regretted that I never told him how much I appreciated his guidance to help me on the project. He was always courteous, willing to help and showed the highest standard of a true public servant, just the opposite of most of his colleagues in the city. It never occurred to him he had the power to harass. I just wondered how could he fit in an environment that was contrary to his standard. Several years later, we met at another inspection, he was working for the City of Morro Bay nearby. The City of Morro Bay is probably the worst place I have ever seen concerning nit picking by bureaucrats. If he couldn't fit in well in the City of San Luis Obispo, he couldn't do better in Morro Bay either. I retired from my teaching job more than 20 years ago, I am sure he has retired from his job too. If I wrote this book ten years ago, I would not mention his name.

If he might still be working; I would not want to jeopardize his job. However, it doesn't mean that every city in the state has nit-picking bureaucrats, I have very good experience dealing with other cities in California including El Cajon, Los Angeles, Grover Beach, Atascadero, South San Francisco, etc.

Take El Cajon as an example, at one time, I owned a motel in the city and wanted to add kitchenettes to 12 rooms. A kitchenette included a small sink plus a small gas burner for cooking. The sink required ½" cold and hot water supplies and a 2" pipe for drainage and the gas burner required ½" gas supply line. I asked my son to draw a set of plans and submitted it to the Building Dept for permit. The city quickly issued building permit. When I picked it up, the person at the counter asked me if I drew the plan myself. I said: "No! My son did." He asked: "What is your son doing?" I said he was a sophomore majoring in Mechanical Engineering at UC Santa Barbara. He said: "No wonder! I know the plan was not done by an architect or a mechanical engineer, but it was good enough for a permit." I am sure that my son's plan would not allow me to get a building permit from the City of San Luis Obispo or the City of Morro Bay.

So, it is not a big deal to build a house, except it is just hard to get a building permit. It is even harder to find a piece of land in this big state to build, even though there is open space almost everywhere in the state.

There are a few other reasons for high construction costs in California, building codes and licensing of the various trades related to housing construction. Architects, civil engineers, (including structural, soil etc.) electrical and mechanical engineers, all need to be licensed. Every one of them needs to sign an application even for building a simple house, bungalow or cottage.

No one would question the absolute necessity of these professionals when designing a high-rise housing structure. For a simple house, these professionals still contribute to the quality of the design. But the questions are: "At what cost?" and "Is it worth the cost?"

Decades ago around 1972, someone estimated that if an automobile were built like a house, it would cost a couple million dollars. One could buy a new Volvo station wagon for under $5000 and a new house for

$20,000 in Los Angeles. Imagine every car is to be uniquely designed like those custom homes. Every step during the manufacturing process requires an inspector to sign off before the next step may begin. Then, of course, these cars would not have been affordable. To lease a luxurious automobile now, the monthly payment costs only a few hundred dollars. In most cities in California, to rent a simple room for a month costs at least twice as much. A few able-bodies with simple hand and power tool and enough building materials can build a simple cabin rather easily in a couple of weeks. Now suppose they're a team of experts with any machine tools of their choice and any raw material they may order with a snap of a finger. How long do you think it will take them to build a Model T? Probably more than a year. It seems rather unreasonable for the cost of monthly rent for a simple room to be more than double the monthly cost to lease a luxurious car. Also, now a Volvo Station Wagon costs about $50,000, can anyone buy a new house in Los Angeles for $200,000?

All trades involved in housing construction are licensed; including footing excavation, masonry, concrete, plumbing, framing, electrical wiring, heating, cooling, mechanical fixtures, roofing etc. Different codes govern every step of the construction. Codes are updated regularly. Some reports claim that one of most important consequences of licensing requirements is to restrict competition and, thus, increase construction costs. Some building codes are definitely necessary. For example, California is in an earthquake zone, we expect building codes to strengthen building against earthquake damage.

To show whether all the requirements are necessary or not, I like to recall a few of my first-hand experiences. Once I called a backhoe operator to excavate the foundation for a small apartment. I asked him if he had a State Contractor's License. He answered, "No!" He explained that he had been in business for decades and never bothered to get a state license. He also said that he did a lot of work for the City. I hired him and he didn't bother to give me a written estimate or sign a contract. But he did the work without a glitch. When he finished the job, I gave him a check. He appeared to be old-fashioned. A handshake was good enough for him, and it was also good enough for me. A few months later, I saw him working on a city street. So what he said was right, the city hired him too.

In 1978, When I built the duplex in the City of San Luis Obispo. The Building Inspector Mr. Nick Nicolas looked at the sewer line I put in. He commented: "This is what we call a country plumber's work. There is a spot that doesn't meet today's codes. But it is OK. It will work!" I could have easily corrected the problem, but Mr. Nicolas didn't think it was worth the trouble and he just signed it off. But I changed it anyway! There are many like Mr. Nicolas, then there are a lot of them at the opposite end of the spectrum, nit-picking for no good reason.

For example, once a building department official in the City of San Luis Obispo refused to accept my application for a building permit, because the paper size of my application was not uniform. In my application, there were standard specifications printed on letter-size paper from a computer file. The rest was in large blue print sheets. Blueprints have a standard-scale requirement, and it is not possible to shrink them into letter-size paper. To print a computer file on blueprint size paper is difficult, admittedly, but not impossible. I could not think of a single reason for requiring uniform paper size. But nobody would dare to challenge a city employee on things like these.

When people in the housing industry put up with this type of abusive treatment from city bureaucrats, they should be compensated properly. No wonder housing prices go up and up. Anyone who doesn't want to take this kind of treatment should contribute generously to mayor's and city council members' campaigns.

I am sure bureaucrats pay attention to campaign donors' lists. When my name was on the guest list to mayor's inauguration ceremony, I felt I got more courteous treatments from city employees. In a housing development project, even if a developer does everything by the book, there are always details for bureaucrats to nit-pick.

I have a lot of practical experience in the maintenance of simple residential buildings. Some were built in the 50s. These were not only a few units of rental properties, but close to a 100. I have not just managed these units for a year or two, but for decades. I don't manage them now. I am over 80 years old. Electrical Codes are updated every three years. I don't know how many changes there have been over the years for simple houses and apartment buildings. Except for one or two, I cannot think of any changes that seem to have a huge benefit.

Over the decades, there have been more and more household appliances. We have to increase the meter size to accommodate these new gadgets. The electrical wiring increases from two wires to three wires. The 3rd wire is for a ground to protect us from faulty appliances.

I have a very personal experience about the need for a ground wire. One day when I was a high school student, my mom tried to move an electrical fan a little. When she grabbed the handle, she was electrified and could not let go of the handle. She cried out. Luckily, I was only a few steps away from her. I grabbed her bare wrist and tried to pull her away from the handle. I got a shock from her wrist. Instead, I pulled her clothing very hard. She fell down on the floor and pulled the fan down with her. The fan unplugged itself and she was saved. If the house wiring had the 3rd ground wire, the faulty fan would have tripped the circuit breaker.

Over the decades, I managed a lot of units were not in compliance with the updated electrical codes, yet I encountered no electrical problems that the new code requirements would prevent. During this time period, I probably paid over a few million dollars in premiums for those rental insurance policies and only filed one claim. A couple of college kids cooked something on an electric stove and forgot about it. It started a small fire and burned itself out. There was no damage except smoke. I got $3000 from the insurance company to clean up and repaint the unit. So, most of these codes have increased housing costs a lot with little tangible benefit. These ever-changing code requirements discourage a lot of do-it-yourselfers from working on any housing projects. So the major consequence of these code requirements appears to be limiting competitions for different tradesmen on home improvement projects and jacking up housing prices. I can honestly say, most electrical codes only protect electricians' jobs rather than protecting the public!

Take insulation requirements for a residential unit as an example. This requirement is necessary to ensure comfortable living for the occupants and to conserve energy for heating/cooling. But how complicated can it be? Why do we need a specialist to do complicated calculations? At any locality in California, the requirements could easily be summarized on a single page of letter-size paper. We just need three numbers for a house: insulation on the ceiling, insulation in the walls and insulation under the floor if it has a raised foundation. But instead of just looking at a simple summary on a sheet of paper, a building permit applicant must hire a specialist to do a lot of calculations. Lighting requirements are very simple in a residential housing unit. It is common sense; each room needs at least one light fixture. If a room is large, it may need more than one. If a room doesn't have enough light, how terrible could it be? One can add a floor lamp or a table lamp any place and any time. If a room has too many light fixtures, no problem at all, one doesn't have to use them. Why do we need any calculation or code requirements for lighting? Believe me, there are! About 20 years ago, after I retired from teaching, I built a house for my family. In the kitchen, I put in 6 recessed light fixtures in the room and an energy saving (fluorescent) fixture above the sink. But the inspector told me to add two more energy-saving fixtures in front of the sink because of a new code requirement. So, two more were added. Why there was no similar requirement for other rooms? Perhaps because we spend a lot of time at a kitchen sink. But before my house was completed, the compact fluorescent light bulb was invented and could be used to replace the regular incandescent light bulbs. So now the kitchen has 9 light fixtures that are all energy saving. The original seven light fixtures now have LED light bulbs that are even better than the compact fluorescent light bulbs. The original fixtures positioned nicely, the two added ones appeared out of place and unnecessary.

This code serves no useful purpose. Instead, it wasted my time and resources, and destroyed a nice layout on the kitchen ceiling. Codes like this one benefit electricians only with the public footing the bill. But perhaps the group of electricians in charge of updating electrical codes had good intention for saving energy. They just failed to predict the invention of compact fluoresced bulbs. These people should be the best in their profession. They should know the future of their profession.

Fluorescent light fixtures were around for a long time. Before the electronic age, fluorescent light fixtures were bulky, because every fixture required ballast about 2"x1"x10" in size and weighted a couple pounds. But with the advancement in technology and electronics in particular, the fixture had shrunken to less than one tenth of the previous size, and the light tube had shrunken to the size of a regular light bulb. It didn't require a genius to imagine the next step.

It should be easy to pack the further miniaturized ballast and fluoresced bulb together into the shape and size of an incandescent light bulb. This advancement turned every incandescent light into an energy saving fixture. Failing to see it ahead of time showed incompetence of those who in charge of updating electrical codes. Were they penalized for their incompetence? No. Their incompetence gave their profession another chance to enrich themselves. I sure hope that they didn't make this mistake on purpose. Usually, in a free-market economy, when anyone cannot predict the future and makes a wrong business decision, the person pays a price for the mistake. The person may lose his shirt or worse. This is the trouble with code requirements. Code writers were never penalized for excessive requirements, also their profession is rewarded with extra profit. So, code writers have no incentive to slow down. Codes are updated regularly in the name of safety, health, energy conservation and quality of life. Who dares to argue against these virtues? All local officials routinely adopt all new codes. Almost nobody would challenge the necessity of these updates, nor would anyone question if the costs were justified. Because none of the decision-makers would bear any of costs, why should they care? So, housing price increases with little benefit to show for. I have done more than my fair share of electrical wiring and repair work in my life. One thing always puzzling to me was the requirement to secure electrical wires at least every 4 feet in the attic. The 4 feet appears to be arbitrary, why not 5 feet? I can think of a few reasons why it should not be secured, but I cannot think of any reason why it should. To go inside an attic is never routine, no one should go in without a good reason. One should always be careful inside an attic, otherwise, one can easily fall through the ceiling. Both the injury to the individual and the damage to the ceiling are serious. So why do we need to secure the wire if no one will mess with it? This code, like many others, is unnecessary. The main purpose is probably to intimidate: "If you don't know the rule, don't try to do it yourself."

Building Codes impose many minimum requirements; bedroom size, space around a toilet or a kitchen sink, etc. Why are they necessary? If we take a toilet from a first-class section of a jetliner and put it in a house in California, I bet it would NOT satisfy building code requirement. If it is good for travelers on a jetliner, most Californians can use it too. In London, Berlin, Tokyo or Hong Kong, one can find a 3-bedroom and 1 bath flat with total square footage around 500. I am sure not every bedroom on this flat satisfies US Building Codes. The US is exceptional, and the US is rich with an abundance of resources, including land. Most of us can afford to live in comfortable houses. But we should let the free market dictate housing demand. We should limit building Codes and other Codes to absolutely necessary requirements for safety and health only. We should not let codes push up housing prices unnecessarily.

I can list numerous examples of unnecessary code requirements, but let us just mention a couple Electrical Codes and Plumbing Codes. In the late 70s, electrical code changed circuit breaker size from 20 AMP to 30 AMP for a residential 30-gallon electrical water heater. Also, the wire size increased from 12 to 10 gage for the wiring to match the circuit breaker size. All residential units built in the 60s or early 70s had 12 gage electrical wires and 20-AMP circuit breakers for 30 gallons of water heaters. Over the decades, I managed over 60 units, apartments, condos and houses built before the new code was adopted with 30 gallons of electrical water heaters. Did I encounter any problems with any of the water heater? Yes! I replaced worn out heating elements, control units, drain valves, temperature/pressure relief valve and connectors. I replaced the whole water heater at least once for every unit I had managed, but none of them had a problem with the supposed undersize electrical wires or circuit breakers. So, the code update mentioned above appeared to be totally unnecessary. I believe one of the reasons for the code update was the rating of the heating elements, most of them are rated at 4500 Watts. The maximum Watts allowed for 20 Amp and 12 gage wire at 220 Volts was 4400 Watts (20x220=4400). Why the manufacturers produce 4500 Watts elements instead of 4400 Watts is beyond my understanding. The difference is less than five percents, it hardly matters. Perhaps the manufacturers just try to give the profession of electrician a chance to update the codes. As I pointed out before that sometimes code update serves no useful purpose except to intimidate outsiders to protect the profession. This is another example. Similarly, about 45 years ago Electrical Codes required GFCI (Ground-Fault Circuit Interrupter) breakers for receptacles in kitchen, bathroom, garage and for out doors. Probably the receptacles in these rooms and outdoors may encounter steam, vapor and water. I installed dozen of them in new constructions and replaced dozens of them in old housing units. I also managed dozens of old units without GFCI for decades. Not a single time in my life did I see a GFCI work as it is designed for.

I also like to mention a couple of unnecessary plumbing codes. Every water heater requires a T-P (Temperature-Pressure) valve on it. The justification is safety. Suppose the water inside a water heater is hot enough, but the temperature control unit on the water heater fails to turn off the heat source. A water heater always has the shape of a huge bomb. If the temperature inside the water heater keeps rising, the unit is virtually a bomb waiting to explode. It is certainly scary! The purpose of a T-P valve is to drain water from over-heated water heater; it is a life-saving safety device. But in my life, I have never seen or even heard a T-P valve working as it is designed for. Yet I have seen numerous times a T-P valve malfunctioned, draining water from a water heater that was not over-heated. Is it worth the pre-caution? Probably not. In my opinion, a water heater would never explode! The water heater is made of steel. The connectors from the water heater to the water pipes are made of a thin layer of copper. Copper is very soft metal compared to steel. Even if a water heater becomes over-heated, the copper connectors will leak long before any explosion.

About twenty years ago, I visited Lincoln's log cabin in Spencer, Indiana. Supposedly, Thomas Lincoln, President Lincoln's father and a skilled carpenter, could erect a cabin from scratch in four days. Abe was tall, he probably was a great helper. Even if the rumor exaggerated the speed, let us give them 10 times of 4 days. It was not bad to spend 40 days to build a dwelling. When Abe Lincoln grew up, he built his own log cabin. It was fortunate for him to build it almost 200 years ago. If he tried to do it now, no local government would allow him to do it in California, especially in San Francisco or in Silicon Valley. The cabin could not meet any code requirements. Yet it didn't seem to have inflicted any harm on him. He went on to be the greatest President of America. I am extremely happy for him that he didn't need to go before an architecture review commission for approval. His "card board box" would never have gotten approval from any of these commissions in most counties or cities in California.

In the past, there was little polarization among the poor and the rich in the US. Social and economic mobility allowed the poor to have a fair chance to join the middle class and to realize the American dream. The poor did envy the rich, but they did not resent the rich. The poor could work hard and had a fair chance to become rich themselves. Now, for a large part of the US population, the dream has turned into a nightmare. For those who have no prospect of shaking off the poverty, their envy becomes resentment. Their resentment may turn into hatred. This is a symptom for possible revolt or even revolution. So, the situation is not politically sustainable.

2.5 Lack of Checks and Balance at Local Level

We occasionally see reports about high housing costs or housing affordability problems on local news media. But don't hear a lot of in-depth analysis from them. Local media for sure understands the problems well and knows who are responsible. Local news media should be part of the checks and balance to curb any local politicians' abuse of power or any other unlawful or unethical conducts. The national new media reporters often confront the President of the US head on, serving the function of checks and balance well towards the most powerful person in the country. But we don't seem to see many local news media reporters confronting local officials similarly. Popular celebrity reporters have a lot of supporters, so they have the courage even to offend the President of the US. Local reporters are rarely powerful enough to offend any local officials. It takes a lot of courage for local new media to report or comment on local housing problems. But they know the limit, they dare not overstep the boundary. We hear stories about news anchors for major networks making multi-millions annually, but journalists at the local level often have trouble to make ends meet. If a city has chronic housing shortage, the high housing costs hurt journalists just the same. Except that journalists know the cause and the responsible parties; the rest of the public don't know the cause and have no idea whom to blame.

People in charge of local media, newspapers and TV don't want to offend local politicians. They are not only the most powerful people in town, but they are also big advertisers during election time. So, don't blame news reporters' failure to expose the housing problems and those who are responsible. All local newspapers around the country struggle to survive, because of dwindling circulation and advertisement revenues. It takes extreme courage to offend the biggest advertisers, local politicians, developers and realtors. Local TV stations' position may be better than the newspapers, but perhaps they are also struggling. There was a time that there were only 6 or 7 channels on TV. Now there are at least 10 times more channels.

When a low-wage worker in the US has trouble to make ends meet, it is local community's responsibility to help the person. If the person has a full-time job, the person is contributing to the community. Should the person be unable to afford housing near where the person works, the person has a right to demand reasonable accommodation. We must have compassion for our fellow countrymen, especially those who contribute to our welfare. To compel anyone to pay 1/3 to ½ of their earning for rent is worse than stealing or robbery. The situation is not morally sustainable.

Last but not the least, the housing problem in California is an environmental disaster. Yet we hardly hear any discussions about the environmental impact of the current housing policy in California. Even avowed environmentalists don't seem to know that there is an environmental problem with low-density housing developments. The environmental problem related to California's housing pattern will be discussed in details later. I just want to point out a simple fact as a preview. It is common in California, a person living in a house may be 2 miles from the nearest shopping center. If the person wants to buy anything, walking will take at least an hour. So most likely, the person will drive. Now suppose the housing density increases 10 times, then the distance between the person and the store shrinks to about one-half mile. As population density increases by 10 times, the distance between two points is reduced to one third of the original distance. As population density increases, foot traffic increases and the efficiency of public transportation increases, many parking lots can be eliminated or reduced. So, the distance between two points will reduced further to about one fourth of the original. It is well within easy walking distance. The person can walk a little for whatever is needed to buy. It is good for the person, and it is great for the environment. Instead of leaving a carbon footprint that adds to global warming, the person's heartbeat increases for a few minutes with no ill but beneficial effect to the person's health.

If we make a simple comparison between Hong Kong and California, we will see how ridiculous that California even has a housing problem. Hong Kong's population density is about 70 times higher than that of California's and land value is more than 70 times expensive than the land value in California. The population density of Kowloon, a peninsula and the most crowded part of Hong Kong, is 6 times higher than that of the City of San Francisco. If people in Hong Kong can manage to get by the housing problem, however hard may be, Californians should not have any problems at all!

Here is an actual example of how local bureaucrats and politicians manipulate land-use processes and regulations. In 1977, City of San

Luis Obispo adopted a new general plan on land use. Department of Community Development, a fancy name for Building Department, published a four-page document to inform developers how to comply with the change:

> "The San Luis Obispo City Council has adopted a new general plan that will change development potential on many properties. Effective immediately, proposed project will be evaluated by the City according to 1977 General Plan policies. For any project that varies significantly from plan policies — even though it conforms to current zoning and zoning standards — City law requires an environmental impact study. This can cause delay in construction and might suggest urgency zoning amendments to prevent projects which are inconsistent with the intent of the plan.
> ZONING ORDINANCE AMENDMENT ARE IN THE MILL
> ----------—
> Unless a building permit has been issued and construction has begun prior to the effective date of these amendments, a project that does not comply with all new standards will have to be revised.
> ————-
> Maximum density in these four zones, R-2, R-3, R-4 and R-H, will be reduced."

The new general plan meant two big headaches for developers: First, it was retroactive. If a developer submitted a set of plans for approval based on the existing zoning, the architect had to redesign the whole project, because there wasn't enough time to get a building permit and start the construction prior to the effective date of this amendment. In fact, the architect could not just redesign the structures. The rule said that even though it conformed to the current zoning and zoning standards — City law required an environmental impact study, this was new. The document stated that this could cause a delay in construction. Second, maximum density in all lots zoned for multifamily housing would be reduced. Every developer for every multifamily housing development always wanted to build the maximum number of units allowed.

ZONING LAND USE DENSITY

WHAT TO DO IN THE INTERIM

CITy of san luis obispo

DEPARTMENT OF COMMUNITY DEVELOPMENT
990 Palm Street • Post Office Box 321 • San Luis Obispo, CA 93406

What's it all about?

The San Luis Obispo City Council has adopted a new general plan that will change development potential on many properties.

Effective immediately, proposed projects will be evaluated by the City according to 1977 General Plan policies. For any project that varies significantly from plan policies -- even though it conforms to current zoning and zoning standards -- City law requires an environmental impact study. This can cause delay in construction and might suggest urgency zoning amendments to prevent projects which are inconsistent with the intent of the plan.

(The City's Environmental Review Committee is the body that determines -- subject to appeal -- whether a variation is "significant.")

ZONING ORDINANCE AMENDMENTS ARE IN THE MILL

Provisions of the 1977 General Plan will not be in full effect until zoning ordinance text, charts and maps are amended to implement the plan policies. The first step, already under way, is amending zoning ordinance text and charts. These amendments will redefine permitted land uses within individual zoning districts and change some development standards. They are expected to be effective by May 19, and possibly earlier.

Unless a building permit has been issued and construction has begun prior to the effective date of these amendments, a project that does not comply with all new standards will have to be revised.

Rezoning of individual parcels -- where necessary to comply with the 1977 General Plan land use map -- will come after text and chart amendments have been adopted. Rezoning is expected to begin in April and be completed in September. Any project not under construction by the effective date of new zoning will have to be revised if it does not comply.

The citywide rezoning program may cause some delays in processing
development applications. From April through August the Planning Commission
has reserved its second regular meeting of each month for rezoning hearings.
All other commission matters during that time must be handled at the first
meeting each month. Because the commission cannot handle its normal monthly
workload in one meeting, agendas will have to be limited. The commission
may not be able to get an item on its agenda as quickly as it normally does.

For these reasons, anyone planning to develop property is urged to
ensure that his project complies with the land use element map and
policies, with uses defined in proposed zoning ordinance amendments, and
with proposed zoning. By October 1, 1977, the City expects inconsistencies
between the new general plan and present zoning to be rectified.

CALCULATING RESIDENTIAL DENSITY

Proposed amendments include two particularly important changes for R-2,
R-3, R-4 and R-H zones, in accordance with general plan policies:

-- Maximum densities in these four zones will be reduced.

-- A new method of calculating density -- based on a two-bedroom
standard -- is to be applied.

Developers are advised to follow these new standards in designing
residential projects. The next page explains the new method of calculating
density and offers examples using the new maximums.

For additional information or
specific advice regarding a project
now in the preliminary review process,
please contact the planning division
representative of the Community
Development Department, City Hall,
990 Palm Street, San Luis Obispo,
or call 541-1000 to arrange an
appointment.

there's more...

It all adds up...

The 1977 General Plan and proposed zoning ordinance amendments set new maximum densities for R-2, R-3, R-4, and R-H zones:

R-2: 12units/acre   R-3: 18 units/acre   R-4 and R-H: 24 units/acre

The plan and revised zoning ordinance also establish a new method for calculating multifamily density: A two-bedroom dwelling is considered a "standard unit" and given a factor of 1.00. A dwelling with more than two bedrooms is calculated as more than one "unit"; a dwelling with fewer than two bedrooms is calculated as less than one "unit". These are the numerical factors to be used in making your calculations of density:

studio apartment	.50	3-bedroom dwelling	1.50
1-bedroom dwelling	.66	4- or more bedroom dwelling	2.00
2-bedroom dwelling	1.00		

TO FIND OUT WHAT YOU CAN BUILD:

(1) Divide the area of your lot by 43,560 sq. ft. (an acre).

(2) Multiply the result of step (1) by the maximum number of dwelling units allowed per acre.

(3) Choose any combination of unit types whose values add up to, or are less than, the result of step (2).

EXAMPLE: 6,000 sq. ft. lot in an R-2 district (maximum density: 12 units/acre)

(1) $\frac{6,000}{43,560} = .138$ acre
(Your 6,000 sq. ft. lot is the equivalent of .138 acre.)

(2) .138 X 12 = 1.66 units
(You can build 1.66 units on your lot.)

(3) To get your 1.66 units you could build any of the following combinations:

One 1-Bdrm + one studio
(.66   +   .50   = 1.16)

or One 2-Bdrm + one 1-bdrm
(1.00   +   .66   = 1.66)

or Three studios (3 X .50 = 1.50)

or One 2-bdrm + one studio
(1.00   +   .50   = 1.50)

and so on......

Figure 3: 1977 San Luis Obispo General Plan update.
(Please notice that "Maximum density in *these four zones, R-2, R-3, R-4 and R-H, will be reduced.*")

Now this number was uniformly reduced for all lots zoned for multi-family structures. Did anyone bother to explain why? Obviously, those who made the changes didn't think anyone dared to question the change, so they didn't bother to give a word of explanation or justification.

This new general plan for the City of San Luis Obispo was a significant change. It added more red tape on every housing development for apartments or condominiums. In the late 70s, it was high inflation time:

Inflation per year from 1977-1980

Year	Inflation
1977	6.30%
1978	9.00%
1979	13.30%
1980	12.50%

Every developer who turned in an application for a building permit based on the existing zoning had to reduce the number of units under the new rule. The owner of a project had to redesign from scratch. Any delay meant increase in budget. This increase inevitably translated into higher rents for renters and higher housing prices for buyers. If this inflation happened to any other life's necessities, consumers would protest loudly and hold government officials responsible. Suppose that Department of Transportation issued new regulations to slow down automobile productions and to restrict the maximum number of cars each factory may produce. Consumers expected higher car prices would demand an explanation from government officials to justify the regulations and restrictions. News media would report the details of the new regulation and editorial would criticize the red tapes and new restrictions, and Congress would hold hearings to investigate. But in the City of San Luis Obispo, the City Council adopted the new general plan without reaction from anyone. Public didn't pay any attention to this land-use regulation, and they might not understand the impact at all. Those who already owned their dwellings only worry about their monthly mortgage payments, they didn't care much about housing prices any more. If housing prices would go up a great deal, it would only benefit them. Their "investment" in their shelter would increase in value. Those who would rent or buy housing in the city in a few years from that time might not be around at all. A future student of the college in town might still be in a high school few hundred miles away.

How would landowners and developers react to the changes? Should they complain about the changes? They didn't like the changes, but they dared not to complain. I was one of them. I was penniless in June 1972. I taught summer school for the first time to earn extra pay. The extra pay allowed me to buy my first house in October 1972. I bought my second house a year later, and third house 2 more years later. The housing price in San Luis Obispo increased about 25% - 30% annually since I bought my first house. By 1976, I had a considerable amount of equity in my first two houses. I refinanced the mortgage on the two houses and took out some cash to invest in additional real estate. By then, everyone knew that housing was a good investment in the city. My limited amount of capital was no comparison to other investors'.

How could I compete against other investors? Since my wife didn't work, I asked her to study everything about housing; from maintenance of a rental unit to new housing construction and from refinancing a mortgage to construction loan for small apartments. In summer 1976, my wife and I added a room in the backyard of our first house. After the addition, we were confident enough to be a small developer. We bought a duplex of two two-bedroom and one-bath apartments; the lot was large enough to add a triplex on it. The seller told me that property came with a set of plans ready to be submitted to the city. I went to the city to check the zoning requirement; the plan for the triplex met the current zoning regulation. The deal was perfect for us. Except nobody told us about the new general plan. Not only I couldn't submit the plan to apply for a building permit, I could not even build a triplex. Should I complain? Perhaps, but I dared not. I attended a few public hearings on housing developments and noticed that no one dared to offend any of the city officials if the person had a project waiting for approval. Some applicants were big developers and long-time residents of the city. If these big players with good connections dared not to object, a little player like me with no connections at all better shut up.

I started my teaching career in Statistics at California State Polytechnic College in 1969. My office was in the Science Building (called Frank E. Pilling Building now) that was part of a new complex, including a division of the School of Architecture. During the first rainy season, (October 1969 to April 1970) the hallway of the brand-new building leaked like a small waterfall. My first impression of the School of Architecture was not spectacular. If the college had a School of Architecture, not just a Department of Architecture, at least the roof of its brand-new building ought not leak so badly! If I were a professor in the School of Architecture, how would I explain this leak to my students? Even if I were not overseeing the building inspection, but I would be a future occupant of the building and building design were my profession. When the construction was going on right under my nose, how could such a defect in the building escape my notice?

When a person starts a life in a new environment, the person always learns a few names. I learned the names of my colleagues in the department and the names of the top administrators of the School of Science and the College. At the time, the campus was not a university but a college. Next, the names of a few big shots in the local government. One of the names I learned was Mr. Kenneth Schwartz, the Mayor of San Luis Obispo and one of the four Directors in the School of Architecture. This was how I got some answers about the leaky roof of the building. It appeared that the faculty of the School of Architecture paid more attention to politics than to building designs. I began paying more attention to the city government and to the School of Architecture. Soon, I didn't like what the Mayor was doing. The City of Santa Barbara imported the Architectural Review Board from London in the 1920s. After a year or two it was suspended and it was revived about 20 years later. Mr. Schwartz copied it to the City of San Luis Obispo. He also promoted the idea to the whole State of California. At the time, the commissioners, especially the chairman, appeared to be power hungry. Every building project, except custom family housing, needed the Architectural Review Commission's or ARC's approval. Everyone who presented a building project to the commission was extremely humble. No one dared to talk back to the commissioners. Whatever the commissioners wanted, they always got it. Architects and project owners were always trying to understand what the commissioners wanted. Basically, the commissioners wanted beautiful buildings, but beauty is a matter of taste. You can never debate a matter of taste. So, Commissioners had the power to impose their tastes on the architects, landowners and developers. The job of the commission had nothing to do with the safety, health or the utility of the buildings. It was all about the attractiveness, elegance and charm of the buildings. We probably understand that an opera house, a gallery or a museum needs to be attractive, elegant and charming. For an apartment building, it would be nice if it was attractive, elegant and charming, but being affordable is probably more important than being pretty. Usually all these commissioners wanted to show off their excellent taste, they didn't want any cost to interfere with their sophistication. You didn't need to be a rocket scientist to know that building cost would explode. It shocked me to notice that, at the local level, there was little or no separation of power in government. In a true democracy, all government employees are public servants. But based on what I observed in the operation of ARC, the commissioners acted more like masters than servants, and landowners and developers were more like slaves than servants. A servant could be assertive if he is right. A landowner, a developer or an architect could not even have an honest discussion with any of the commissioners. These commissioners dominated the processes. Since landowners, developers and architects always tried to please the commissioners, instead of behaving like a public servant, commissioners acted like a bunch of spoiled kids. They would never take a 'No' for an answer.

The year 1977 was Mayor Kenneth Schwartz's 8th year as the Mayor in his ten-year rein. So, the new general plan had to be his idea. San Luis Obispo's housing prices increased about 10% a year during his first three years as Mayor. The rates of increase were high, but not much higher than annual inflation. He could also blame previous city council for the increases. But the next four years, San Luis Obispo's median price of a house had more than doubled. He could blame no one but himself for the increase. He didn't blame himself, and no one else seemed to blame him either. If the housing prices were out of control like a wildfire, what Mayor Schwartz did to the General Plan of the City of San Luis Obispo was adding gasoline to the fire. If anyone did similar things to any other life's necessities as Mayor Schwartz did to the housing prices, the person would have been castrated and ousted from the office. If food prices had doubled in four years, could those who were responsible get away free? Mayor Schwartz not only got away, anyone who didn't know about him would have believed him to be a saint from media reports.

His policy benefited all local architects, I knew the fact personally. The land that I bought in 1976 with a set of plans to add a triplex was also down-zoned from R3 to R2, I had to hire an architect to design a duplex from scratch. If it happened in Federal Government or any state governments, it would have been a scandal. But in San Luis Obispo, neither his policies, conflict of interest, nor the consequences of his policies, the sky-high housing prices, created a ripple or a whisper. I can imagine that during every gathering of architects in the City of San Luis Obispo in the last few decades when Mr. Schwartz attended, he had to be the most popular person and the center of attention.

In the middle of 1972, except the bare necessities for my family of four, I was practically penniless. In less than eight years, or before the end of the decade, I was a millionaire because of Mr. Schwartz's policies. I took advantage of his policies and invested in local real estate aggressively. I probably should thank him for making me rich. In fact, I did not care much about being rich or not. I just didn't want to work for minimum wage the rest of my life. When I became a college professor, I wanted a fair chance to realize my American Dream. I would hate anyone who blocked my way. It was amazing that I never heard a word to criticize Mr. Schwartz for his policies to push up housing cost, neither did I read a single report, editorial or letter to the editor in local new papers to hold him responsible for the high housing cost. The only exception was my letter to Editor on San Luis Obispo Telegram Tribune November 1, 2019:

"As a resident of San Luis Obispo for more than 50 years, I have never seen a single bad word published in The Tribune about Mr. Ken Schwartz. Now he has passed away, praise upon praise has been heaped on him. Would it be possible for a different opinion to be heard?

As a newcomer and an assistant professor in 1969, I soon learned that the friendly and distinguished looking gentleman was the mayor of San Luis Obispo as well as one of four directors of the School of Architecture.

Mr. Schwartz was a huge proponent of the Architectural Review Commission (ARC) in the City of San Luis Obispo and he promoted it to the whole state of California. The ARC oversees the appearance of new buildings.

When a city government made beauty an official business, it didn't take a rocket scientist to figure out what would happen to the housing costs in SLO.

It worried me to death: could I save fast enough before the housing prices in SLO rose 25% to 30% annually? I was lucky to be able to buy one of the last inexpensive track houses in 1972.

Ever since colonial times, every generation of Americans has been able to live a better life than their parents until now. Try to convince young Americans today that they will have a better life than their parents.

Singchou Wu, San Luis Obispo"

Why didn't the local news media discuss housing affordability? They didn't understand the problem, or they didn't care? Why didn't the local media do its duty of checks and balance when Mayor Schwartz's policies were self-serving and had a conflict of interest? When housing prices jumped far above inflation, all homeowners reaped a windfall. Almost all homeowners were voters, so Mayor Schwartz was very popular among voters. It was almost impossible for news media to criticize him. Homeowners were also TV viewers and newspaper subscribers; local news media just could not criticize a popular politician and offend most of their viewers or subscribers.

Now the damage of high housing costs is plainly visible just about everywhere in California and beyond. In 2020, we could even blame the high housing cost for the spreading of the Covid-19 virus in America. In Spring, 2020, many politicians hesitated to close public schools because a large portion of school children needed the free or discounted school lunches. Many workers hesitated to stay home because they needed a paycheck to pay rent and other necessities. Many small business owners hesitated to close their business, because they needed to stay in business to survive. Their hesitations contributed to the rapid spread of the virus. If housing cost didn't explode out of control in the last few decades, most people would have built up considerable savings for the rainy days. If the total lockdown was the proper policy to stop the spread of the Covid-19 Pandemic, nobody needed to hesitate to carry out the right policy. The policy makers' hesitations killed. But don't just blame the current policy makers, those who pushed up the housing costs sky-high should bear the responsibility.

In the late 60s, when President Lyndon B. Johnson declared his "War on Poverty" to build a "Great Society", his administration estimated that a poor family spent on the average one fifth of the income on food and about the same on housing. Half a century later, poor families in America spend only about one eighth of their income on food. Yet the housing costs just have exploded out of control. In many places, low-income workers cannot afford to live where they work. If local politicians didn't push up the housing costs, there was no reason a poor family couldn't reduce their housing budget from one fifth to one eighth of their income as their food budget did! If poor families spend only one eighth of their income for food and one eighth for housing, they could save at least 25% of their take home pay for the rainy days.

After 25% income for food and housing expenses and 25% for saving, poor families still have 50% of income for other expenses. If poor families spend 50% of income for housing, they have only 50% of income for food and all the other expenses. They end up with nothing for savings. So, the high housing cost is cause for most Americans' social and economic troubles; local politicians are solely responsible for the cause.

If a low-income family can save 25% of disposable income, then these families can put 3 months' paychecks as saving for every year on a job. After a few years, most workers should be able to realize their American Dream. This is what the land of opportunity used to be and should be now. During Covid-19 crisis, Federal Government budgeted more than a trillion dollars to help low and middle-income families to survive the crisis, because unemployment rate shot up and many low incomes and middle-class families couldn't make ends meet without their monthly paychecks. If housing costs didn't jump up in the last few decades, workers who have a steady job also have a sizable saving. Their savings and unemployment benefits should allow them to endure the crisis easily without Federal aids.

CHAPTER 3

Justifications for Low-Density Housing Developments

3.1 City of Irvine: A Case Study

We can look at the City of Irvine to get some idea about how housing supply and land use may be manipulated. Irvine is a unique city in California, but the tactics to drive up housing prices are quite typical. In the 50s, the Irvine family and company controlled a large tract of land in the southern part of Orange County. Orange County was a rural area with mostly olive and citrus orchards and farms at the time. After Disneyland was opened in the northern part of the county, the population of the neighboring area started to grow. In the '60's, the median house price in Orange County was not much higher than a typical house in any suburb in the US. How did I know and remember things like this? The friend who picked me up when I arrived in Port of Los Angeles helped me find the boarding housing to settle down. Both my friend and I worked for low wage. He saw a TV commercial about a land sale in Orange County and was interested in buying one lot. After he talked to a salesman, he found he was qualified to buy a lot with a few hundred dollars down-payment. He told me that, if he was qualified to buy, then, I should be too. I told him I was not interested; my priority was to go to graduate school. A few days later he told me, instead of just buying a lot, he was qualified to buy the land plus a house on it. Apparently, with a few hundred dollars saving and a minimum wage job, he was qualified to buy a new house. Why cannot anyone with a few thousand dollars saving and a minimum wage job buy a new house in California now?

The early urbanization of Orange County was around the amusement park Disneyland. But the southern part of Orange County was even better suited for growth. Construction of Interstate 405 had begun. Orange County Airport, later renamed to John Wayne Airport, was nearby. Ocean breeze kept temperatures cool in summer and mild in winter.

Many housing and commercial real estate developers noticed a great opportunity in the area. They all started looking for land. Since the Irvine family or Irvine Company was the largest landowner in the area, developers approached the Irvine Company to buy land in droves. It didn't take the Irvine Company very long to recognize the lucrative potential in real estate development. Why let others make money off their land, if they could make money themselves? Better yet, why couldn't they make sure there would be steady needs for developments? That was exactly what the Irvine Company did.

When the University of California identified the area for a new UC campus, the Irvine Company donated 1000 acres to the UC and granted them the right to purchase 500 acres more for UC Irvine. Legally, the Irvine Company sold 1000 acres to the State of California at 1/10 of a penny per acre, or $1 for 1000 acres. Meanwhile, the Irvine Company drew up a General Plan for the City of Irvine to accommodate a population of 50,000 around the campus. So, the Irvine Company developed the City of Irvine in a closely controlled fashion.

The way the Irvine Company carried out their plan was very clever. Orange County, like most places in California, has rather high housing prices now. But in the City of Irvine, the price is even higher than the neighboring areas, such as Laguna Woods and Laguna Hill to the south-east, and Fountain Valley and Westminster to the north-west.

It is not necessary for the Irvine Company to sell anything cheap in Irvine. Faculty, staff and students of UC Irvine all like to live near the campus and the Irvine Company has no competitors. Time is money. Those who don't want to commute far from the university need to pay a little more for housing and they are willing to do so. So, the Irvine Company always sets the price as high as they can get away with, but not so high that they force the buyer to go to neighboring towns. Here are the median prices in 2018:

Table 4: Median Housing Prices in Irvine and Surrounding Towns

City	Median House Price
City of Irvine	$919,000
Laguna Woods	$385,000
Laguna Hills	$450,000
Fountain Valley	$810,000
Westminster	$680,000

Laguna Woods appears to have rather low housing prices, because it is a retirement community with median age of 78 according to 2020 census data. Also, there are many mobile homes in the city.

The Irvine Company also tightly controlled the release of any new housing units, so that there was never an oversupply of housing units on the market. House prices usually always creep up in Irvine. Only during the financial crisis in 2008, the housing bubble burst and housing prices in Irvine dropped off like everywhere else in California. If a person bought a house in Irvine and held onto it for several years, the person could expect to make a good profit on the house.

So, the voters in Irvine don't want to change anything. They especially don't want the Irvine Company to flood the housing-market with many inexpensive units to drive down the housing prices. The Irvine Company can continue to control the city government and its general plan on land use. So, the housing situation in Irvine is about the same as everywhere else in California. Prices are going up and up. It is just impossible for minimum wage earners to even afford a room in Irvine.

The Irvine Company enjoys an advantage that no other developer may have. The Irvine Company controls the general plan of the City. It is not necessarily bad. For example, one cannot find any house in Irvine sitting on a three-acre lot. Some multi-million-dollar houses in Irvine have only 5000 square feet of land, others from 1/3 to ½ of an acre. Even in Silicon Valley which has one of the most severe housing shortages in the US, there are many large lots, three acres or larger. The Irvine Company drew up the General Plan even before the City existed. Buyers of single-family houses in Irvine not only pay more for the houses, they also get smaller lots. Usually a house buyer prefers a large lot to a smaller one. The advantage is obvious. A big lot means a big backyard. One can plant more trees, have a big garden and have a lot of space for children or pets to play. Also, large lots keep houses far apart. Thus, occupants have more privacy. But small lots have some advantages too. Small lots require very little maintenance and reduce the distance between a house and a school or a shopping center. Small lots allow public transportation to run efficiently. Most of all, small lots allow more houses to fit on a tract of land, so small lot may help to ease the problem of housing shortage in California.

Imagine your house is sitting on a lot about 50 feet by 80 feet, or 4000 square feet, about one tenth of an acre. Now imagine again, a friendly genie snaps his fingers and your lot suddenly increases about ten times to an acre. Is it a blessing or a curse? It depends on how you want to use the land. There are obvious benefits. You have more privacy, because your next-door neighbors are far away. If you have children and they like to play outdoors, now they have a big play ground at home. If the local government allows you to build 9 more houses on the lot, you may become an instant millionaire. Now imagine the opposite. You have no use for the big lot, so the big lot may be a curse. If you need to build a fence, then it is a big project and very costly. You need to spend a lot of time to take care of the big lot, or hire a gardener to do it for you. If you want to maintain a beautiful garden, the water bill will go up plus all the other costs-the investment on an acre of landscape can cost a fortune. Suppose all your neighbors get the same big lots, then it will be a drawback for all the residents in the area. Your children could walk to school in about 10 minutes before; now, it would be at least 3 times longer. Any other destination that used to be within walking distance is also 3 times longer. This is the reason why Irvine Company can get away with building many houses on small lots and sell at higher prices than in neighboring cities.

I bought a new house on a tiny lot for my younger son when he got a job in Newport Beach after he graduated from law school. I asked him if he would mind the tiny lot. He said why would he want a big lot. He had no children and no pets, so big lot would be nothing but trouble.

In recent years, lots and houses have all grown bigger in the US. It appears that the trend is not the buyers' choice but the result of local government policy.

3.2 Why are there so many single-family houses on large lots?

Usually, lot size is a compromise between the landowner and the local government. A landowner always likes to put as many housing units as possible on a parcel of land, because land value is about proportional to the number of units allowed on the parcel. Local government or the elected politicians usually don't want too many housing units on any particular parcel. Suppose we look at a small city that needs 100 new houses a year. If one landowner builds 300 houses on a large parcel, in three phases and completed in three years, the project will satisfy the local housing needs for three years. Most likely, no one else needs to build any more dwellings in the city at the same time. Thus, not many landowners or developers need to ask for favors from elected politicians. If they cannot handout favors, they cannot get many campaign donations. So, politicians don't like it. This may not even be fair to other landowners or developers in the city. Why let one landowner or developer enjoy a monopoly as the sole supplier to the city's housing needs three years in a row?

For the local politicians, it would be better to approve only 20 or 30 units for the parcel. This allows other landowners to have a chance to get into the housing business. It is good for the free-market economy to promote competition and lets buyers have choices. It also promotes another type of competition as landowners and developers vie to buy access to politicians. When there is plenty of competition, local politicians become more powerful and get more campaign donations. One of the results of this competition is a lot of single-family houses in California. Also, lot size for single-family houses gets bigger and housing prices soar. This is why, as California's population doubled in the last few decades, lot-size and living space of a typical single-family house didn't decrease but instead increased.

Severe housing shortages and soaring housing prices have slowed down California's economic and population growth. In recent years, there are more people moving out of California to other states than from other states to California. If it were not for natural births and more immigrants from abroad, California's population would decrease. Most emigrants moving out of California blame high housing costs as the major reason for leaving. But how did local politicians get away with building so many single-family houses on large lots? Politicians will never admit they are the ones responsible for housing shortage in California. They would especially deny creating a housing shortage to extract campaign contributions. Then, how do they justify the abundance of high-priced single-family houses and the lack of affordable dwellings?

Right after World War II, simple and inexpensive tract houses sprang up in suburbs around the country for returning GIs. Automobiles became widely affordable. Residents in suburbs had no trouble commuting to work in the cities. It was a pretty picture in the suburb. The houses were simple but with garages and neatly manicured lawns. Kids and pets played in the yards. Tract houses were very affordable everywhere in the country. Even nowadays, these houses are still affordable in most states. It just has a wrong name! It is not an environmental impact report, it is a LOCAL or NEIGHBORHOOD impact report. How can we minimize the local impact? Easy! No housing development at all! Then the impact would be zero! The trouble is, where would people live? So, let us build a few nice houses on twenty acres of land! Now the impact is negligible for the track. This is close to what we have in California!

In California, housing prices soared in the 70s. If local politicians need to find a reason to promote low-density housing developments, they will find one easily. They want residents to have "quality of life". Given a choice between a delightful house on a quiet street and a flat in a crowded complex, most people would choose the house. If they can justify building a bunch of houses rather than apartments or condominiums, then it is easy to justify the large lot-size for a single-family house. In their eyes, a house on a large lot is definitely better than a house on a small lot. Local politicians claim that they want families with children to have large yard, so kids have a big playground and pets have enough space to run around. They claim that they are also concerned about the environment. They want low environmental-impact from every housing development. Who could argue against that goal? Every big housing development needed to provide an environmental impact report including but not limited to: the impact on local traffic congestion, air quality, noise, water usage, sewage treatment, storm drains, school enrollment, etc. It sounds great! Any problems? Yes! Can everyone afford to live in a big house on a large yard? No! Many people cannot afford to live where they work. For example, not every homeowner can take good care of a large yard, so many homeowners need gardeners. Can gardeners afford to live in a house with a big yard? What is the environmental impact if all these gardeners live an hour away? Some politicians complain about the low Federal minimum wage. For example, San Francisco's minimum wage is about double the Federal minimum. If a person has a minimum wage job in San Francisco, can the person afford to live there? What is the purpose of the $15 minimum wage? Some politicians call it a 'living wage'! It is just a big laugh! You need two full-time living wage jobs just to pay for the rent for a one-bedroom apartment in San Francisco. How could politicians call that wage a living wage? If a supervisor in San Francisco truly wants to help a low-wage worker, just allow developers to provide real affordable housing. We don't need lip-service, posturing, rent control, or budget for affordable housing. I have my experience as proof.

When I came to the US in 1962, to me, America was the land of opportunity. I could save about 60% of my take-home pay. In the boarding house, my housemates included World War I veterans, retired grocery store clerks, restaurant workers, etc. Some retirees were on wheelchairs, but they lived there happily and comfortably. Some of them told me they could live independently on Social Security alone. In today's California, all residents in the boarding house would be homeless, because today's local politicians in California would not allow this boarding house to operate. At the time, LA had homeless people. Most of them were drug addicts and winos. They lived on skid row and some of them took advantage of mid-night missions. But there was no such term as 'working poor'. If one had a job, one couldn't be poor. I never felt I was poor, even though I earned less than minimum wage. There was no such term as 'affordable housing', most housing should be affordable. Just like today, we don't hear 'affordable food'.

There is abundant food, most food is affordable. Now we have a housing crisis, there is not enough affordable housing. Can rent control, state wide or local, solve the problem? I think no one is ignorant enough to answer 'Yes!' Can billions of dollars in the state budget for housing assistant and affordable housing solve the problem? If the state can budget trillions of dollars instead of just billions, it may be enough. In the last 50 years, local politicians in California got rid of affordable housing. American exceptionalism allows only decent, comfortable and pretty housing, American exceptionalism cannot allow cheap housing like boarding house. Does this exceptionalism make every city like Beverly Hills? Does San Francisco look like Beverly Hills? Maybe, if they can get rid of all the homeless camps and clean up all the human feces on the streets!

If I arrive in the US and land in San Francisco today, what could I do to move up? If I started a job paying below minimum wage, how could I afford to rent a room in San Francisco? If I couldn't afford a room, I would live in homeless camps the rest of my life. In fact, the homeless never call themselves homeless. Your home may be a palace, my home may be a cardboard box. But it is still a home to me. Those who live on the street call themselves 'street people.' It is wrong for local politicians to push anyone with a full-time job to live on the street with or without voters' approval. Therefore, every democracy has a constitution, so politicians with voters' support still cannot do everything they like.

Now let us suppose that there is a parcel of ten acres of land. It is appropriate and big enough to build a complex of 200 units of condominiums. Even though the county or the city is badly in need of more housing units, this project has no chance of getting approved in most places in California.

Because of the large number of units, a lot of cars will be in and out of this complex daily causing traffic jams in the adjacent streets. Because of the large number of occupants in the complex, noise will ruin the quiet neighborhood. A large group of the residents will use numerous cars, truck, gas appliances, etc. Thus, exhaustive gas and fumes will harm the air quality at the location. The increased area of roofing in the complex, parking areas, sidewalks and patios will result in excessive water run-off during heavy storms, overwhelming the drainage system. Large numbers of residents will use large quantity of water, so water pressure will drop and sewer mains may overflow. Any one of these excuses is enough reason to stop the project.

OK! Let's come up with a compromise. Maybe it is acceptable to the local government to build ten houses, each on a one-acre lot. Or perhaps it is acceptable to build thirty houses, each on a third of an acre lot. The result of the compromise depends on the relation between the developer and local politicians. The politicians can vote any way they like and they can always justify their votes. Yet the way they vote can make big differences in the millions of dollars that would go to the landowners and developers. Landowners and developers don't have to be geniuses to figure out how to please local politicians, and the politicians don't have to be geniuses to figure out how to get the most campaign contributions legally. For a small county or city, their land-use decisions may be the only way to get major campaign contributions.

All levels of government in the US have well established-operational procedures based on rules of law. In other countries, democracies or not, corrupted government officials can get rich fast. But it is unheard of in the US for government officials to get rich on the jobs. Being honest and upstanding are virtues we admire for everyone, especially for government officials. We all want clean and efficient governments. But even the best medicine may have a little toxic side effect. Most local governments are so clean that there is little room for any misconduct or corruption. It is great! But there are also some side effects. For local elected officials, campaigns cost money and are getting more and more expensive. In a national election, a candidate's position on various issues will always generate contributions. But local elections involve only local issues which most voters pay little attention to. Local candidates have no chance of getting many contributions from the public. Candidates cannot rely only on friends and relatives for contributions. In small cities and rural counties, the only reliable source of campaign contributions is from landowners and real estate developers. What is the toxic side effect of this situation? Soaring housing prices are common in California, even in rural areas where there should not be housing shortages at all!

As it is true in any functional democracy, every problem will be solved sooner or later by the wish of the people. If a problem is serious, voters will demand change. If politicians don't act according to the wishes of a majority of voters, voters will vote them out. California's housing shortage has been serious for years. Why is there no solution in sight?

To justify slow growth policies, local politicians often use "preventing urban sprawl" and "preserving small town characteristics" as their goals. Who wants traffic congestion and smog like Los Angeles? To anyone who wants more housing, they ask "Why don't you just move to LA?" Many new-comers complained about high housing costs. But as soon as they bought their houses, they no longer wanted housing prices to come down any more. They would like the housing prices to stay high or even go higher, so that their purchases would be good "investments."

When local politicians push for low-density housing developments, they are not doing it against voters' wish. In fact, most of the homeowners support local "slow growth" policy. In the name of promoting quality of lives, preserving small town characteristics etc., they trick most voters to believe tight housing supply and slow growth are good for everyone. Soaring housing prices may be bad for the economy of the state and terrible for all the newcomers. But it is not necessarily bad for most homeowners in the state. In fact, when housing price goes up, a homeowner's equity in the house increases. For many homeowners, the equity on their houses may be the most important part of the family savings. Many Californians sold their houses after retirement, move to other states with low housing prices. After they bought houses that were better than the ones sold, they still ended up with a lot of cash on hand. Many reports show that Texas got the largest share of emigrants from California in recent years, about one third of emigrants left California for Texas!

As local politicians push for slow growth, at first, nobody would pay much attention to it. But a policy of slow growth always leads to higher housing prices. As soon as housing prices increase above inflation rate, local homeowners reap a windfall. Most homeowners are voters. Once they get a taste of the windfall, they want more. As the politicians continue to push for slow growth, they usually get voters' support, so they are on solid political ground. No one can do anything to them. We must give local politicians in California some credit. They have pushed housing prices in the state to unreasonably high levels, yet they can still resist the pressure to change. Realtor Coldwell Banker reported in 2018 based on its nation-wide listings, that the eleven most expensive housing markets were all in California.

We have all heard about a few high-tech giants that had a humble beginning out of garages in Silicon Valley. Now, this is no longer possible. First, most young entrepreneurs cannot even afford a garage in Silicon Valley. Besides, code enforcement officers in California's local governments make sure that no one lives or works in garages anymore. Once a Code Enforcement Officer in the City of San Luis Obispo told me that legally a garage is for automobiles only, and it was illegal even for storage. I told him I sure liked to see how he would enforce the code. If we may not use a garage for storage, don't even try to start a company in a garage. What were the excuses for government interference? Government had "good intention for the occupants' health and safety." A garage is not a living space. Many of California's local politicians make sure we spend big money on housing, they make sure we don't find any ways to get around it. As if a resident in California saved a buck on housing, there would be a buck less going directly to their pockets. I had first-hand experience sleeping in a garage. In 1962, a kind coworker understood that I was doing manual work to save money to go to graduate school, he offered to let me live in his detached old garage for free. I took the chance to save about a hundred dollars in a few months' time. A hundred dollars is not a sizeable amount now, but it made a big difference for me. I didn't know it was illegal to live in a garage.

I can honestly testify that neither the substandard boarding house nor the illegal living quarter in the garage harmed me a bit. I am glad LA didn't have code enforcement officers wandering around to evict me from my living quarter! I suppose they would tell me it was for my own protection from unhealthy and unsafe conditions. Thanks a lot! Where was I supposed to live? In a tent at a homeless camp! Would I be better off in a tent? I don't think so. I am literally a living proof. Choosing between my life and living in tent for my whole life, I choose my life every time. I am in my middle 80s now and I don't have any conditions that may threaten my life. I lead an active daily routine and often don't feel I have enough hours during the day to do things I want to do. When I was about to retire from my teaching job, my colleagues gave me a small farewell party. At the gathering, I told my colleagues that: "We are all statisticians and we know what statistics say about retirement. Most people don't live very long after they retire. There are two possibilities; one, retirement is hazardous to one's life, two, most people work too long. They work until they are about to die. So I choose to retire a little early and let us see how long I can live." My colleagues had a big laugh, and that was more than twenty years ago. In the US, men live an average 8 years after retirement and women average 12.

A friend told me his son bought a three-bedroom and one-bathroom house in Silicon Valley years ago and paid more than a million dollars. The house is at a great location, but has a drawback. To go to the bathroom, the occupants in one bedroom must go through another bedroom. It should not be a problem at all, the common sense solution would add a bathroom or a passageway. But none was possible, because the house was a historical monument. The city would not allow addition or modification to the house. I wonder if they built the house with gas lights inside, would the city allow electrical lights to replace the gas lights? I visited the house where Mozart was born in Salzburg, Austria. It is a big tourist attraction. Every day thousands of music lovers visit the city to see the Mozart House. But in Silicon Valley, my friend could not even tell me the reason his son's house was a historical monument. We probably don't want to tear the house down, but why do we mind letting the present occupants adding a bathroom? If we turn a house into a museum, that is fine to preserve the interior as it was. If the local government doesn't want to put up the money to preserve the house as a museum, then government has no right to dictate how the current owner wants to live.

But local politicians' control over housing seems to be limitless. They started with city or regional planning that controls the general direction of the local land-use and housing developments. The next tool of control is zoning, which controls specific numbers of units or dwellings that may be constructed on each plot of land for housing developments. Before any buildings may start developers need to get building permits. For a common one-family house, the process usually takes about a year. This is the simplest process, because local politicians like single-family houses. For a big project, it may take several years even decades. They don't like large development. The bigger the housing development, the more red tape. The reason for this is simple and straightforward, because they like to have a lot of small developers instead of a few large developers. The more developers, the more campaign contributions for local politicians.

The exceptionally high housing costs in a region of plenty of open space and endless rows of single-family houses on spacious lots are self-evident that all these so-called general plans have failed miserably. It is equivalent to a country that has overflowing food in storage and lets some of its people starve to death.

3.3 My Fight Against ARC

Mr. Kenneth Schwartz was the mayor of San Luis Obispo from 1969 to 1979. The median housing price in San Luis Obispo increased from about $20,000 to $95,000. He not only installed the Architectural Review Commission in the City of San Luis Obispo, he also promoted it to the whole state of California. He preached in the School of Architecture what he practiced in the City of San Luis Obispo.

I saw an enormous problem! Mr. Schwartz was an architect, yet he used his political power to promote his profession. There was a conflict of interest! If it happened at federal or state level, there would be an outcry and a backlash. But at the local level there was no criticism of any kind. Newspapers were full of letters and commentaries praising Mr. Schwartz's accomplishments from his proteges, students, colleagues, or citizens who reaped a windfall from rising housing prices. Undoubtedly, some of his admirers might truly appreciate his policy that resulted in a beautiful downtown, but unfortunately, they didn't know what price they had to pay for Mr. Schwartz's other policies.

Attending a couple of Architectural Review Commission meetings, one can quickly understand what the Commissioners don't want. They don't want houses that are look-alike on the same street, they call these houses cookie-cutter houses. They don't want a simple rectangular building anywhere either. They have a term for that too, they call them card-board boxes. In other words, they want the buildings to be as complicated as possible. Unfortunately, all building materials are designed for rectangular buildings and rooms. All plywood sheets and gypsum boards are rectangular. Roof panels, tiles and shingles are all rectangular. Standard vanity tops and cabinets are mostly rectangular. So are most bathtubs. We spend about one-third of our life in beds that are almost always rectangular.

In fact, the most economical way to build a house or a room is a simple rectangular shape. The most efficient way to top it off with is a gabled and centered rectangular roof. So here is a bureaucratic red tape that serves almost no useful purpose except jacking-up construction costs and give city governments more power to regulate the housing industry.

I remember visiting a few resorts in the Swiss Alps. It surprised me to see a lot of identical and simple rectangular cottages that I had not seen in the US, especially in California, for a very long time. In fact, the average income was higher in Switzerland than in the US. The minimum hourly wage was also higher in Switzerland.

Perhaps the Architectural Review Commissioners may not want to live in a cardboard-box like cottage, but why not let a minimum-wage earner live in one? In California, almost all of the cities and the counties have some regulation about architectural design, because this kind of regulation is contagious. If one city or county started it, other cities and counties would follow immediately.

Figure 4: A granny unit built in 1960s before ARC in San Luis Obispo

Figure 5: Apartment moved here in 1960s
before ARC in San Luis Obispo

Figure 6: Built in the 90s after ARC in San Luis Obispo

Figure 7: Built in 90s after ARC in San Luis Obispo
Note: The last four photos show structures
with in 50 feet of one another.

Figure 8: Fancy rest area's restroom in California, 2019

Figure 9: Rest Area in Oregon, 2019

Figure 10: Swiss Alps, 2005

Figure 11: A simple and magnificent building in Switzerland

In 2005, I took the last two photos in Switzerland. Not only I saw many simple cottages that you would not find in California, but I also saw many large simple structures which were beautiful, practical and efficient. By every standard, Swiss are richer than Californians, but they don't live beyond their means!

Most citizens really pay little attention to the appearance of new buildings. But, of course, they don't mind all new buildings looking great as long as they don't have to pay for them. At ARC hearings, I also noticed that developers and architects dared not offend any commissioners. Commissioners usually competed to show off their great taste. Beauty is in the eye of the beholder. When a city government made beauty an official business, we could expect what would happen to the housing costs in SLO.

It worried me to death: could I save fast enough before the housing prices in SLO rose 25% to 30% annually? I was lucky to be able to buy one of the last inexpensive new track houses in 1972 at $23,000, 1.5 times my assistant professor's gross annual salary. I made about $8000 improvements plus $2000 for down payment and sold the house in 1978 for $80,000. Of course, those were the high inflation years; the cumulative inflation from 1972 to 1978 was only about 65%, it was a lot. But my profit from the house was $49,000 in six years for an investment of $10,000-or about 390%, or 325% more than inflation. Actually, the rate of return was much better than what is shown here. I didn't put down $10,000 in 1972. My original investment was only $2000, the rest of the investment of $8000 was spent in 1977 for the room addition and in 1978 for preparing the house for sale.

If food price increased 100% faster than inflation in 6 years, there would be thundering outrages. Yet housing, like food is a necessity for survival. During the time, there was no protests of any kind. Housing was a local issue, so there was no congressional investigation and nobody would blame federal government or state government for outrageous price increases. Most voters in the city were homeowners. When housing prices increase 325% in 6 years, would they protest? They would not, they reaped a huge windfall. Their mortgage payment may increase a little to pay for higher property tax, but it was a small price to pay for the huge profit on the house. So, Mr. Schwartz was re-elected again and again until term limit prevented him from serving. Did anyone in the local media investigate the high housing costs? Mr. Schwartz and city council members obviously had majority of the voters' support. Local media could not offend the popular politicians and the majority of its readers and audience.

There is a simple rule: "Power corrupts, absolute power corrupts absolutely!" All levels of government need checks and balance. Good and aesthetic taste in housing development is none of any government's business. How could some local politicians think it is their job to appoint a few well-to-do residents to dictate the looks of the new buildings better than the architects and owners can? Who gets appointed to ARC? It is difficult to answer. But at least we know who will not get the job. For example, a city will not appoint a person earning only minimum-wage. A person working for a minimum-wage cannot make any good decision for others. If the person is smart, how does the person end up working for a minimum wage? The person will be more concerned about making ends meet than anything else. Definitely the person has no time to impose his or her taste on anyone else. People earning a minimum or low wage are the ones in need of affordable housing. Too bad they will never have a voice in local land-use decision. Architects, landowners and developers dare not to offend the commissioners. They are all trying to please the commissioners. If an architect offended any bureaucrats and word got out, who would hire the architect for any future project? If a developer or landowner offended any bureaucrats, the person could count on project delay and cost overrun. Who may attend a public hearing of ARC other than architects, landowners and developers of building projects? Normally, public doesn't attend this kind of hearing. The architects, landowners and developers may invite their local friends to speak for them at the hearings. But they always warned their friends not to offend any commissioners. Usually, ARC commissioners are just getting bolder and bolder. They serve no useful purpose except pushing up building cost, delaying building projects, creating job opportunity for architects and giving more power to the local politicians.

Figure 12: A typical house in Narvik, Norway, February 2020

The ARC in the City of San Luis Obispo is a typical example of local government out of control. There is no checks and balance on the authority of the Commission. Nobody dared to offend any of the commissioners, so they have absolute power. After I attended a few public hearings of the commission, I figured that the housing price in San Luis Obispo would rocket up. Mayor Kenneth Schwartz was also one of 4 directors in the School of Architecture at California State Polytechnic College or Cal Poly in short. What he practiced in the City government; he taught his students in the School of Architecture. Cal Poly had a well-known motto: "Learning by doing!" Mayor and Director Schwartz practiced "learning by doing" to perfection. The School of Architecture has an important major–City and Regional Planning. It is like a training camp for future bureaucrats in Planning Departments. Cal Poly graduates have a renowned reputation to be very capable to put in outstanding work from day one. Cal Poly's City and Regional Planning graduates can find jobs in local governments easily. Not just because their ability makes them welcome additions to many planning departments in California, but also because the bosses of those departments are often Cal Poly alumni. It didn't take a genius to figure it out. Any red tape on housing developments started by Mr. Schwartz in San Luis Obispo would quickly spread to the rest of the state and beyond. So, I predicted that housing price would soon rise in America because of rising crude oil price and inflation. But California's housing price would rise much faster than anywhere else in the US. Thanks to the examples set by Mayor and Director Schwartz, his disciples spread his teaching to the entire state.

My bachelor's degree was in economics and my Ph.D. was in statistics. There is a discipline in economics called econometrics that applies some statistical methods on economic forecast. It was part of my interest. As an immigrant, I always thought about how to realize my American Dream. So, I paid attention to the local housing prices. When I had spare time, I often went to the library. I tried to get as much information as I could about business forecast and housing prices in California in particular. American Petroleum Institution, a trade organization of oil and gas producers in the US, published a report about oil production and the likely impending shortage. It also discussed the military tension between the Arabic counties and Israel might turn OPEC, Organization of Petroleum Export Countries, against the US. Housing construction relied heavily on lumber, asphalt and cement. The productions of these materials were energy intensive, or a by-product of oil refinery. The report predicted that the crude oil price would rise, and so would inflation. I expected housing price would rise above inflation in the US and above inflation a great deal more in San Luis Obispo and California. I made the prediction because I had a front-row seat to observe Mayor Schwartz's housing policy in action and his teaching position to promote his policy to the state.

His ARC definitely made San Luis Obispo a very pretty place. The City was often named as one of the best little cities in America. However, there is a price for every thing. The price in this case is high housing cost! For example, in 2018, "realtor.com" listed San Luis Obispo as the most expensive retirement town. The expensiveness is defined as the ratio of median house price over median income. The retirement town is defined as having a minimum 20% of the population at least 65 years old. San Luis Obispo had 25% population over age 65. Who pays for the high housing cost? New comers and renters. I was both in 1969. I was a newcomer, and I rented a two-bedroom apartment for my family of four. I didn't like Mr. Schwartz at all. I knew what he was doing to me; he did nothing but push up housing cost. I didn't care if I lived in the best little city in US, the best retirement town or the city with the charming Mission Plaza. For most voters in town, they already owned their houses. Why should they mind rising house price? To make the city more beautiful, charming, livable and more expensive suited them just fine, as long as they did NOT pay for any of these. Not only they didn't mind rising house price, they profited from it. Rising house value made their "investments" in their houses appreciating in value. So, I was a minority in every sense of the word. I was an ethnic minority. I was a minority in the term of public opinion on the city's housing policy. Mr. Schwartz was very popular with voters and with the faculty and students in School of Architecture. There was another point, politicians and voters didn't talk about. That was, high housing cost kept poor ethnic minorities out of the city and, some minorities are perceived to be more likely to commit crimes. So, the high housing cost might make the city safer.

At my job, I heard my colleagues talking about the rising values of their houses, $1500 or more a year. Since they had to live in the house, the increase in value didn't do them much good. Some of them even complained about the increase, because they had to pay higher property tax as their house value appreciated. That was the time before California had Proposition 13 that limited property tax to

1% of the value of the property in 1978. The Proposition also limited the annual increase in property tax to 2% from the base value in year 1978. The base value of a property changed to the fair market value of the property, if the property changed ownership after 1978. When my friends talked about their houses, I kept my mouth shut, but I said to myself: "Why didn't they buy more houses?" They could have made some real big money. I told some of my friends and relatives that the 10% annual increase in housing value in the early 70s was mild comparing to what would come. Since I didn't even have a house, none of them listened to me. They probably were thinking: "If you are so smart, why are you so dirty poor?" Some politicians blame Proposition 13 for high housing prices in California. Proposition 13 limits property tax revenue local governments may collect, so local governments try to push up the price of new housing developments to get more tax revenue. Proposition 13 creates a strange phenomenon in California. For two identical houses sitting side-by-side, one owner may pay three or four times more property tax than the other. It is unfair, but it cannot be responsible for high housing cost. California's housing price jumped up years before Proposition 13 was even on the ballot.

Luckily for me, by September 1972 I bought my first house. It was the very last batch of inexpensive tract houses the city allowed. It was a brand-new house for about $23000, affordable by any standard. It had 4 bedrooms, two bathrooms, double-garage, 1200 square foot living space on a 6000 square foot lot. My assistant professor gross annual salary was about $16,000. It was still affordable even though the City's housing price had gone up about 10% a year for 2–3 years in a row. The loan officer at the local bank gave me a hard time. I applied for a 30-year mortgage before the summer. The loan officer asked me how long I had been on the job. I answered that by the end of the school year, or about the end of June 1972, it would be 3 school years. He asked me did I have any saving for the 10% down payment. I answered: "No!" He asked me if I had any investments. I answered: "No!" Then he asked how could he be sure I would come up with a couple thousand dollars to close the deal. I told him I would save my summer's extra pay for the down payment. He said that for almost three years I couldn't save anything, then how could I save more than $2000 in one summer. I had to explain to him how I paid off $3000 loan in less than 3 years. Also, I explained to him that the College allowed professors to teach summer school once every 3 years and the next summer was my first chance to teach for extra pay. Finally, he reluctantly approved my application.

I bought my house at the nick of time. Right after I bought it, the increase in housing price in town was no longer 10% or 15% any more. It was more like 25% to 30% a year. My first house was a cheap one in the development. I didn't pay $500 for a fireplace, but I paid $900 for wall to wall carpet and $100 for a garbage disposal. The next year, I bought my second house just across street from my first house. It was even worse than my first one. It was in the same development. The original owner of my second house paid only $22000, $1000 less than I paid. My second house didn't have fireplace, and neither had garbage disposal nor carpet. But I paid the original owner $31,000 for the house, or $9000 more than the original price a year ago. Almost everyone who knew about my purchase thought I overpaid for it. But I was certain that the enormous increase in price was no aberration. It would continue for years.

I also believed the developer of the track houses made a big mistake by pre-selling these houses before they were completed. During this high inflation time, the pre-sale price was too low without accounting for the inflation during the construction. Being a statistician and an economist, I luckily figured out what most businessmen overlooked. No surprise to me, in the next few years, price increased 25% to 30% again and again. This kind of increase was exactly what I worried about before I bought my first house. I knew what the Mayor Schwartz did would push up the housing value in town. I just didn't know if I could buy my first one before the price jumped 20% or 30% a year. I bought my 3rd house in 1974. It was much worse than my first two houses, but I paid $36,000 for it.

After I bought my three houses, my financial welfare made a big turn to the better. After three to four years over 20% price increases, I had solid equity in my houses. I started to refinance my mortgage loans or take out second mortgages whenever I could. Banks were quite willing to make loans to me. Being an ethnic minority definitely helped me. At the time, banks were required to make an effort to make loans to ethnic minorities. They particularly liked my applications for loans. I had a steady job with considerable equity in real estate. I was a perfect candidate for loans. I put all the cash I got from refinancing and second mortgage back to real estate, so my real estate portfolio grew rapidly.

After I bought my first house, like most homeowners in town, I probably should thank Mayor Schwartz for pushing housing prices sky high. By observing and studying what he did as a mayor and a director of the School of Architecture in the College allowed me to predict the housing trend in the City and in the State of California. Even though I benefited from the trend, I didn't change my opinion about what he did to the city and to the state. I never forget the time I worked for less than minimum wage when I first arrived in the US. I needed an inexpensive room to live, so I could save and go to graduate school. If I were to start my life in US now, I would have to spend more than one half of my income for a room and would never have saved anything to go to graduate school. Neither could I forget the time I was an assistant professor with a family of four. My family and I never went to any restaurants in three years. Except a pair of new laundry machines for my two children's diapers, the most expensive furniture I had was $5. Yet I could only save about $1000 a year, while the prices of the least expensive houses in the city were rising more than $1500 a year. I can never forget the dread and anxiety I had, worrying whether I could ever buy a house before the prices really took off. When I see young people struggling to pay rent and young professionals struggling to buy house, I just feel lucky it is not me. I sympathize with them, and I could never forgive those who were responsible for the high housing costs. I could have been one of these unfortunate people if I did not come to US over one-half century ago.

Nothing is worse than destroying young people's upward mobility. When I came to this country, I had no special talent, knowledge, skill or ability. All I had was a willingness to work hard and it was enough for me to move into middle class and to realize my American dream. But unfortunately, it is not enough nowadays if the rent of a room costs one half of a full-time worker's pay check. How can we expect anyone to work and live like this his or her whole life?

Many think the housing crisis in California is the failure of free market or capitalism. It is definitely a failure for the State. California is a big state, there are open spaces just about everywhere. If there is not enough affordable housing to go around, we need to blame someone. America is a free market economy; it should keep housing supply and demand in balance. Now, if house supply and demand is out of balance, shouldn't we try socialism? If we do, then we couldn't be more wrong.

First of all, the housing crisis in California is not the result of a free market system. The housing crisis in California did not just happen, it took a lot of meddling and arbitrary restrictions to make it happen. It is not the failure of capitalism, but the lack of it. The housing market is not functional because local politicians choke it to death.

For Capitalism to work in a housing market, consumers must be allowed to choose. If local politicians and bureaucrats go as far as invading bedrooms to enforce zoning laws, such as the rule that prohibits two people from sharing a bedroom or the rule requiring one bathroom for every 3 occupants, how could we expect Capitalism to work in housing market?

In June of 1972, my net worth was a big zero. By the end of the year, I bought my first house and realized my American Dream. The next year, I bought my second house and put it for rent. My wife and I became landlords for the first time. My wife could never find a job in town. She went into the housing business full time. In 1978, we built a duplex of two three-bedroom townhouses. In 1979, we built a 4-unit townhouse and my wife got her California State General Building Contractor's License. In 1981 we completed a small condominium complex. The year 1981 was the year that annual consumer price index increase went over 10% and prime interest rate was 20.5%. This interest rate was the rate banks charged their best cooperation customers. An average consumer had to pay a much higher rate to borrow from banks. Almost all constructions in town, housing or commercial, ground to a halt. I had money to build because I sold two houses. At the time my wife and I owned about 50 units of rental housing and my wife managed about 80 units. My condominium was one of the few new constructions in town. Before the Final Inspection the Building Inspector noticed a couple of deviations from the approved plan. The Building Department sent a team to fine comb through the building carefully, the team came up with a dozen more violations in the project. If the Building Department just stuck to the two deviations, I would be in big trouble. Their nit picking backfired and thus helped me. When I appeared before the Architectural Review Commission, I didn't expect any sympathy. Seven Commissioners voted 0-7 against me. This was the chance I waited for since the first time I went to an Architectural Review Commission Hearing about ten years ago. I suspected that I was the first person who dared to appeal a 0-7 decision by the

Commission. Their nit picking exposed the excessive intrusion of local government. I told the Commissioners that even though the project is a condominium, I would keep them as rentals. When the meeting ended, I overheard one commissioner asking others that: 'Who are we protecting, he is the owner, builder, contractor, lender and landlord." I called commissioners' impositions on architects, landowners and developers to be power hungry. Apparently, they usually justified their demands with excuses. In my case, they couldn't find one. This was exactly what I wanted to tell them: 'You are not protecting anyone; you are just power hungry!'

I appealed their 0-7 decision to City Council of San Luis Obispo. I had no trouble to explain or defend against those nit pickings. Based on audience's reactions, they appeared sympathetic to me. For the two serious violations, I put up a strong fight.

The first violation was that I painted the building instead of staining the shiplap exterior to show the wood grain. I explained that I was a small builder and didn't have a big volume in business. Local lumber suppliers usually shipped the leftover material to me and saved the best material for the large volume buyers. If I kept returning shipments to suppliers, I might become an outcast to the suppliers and might not be able to buy anything from them. So, I just did the best I could to patch up all the defects. If I stained the wooden exterior, all the patches would show through, so the best way to finish it was paint. I also told the City Council that my wife always insisted on how to finish the exterior and I never dared to disagree. The audience burst into a big laugh. I invited several friends to the hearing to support me, my friends probably were the ones who laughed the loudest.

The second offence was more serious, I cut down a big tree without a permit. My architect didn't measure the location of the tree correctly. Instead of 2 feet outside, the tree was 2 feet inside the building. The excavator digging the foundation noticed the problem. He gave me 24 hours to have the tree removed. I hired tree service to cut down the tree and removed the root. One member of the City Council said that I should apply for a permit to remove the tree and to sue my architect for the loss due to any delay. I said I didn't want to sue anyone for an unintentional mistake. I said I paid the City to check the building plan. Apparently, the plan-checker didn't catch the mistake either. If I wanted to sue anyone, I probably should sue the city. Of course, this accusation was far-fetched. Yet nobody came up with a creditable rebuttal, so I got away. City Council voted 3-2 to reverse the ARC decision. Before the vote, the Chairman of the Architectural Review Commission pleaded to City Council to send the case back to the Commission for a settlement. I pleaded that if the City Council sent the case back to ARC, they were sending a lamb into tigers' den! The proceeding was live broadcasted on radio and the major local newspaper published the news on page 2 the next day. It surprised many listeners and readers that the city even dictated the color of a building. The shocking part of the news was the comparison of a branch of democratic government to a wild beast. The worst part was the comparison had a trace of truth in it. If the Building Department didn't nit-pick to come up with a dozen violations, my comparison might be groundless. Now public attention was focused on things that most bureaucrats wanted to cover-up. I was sure there were people who cheered me in private. I was also sure that many called me a troublemaker and hated me. City Council voted 3-2 to deny ARC Chairman's request to send the case back to ARC, instead, ordered Building Department to resolve the issues. In addition, The City Council voted 5-0 to investigate if ARC treated me fairly.

Figure 13: The Condo at the issue, August
2020. After 40 years, it is still fine.

Fire burns SLO house

A fire that sent smoke billowing 500 feet into the air over San Luis Obispo Wednesday night destroyed a garage and damaged an adjacent house and carport causing $60,000 damages city Fire Department officials said.

The fire started between the garage and carport on Chandler Street south of Mitchell Street, and both buildings were completely aflame by the time firefighters were surrounded it at 10:27 p.m. said Fire Capt. Steve Smith.

The blaze also damaged the house next to the garage said Capt. Ed Marcuno. The cause of the fire was being investigated this morning, Smith said.

He said the fire had burned through electric lines behind the garage, creating a shock hazard that hampered firefighting efforts. Despite this, the fire was controlled by 10:48 p.m. Smith said.

Marcuno said the damaged house was arranged by Steven Cowen and Bill Dilley and the adjacent house with the damaged carport by Thomas Knapp.

Meanwhile, a California Department of Forestry spokesman said the cause of a Wednesday morning house fire on the Nipomo Mesa was found to be an electrical problem. That fire caused $60,000 damage to the home of George on Valdez at Pomeroy and Willow roads.

Council hears complaint on SLO review board

A self-described amateur contractor pleaded to the San Luis Obispo City Council Tuesday that sending him to the city's architectural commission to do battle with that board would be like "sending a lamb into a tiger's den."

Dr. Sing Chou Wu said Architectural Review Commission Chairman Donald J. Kahn yelled at him and "practically called me a liar" when Wu went before the commission on Feb. 2 to request approval for several changes in the design of a condominium project during construction.

Wu, a computer science professor at Cal Poly, is the builder and sole owner of the four-condominium complex located at 178 Stenner St.

Kahn told the council Wu's conduct in making unauthorized design changes was "a blatant violation of everything the ARC stands for."

Occupancy permits were held up after the city discovered that the condo rooms were painted ivory rather than left a natural wood color, as stipulated by the ARC. Wu also cut down four pepper trees he had agreed to preserve, used red concrete in the place of the brick called

for by the ARC, and modified a stairway.

Wu asked the council to overturn the commission's decision to deny approval of the project as it was built and block the sale or rental of three of the four condominium units.

Kahn called Wu's appeal groundless, and the condominium project marginal and a comedy of errors.

Kahn said he was not satisfied with a planning staff proposal that they work out a compromise with Wu. Essentially, the staff suggested that Wu repaint the project and replace several of the trees.

"We want to see this project come back to the ARC," Kahn said.

Wu responded that the ARC had refused to give him a fair hearing. He charged that the plans agreed to by his architect — Ray Hilary Adcock — and the commission contained numerous errors, inconsistencies and omissions.

The council ultimately voted 3-2 to continue the hearing on the appeal until Wu could sit down with city planners and work out a compromise. It then voted 5-0 to investigate the Feb. 2 meeting of the commission to make sure Wu was treated fairly.

Restaurateur still hospitalized

San Luis Obispo restaurant owner Pei Kai Sun Lee, 33, remained in a Fresno hospital this morning, being treated for serious facial cuts suffered Tuesday in a traffic accident near Kettleman City.

Lee's wife, Bay Lin Lee, 30, a biologist with the San Luis Obispo County Health Department, was killed in the accident and their daughter, Karoon, 4, suffered minor injuries.

Lee's restaurant, the Peking Palace, was closed today and was not expected to reopen until Lee recovered, a

arrangements.

A native of Hong Kong, Mrs. Lee was born March 15, 1950, and graduated from San Francisco University where she earned her degree in medical microbiology. She had worked at San Luis Obispo County Health Center since 1974.

Besides her husband and daughter, she is survived by her father, Tad Ho, and another Sau Ying Mok of Hong Kong; two brothers, Ying and Sin Chang, also of Hong Kong.

Also surviving are a sister, Sui Kuen Ho and brother, Yiu Chung Ho, both of San

Figure 14: Newspaper report about my appeal
of ARC decision, February 19th 1981

I fully expected the bureaucrats' retaliation against me. I wasn't sure what I would do! But something happened a few days later, my condominium quickly passed the final inspection.

It was drizzling in the morning; I went to an 8 o'clock class on campus. After I parked my car, I took out my umbrella. One of my colleagues in the same department parked right next to me. He didn't have a raincoat or an umbrella, so I invited him to share my umbrella and walk to our office. While we were walking, a young man took a few photos of us with a big camera, the professional type. He also stopped us to ask for my name. I asked why. He identified himself as the photographer for the local newspaper. He said he found my oil paper umbrella unique and interesting. He hoped that the editor would use one of his photos. I gave him my name and also introduced my colleague to him and insisted that he got my colleague's name too. The next day, a photo of my colleague and I appeared on the front page of the local paper. A friend at the college campus told me that my name appeared twice in a few days on local news did not escape administrators' attention. The first time, I was a fearless troublemaker and dared to challenge the establishment. The second time I was showing the soft side of my characteristics. What they didn't understand was how did I direct the scene and managed to put the photo on the front page of the paper. The first part was plain coincidence, I couldn't do better if I wrote the script. The second part that the editor put it on the front page was not merely coincidence. I was sure the editor didn't forget about the clash between ARC and me only a few days ago. I always believed that the editor knew about the impact of city's housing policy on housing prices. If the newspaper wanted to have an in-depth discussion of the problem, the paper would offend the most powerful people and biggest advertisers in town. So, the editor used me as a pawn to exercise a little checks and balance. I didn't think the photo belonged to the front page; perhaps, it was more appropriate to be in the local section. The news about the City Council's meeting showed the ugly side of the city, bureaucratic nit-picking against a minority. The photo on the front page seemed to portray the harmonious side of city life: two teachers walked in the rain, sharing an umbrella and chatting pleasantly. The photo also portrayed college professors as a bunch of thrift and hardworking individuals, because both of us had brown bag lunch and a stack of paper in hand showing that we had lunch in office and always brought work home. Building Department officials took notice too; they realized they were not dealing with a common troublemaker and they should leave me alone.

Figure 15: A photo showing the author
holding an umbrella, Feb. 25, 1981

The incident happened about 40 years ago. Now, I know more about trees. The fact was that a tree could not be saved if it was in the middle of a building. In fact, even if the tree was two foot outside the building, it could not be saved either. It would be extremely dangerous to save it. In order to put in the building foundation properly, the roots of the tree would have to be cut a foot from the trunk on the side of the building. So almost half the roots of the tall tree would be completely gone, and any strong wind from the side that roots were cut could topple the tree easily.

CHAPTER 4

—

Consequences of the Housing Crisis

4.1 The Destruction of the Upward Mobility of Low-Wage Workers

The most serious effect of the high housing costs in California is the destruction of upward mobility for a significant part of the population. I have the firsthand experience. When I came to the US in 1962, my first job paid only one dollar an hour. I found out years later that the minimum wage was $1.15 an hour. The rent of my first room was $17 per month in Los Angeles. I worked long hours, about 50–60 hours per week. I could save about 60–70% of my take home pay. The savings allowed me to start a full-time graduate school education in 1964. After five years earning two degrees in 1969, I began my teaching job in San Luis Obispo, California. I was well on my way to move from a minimum wage worker into the rank of middle class. I was very proud of myself that my diligence and thrift allowed me to move up the social and economic ladder. Only decades later do I understand and relish my good luck that I started my new life in the US when housing was very affordable in California.

In 2019, the minimum wage in California was $10.60, less than

10 times the minimum wage of 55 years ago. Yet in California, one cannot rent a room for $200 that is over 10 times higher than what I paid 55 years ago. If I were to go back to the same area where I lived 55 years ago, the least expensive room would be about $800 per month. I feel fortunate that I didn't arrive in the US today to start my new life. I could not save any money by working a minimum wage job. Instead of saving 60–70% of my take home pay, I would need to spend 60–70% of my pay for a room. How could I save anything at all? The high housing price is the largest stumbling block toward upward mobility in the US today.

Throughout the US history, up to about 30 or 40 years ago, each generation could expect to have a better life than their parents. This is the first time in the entire US history, including colonial times that this expectation may be in doubt. Take the first group of pilgrims on the Mayflower from England as an example. When they landed in Plymouth, one half of the group, including the crew, didn't survive the first winter. They had little to start their new lives except their hands, and some simple hand tools. They had to build their houses from scratch. They had to clear fields to raise their crops from scratch. The second generation had to be better off, they had nowhere to go but up. They didn't have to build their houses from scratch, they just needed to add on. They didn't need to clear fields from scratch; they needed only to expand. My personal experience is similar. My wife and I both started out working minimum wage jobs. Our two sons never needed to take a minimum wage job to support themselves. When I look at the history of the country, everything seems to get better generation after generation.

A country's GDP, gross domestic production, depends on workers' productivity, innovation, capital formation and management. America should be the land of opportunities with a free market economy. American workers put in longer hours than most workers in other rich countries. The American spirit of entrepreneurship is second to none. America is blessed with rich natural resources, including vast land in rather mild weather. It is also the leader in innovative technologies, and because it is a country of law, it is a haven for liquid assets and investments. Americans have no reason not to enjoy the highest standard of living among all countries. Every worker with a full-time job should enjoy a satisfying life and have a fair chance to realize the American Dream.

Unfortunately, this is not true for those who work for minimum wage or close to minimum wage. Although most vital services and everyday necessities are becoming more affordable, there are three exceptions: housing, medical service and college education. These are expensive and unaffordable.

Medical service is expensive in the US; this topic it is not within this book. I only discuss it briefly here. Americans spent 17.8% of the GDP on medical services in 2016. That is over $9400 per person per year. This amount is about twice as much as the average medical expenses of the people in the next 10 countries with the highest medical expenses. American medical professionals and researchers are responsible for a large part of the advancement of medical practices, procedures, and equipment. American pharmaceutical companies also develop most new drugs. So, inevitably, the American public bears part of the cost of for these advancements and innovations. However, the private medical insurance companies are over extended and bloated, thus, the industry supports an enormous group of employees unnecessarily. The compensations for these employees count as medical expenses, but they contribute little to the medical service. Not only do they not contribute to medical service but they also force medical professionals to waste time on paperwork.

An insurance policy makes sense only for protection against catastrophic events or incidents, but medical insurers have taken over even routine check-ups and office visits in the US. If any routine medical service is necessary, a patient could easily pay the provider directly as the service is rendered. It would be only one simple transaction, under the present system, a simple transaction becomes a complicated process:

Step 1, We pay a premium to insurance companies. Insurance companies spend money to advertise their services, hire many people to sell health insurance policies to the public, and hire an even larger number of individuals to collect premiums and keep records;

Step 2, Medical providers hire people to file insurance claims and insurers hire people to process and to check the validity of the claims;

Step 3, Insurance companies hire a sizeable group of people to keep records to track every insured individual's office visits and routine check-ups. Insurance companies also hire various levels of executives to keep tracks of their employees;

Step 4, Insurance companies do not provide free services, these companies want to make money off every routine office visit or check-up;

Step 5, Medical provider gets paid by an insurance company.

Many people are making a living out of this process. Even though they contribute little directly to our health, their income is counted as part of our medical expense.

If this medical insurance practice makes sense, why not let automobile insurance policies take over routine car washes, oil changes, tire rotations? Why not let home insurance policies cover a gardener's yard work or a plumber's minor repairs?

Another problem of medical cost is lack of transparency in hospital charge. Once a tenant's dog bit me on my right thigh. I went to a hospital emergency room to see if I needed a Rabies shot. I waited about an hour, and a nurse examined my wound for a few minutes. There was a bite mark, but the heavy blue jeans protected me from infections. The emergency room had my records, and charged Medicare for the treatment. I waited for the bill because I wanted the dog owner to pay for the examination. When I didn't get one from the hospital, I went to hospital and paid $2,055.07 for the one-hour waiting and a few minutes examination by a nurse. Also, I noticed the hospital billed my supplement insurance to Medicare for $266.00 but got a payment of $42.10 for the visit. This amount is usually 20% of the total bill. So, the hospital got a total of $210.50 from Medical and supplement insurance. Yet when I offered to pay for the bill, the hospital charged me 876% more. Why did the hospital charge patient at such inflated amount? I had no idea! If a patient pays a hospital bill directly, there is little paper work to do for the hospital to get paid. Yet instead of a discount, the hospital charged a big inflated amount. This is unfair to the patient, and in a free market, no provider of any service can get away with this kind of practice. President Trump signed an executive order on June

24, 2019 demanding transparency from hospitals and doctors on price. He is the only president in recent history who has made an effort to control the run-away health-care cost.

P.O. BOX 70000
VAN NUYS, CA 9°470-0001

EXPLANATION OF BENEFITS   000726

ISSUE DATE	PAGE	E001882
February 28, 2018	00001 OF 00002	

Subscriber's Name: SINGCHOU WU
Identification Number: 997A54874
Group Number: KS030A
Group Name: PERSCARE-CALPERS
                      STATE RETIREES CA MED SUPP
Product: Medicare Supp PBP Plus

***************SCH 5-DIGIT 93402
18490 1 AV 0-378   8b
SINGCHOU WU
775 VIA LAGUNA VISTA
SAN LUIS OBISPO CA 93405-4729

Patient's Name: SINGCHOU WU
Claim Number: 18059GD435I
Claim Processed Date: 02/28/18

Sequence Number: 1972535557   201800271
Provider of Services: CENTRAL COAST EMERGENCY
Place of Service: Outpatient
Patient Acct. Number: 0071886391

Paid Amount: $42.10   To: CENTRAL COAST EMERGENCY

It is your responsibility to pay: $0.00 It is not your responsibility to pay: $223.90

Thank you for using a Network Participating Provider.

SERVICE DATE(s)	TYPE OF SERVICE	TOTAL BILLED	OTHER AMOUNT(S)	PATIENT SAVINGS	APPLIED TO DEDUCTIBLE	COINSURANCE COPAYMENT AMOUNT	CLAIMS PAYMENT
02/12/18	Emergency Service	266.00		223.90/01			42.10
	TOTAL THIS CLAIM	266.00	0.00	223.90	0.00	0.00	42.10

DETAIL MESSAGE:

01 - This provider has accepted Medicare's or Medicaid's allowed amount as the total amount due. The member, therefore, is not responsible for the balance.
++ - According to your Medicare EOB, the Medicare allowed amount was $42.10, and $42.10 was applied to your Medicare Deductible

HAVE QUESTIONS?

Check out our Website at www.anthem.com/ca/calpers
Order I.D. Cards / Check claims status / Review benefits /
Verify family members covered on your policy / Find a participating provider
OR call our CUSTOMER SERVICE DEPARTMENT AT: 1-877-737-7776

MAIL ALL INQUIRIES   ANTHEM BLUE CROSS LIFE AND HEALTH INSURANCE CO
OR CLAIMS TO :   P.O. BOX 60007
                     LOS ANGELES, CA 90060-0007

WE SUGGEST THAT YOU RETAIN THIS COPY FOR YOUR INCOME TAX RECORDS.

THIS IS NOT A BILL

Figure 16: CalPERS, supplement insurance to Medicare, paid 20% ($42.10) for the Sierra Vista Hospital emergency room bill.

```
RUN DATE: 02/23/18    SVM - SIERRA VISTA REGIONAL         PAGE   306
REPORT: SVMFU0535 A484 UB04 ITEMIZED STATEMENT FOR - 02/22/18
FORM: MUBO  ACCOUNT: 017225319 WU SINGCHOU      SERVICE DATES: 02/12/2018-02/12/2018

REV                BILLING                                     CHARGE    SERVICE
CODE HCPCS         DESCRIPTION            QTY       AMOUNT      NUMBER    DATE
---- -----  --------  --------------------------  ----  ------------  -------  ----------
0450 99283         ER VISIT LVLIII          1      2,055.07  006100524 02/12/2018

TOTAL                                             2,055.07
```

SimpleePAY - Payment Confirmation   Page 2 of 2

Customer Copy

Sierra Vista Regional Medical Center
1010 Murray Avenue
San Luis Obispo CA , 93405
(866) 904-6871

Transaction Date: 06/06/2018
Transaction ID: y4uhdmqx

Card Type: Visa
Card Last 4 Digits: XXXXXXXXXX-9578
Total Amount: **$2,055.07**

Amount	Patient Name	Bill Number	Payment Type
$2,055.07	SINGCHOU WU	017225319	Patient Payment

Cardholder Name: Singchou Wu

I AGREE TO PAY THE ABOVE TOTAL ACCORDING TO MY CARD ISSUER AGREEMENT.

Figure 17: Sierra Vista Hospital emergency
room bill and payment record

In early November 2020, California Governor Newsom issued a stringent order of "stay at home" to slow down the spread of COVID-19 virus. One day I watched an evening new report that the Governor violated his own order and went to a dinner party in Napa at French Laundry, a Michelin 3-star restaurant. The news report mentioned that the restaurant was the most expensive one in the US and the group included two lobbyists. The news report cited The New York Times headline: "Governor Newsom asked people: [Do as I say, not as I dine!]" I posted the news on Nextdoor, San Luis Obispo, an internet messaging board. I knew I would offend many of Governor's local fans. Sure enough, some responded in disgust and some ridiculed my posting. One neighbor replied that, since the Governor apologized, it should be the end of the matter. The reply included a link to Governor's YouTube posting of the apology. The apology actually backfired. When I looked at it, the posting got fewer than 50 approvals and more than 500 disapprovals. But as usual, my posting on Nextdoor got more positive responses than negative ones. Since my original posting didn't include any comments of my own, my follow up posting added a few of my thoughts. By then additional information about the dinner was available. The dinner cost $850 per person, the high price even turned many Democrats against the governor, and the two lobbyists were hospital lobbyists. So, I got at least a partial answer to my question about my Sierra Vista Hospital emergency room charge. Since hospital lobbyists got governor's ears, don't expect California hospitals to treat common folks like me any better soon.

Here's my follow-up posting:

"My original posting about the French Laundry dinner party was only a news item without any of my comments. Those who criticized me for the posting appeared to have the intention to silence the messenger who brought the bad news, yet leave the culprit alone. We should question who paid for the dinner, I couldn't imagine that they would go Dutch and French Laundry would do separate checks. If the Governor paid his own tab, was it paid at the dinner table or a few days later after the news broke? I also posted the responses to Governor's apology and the numbers of disapprovals against that of the approvals being more than 10 to 1. Clearly, the public didn't think his apology was enough.

Also in my posting, I didn't just express my opinion about the governor, I provided justification along with my criticism. I listed three facts; what he didn't do, what he did do, and how he wasted tax payers' dollars.

First, what he didn't do. He occupied the governor's mansion and his party controlled both houses of the legislature with super majority. Yet he didn't do a thing about the high housing costs in the state.

Second, what he did do. In 2018, California voters rejected Proposition 10, Local Rent Control Initiative overwhelmingly (7,251,443 59.43% for NO and 4,949,543 40.57% for YES). Yet, right after the election, California legislature led by Assemblyman Chiu (Democrat San Francisco), in 2019, proposed new rent control bills. The Democrats controlled legislature quickly passed AB1482 and the Governor immediately signed it into law. Did our votes mean anything to Assemblyman Chiu and Governor Newsom?

Third, how he wasted tax payers' money. In the last 20 years, Gavin Newsom rose from Supervisor of San Francisco to Mayor of San Francisco to Lieutenant Governor of California, and in 2019, he became the Governor of California. The number of homeless people in the City of San Francisco stayed around 5 to 8 thousand, regardless billions of dollars spent on them by the city and the state. Yet during the same time, Tokyo's homeless population reduced by 80% while the City of Tokyo didn't spend a dime on them. What did the city do? The City of Tokyo just relaxed its zoning regulations on housing development.

My posting was an instant favorite on Nextdoor, San Luis Obispo. After about two hours, Nextdoor Leads censored my posting and accused me of being a bully. I posted a reply and challenged the Leads to have an open debate and let neighbors to decide for themselves who was the real bully. I told them that I was a mathematician and English was not part of my strength. In fact, English was not even my first language, so they should not be afraid of me, but the Leads chickened out.

Young people are usually healthier than the average person, so they spend much less than the average of $9400 per year for medical expenses. Their expenses for college education may be more than $9400 a year, but it is only for a few years. A significant part of that expense is for housing, so the housing cost is the actual problem that we need to focus on.

However, even if we exclude the cost of housing from the total cost of college education, the increase in tuition still far exceeds the inflation. I had been a college professor most of my adult life. Maybe I have a little understanding why college tuition increased a lot. When I started my teaching career, the dean of my school complained that his annual compensation was less than that of any top rank full professors who taught summer school besides regular school year assignment. This appeared to be rather unfair. A dean worked a full year and didn't get the summer off. A dean's responsibility and a full year work should deserve at least as much as, if not more than, the salary of a full professor for the same work schedule. So, it changed. By the time I retired from teaching, exactly 30 years later, a dean's salary was two to three times more than a full professor's. Also, university administration appears to be top heavy. Most college tenured teaching faculty are a bunch of rather independent intellectuals. They don't need a lot of supervision at work and they don't consider their department head or dean to be their supervisor and they rarely listen to department head or dean, let alone other administrators. Perhaps this is why some universities have bloated and top-heavy administrations.

If a president cannot give orders to professors, at least they can command the attention of other administrators. In many Asian countries, such as Japan, South Korea, Singapore, Taiwan or Hong Kong, etc., a university's director of admission's or a registrar's salary is less than an assistant professor's. But in the US, it is comparable to a dean's salary. In these Asian countries, university admission process is clear, simple and totally transparent. Thus, the process of evaluation of the eligibility of an applicant for admission is simple, straight forward and routine. Since it doesn't require tough judgement calls, and it does not involve intricate business decisions, admission officers' compensation should be comparable to an office clerk's salary instead of a dean's. Perhaps one of the American universities' problems is that there are not enough clear rules governing the admission process for undergraduate students. So many universities give admission officers tremendous power to decide who get admitted or rejected. More power leads to higher pay, and more power leads to more corruption. In 2019, the FBI investigated admission scandals involving $25 million in bribery from 2012 to 2018. Wikipedia Website stated: "The investigation and related charges were made public on March 12, 2019, by United States federal prosecutors. At least 51 people were alleged to have been part of the conspiracy, several of whom had pled guilty or agreed to plead guilty. Thirty-three parents of college applicants were accused of paying more than $25 million between 2011 and 2018 to William Rick Singer, organizer of the scheme who used part of the money to fraudulently inflate entrance exam test scores and bribed college officials." August 22, 2020 AP reported:

> "'Full House" actor Lori Loughlin must serve two months in prison and her fashion designer husband, Mossimo Giannulli, must serve five months for paying half a million dollars in bribes to get their two daughters into the University of Southern California as rowing recruits, a federal judge ruled Friday.
>
> U.S. District Judge Nathaniel Gorton accepted Loughlin's plea deal with prosecutors in a hearing held via video conference because of the coronavirus pandemic after sentencing her husband in an earlier hearing.'

On Sept. 27, 2020, about a month before the 2020 election date, Telegram Tribune published the result of a survey in San Luis Obispo County. The survey was based on more than 200 responses from young voters under age 40. The number one issue was the housing affordability, the survey showed that almost 87% of the respondents wanted elected officials to make affordable housing their priority.

Except housing costs, medical insurance and college education, most services and goods have become rather affordable over the years. We can look at a few examples. Today's laptop computers have more computing power than a mainframe computer had half century ago and cost only a tiny fraction of that the mainframe computer cost before.

An average TV set today is lighter, has a bigger screen with better picture and sound, is more energy efficient, has at least 10 times more channels, and last but not the least, costs much less than a typical TV set did half a century ago. Even gasoline, a product refined from the very limited natural resource of crude oil, costs about the same today, after being adjusted for inflation, as it did one-half a century ago. The cost to explore, produce and transport crude oil have exploded, yet the free market-place and technology have kept the gasoline prices rather stable in the US.

Throughout history, countries often spend half of their labor forces to produce food. We have seen no country, community or group of people spend one half of the labor force to erect shelters. Yet today, in

California, it is common for low-wage workers to spend more than half of their income on housing. History recorded many mass starvations, and the last one happened in China during the Great Leap Forward (1958-1962). The Irish Potato Famine killed about one million Irish out of a total population of about 6 million or 12.5% of the population. This was the highest recorded proportion of people who died from famine in a country on the record. During Great Leap Forward, between several million up to 55 million Chinese died, most of them because of lack of food. If one accepts the mid-value of the estimates of about 30 million who died in China, this number would be the largest absolute number of people who died because of famine. Yet there were no records of death of many human beings due to exposure or lack of shelter. California's high housing costs don't kill many people directly, except a few deaths of homeless people because of lack of shelter. But high housing costs kill many people's upward mobility and thus, kill people rather slowly. Lack of upward mobility means lack of hope. We can agree that desperation kills.

According to the Center of Disease Control's National Center for Health Statistics (NCHS), on average, adjusted for age, the annual U.S. suicide rate increased 24% between 1999 and 2014, from 10.5 to 13.0 suicides per 100,000 people, the highest rate recorded in 28 years. By 2018, WHO, World Health Organization reported that US suicide rate continued to increase to 15.3 suicides per 100,000 people and ranked 27th among 183 countries. Now, the land of opportunity may become the land of hopelessness if we don't solve the problem of high housing costs. Those who push up housing costs are also responsible for destroying people's lives. To destroy people's lives cannot be just a minor crime, it is a crime against humanity! As people pay one half or more of their income just to rent a room, how can they look forward to their future? Would their future be better than their present lives? Can they ever afford to get married and to raise a family? The answers are probably no! Then, one more question: are their lives better than the slaves living in the deep South over two hundred years ago? We outlawed slavery, yet, we allow some politicians to treat a group of workers probably worse than slaves today. I know a young couple with three children. In 2019, the family left San Luis Obispo for a place where the housing cost was more affordable. They spent about two-thirds of their take-home pay for housing cost in town. Yes! Weren't they at least free? But they were never free from worries. They always worry about how to make ends meet.

When we look at the housing price, it shocks us. In the early 60s, California's median house price was $15,300. Adjusted for inflation, the median price of a house should be $124,696 in 2017. House sizes have increased, and the quality of the houses has improved. Let us double the amount to $124,696 x 2 = $249,392 to account for the improvements. However, housing industry has not been standing still. The construction industry has numerous new products and tools contributing to savings in labor, material, time and cost. Taking all factors into consideration, $249,392 should be the fair median house price in California. This number, $249,392, is close to the national median, but it is not near the price of a house in California. The actual median house price in California in 2017 was more than double of $249,392. It is fair to conclude that California's local politicians double the housing prices in California. California is a big state, and their meddling and manipulations vary from location to location. The variations of housing values within the state are wide and extreme. Since Silicon Valley has the highest housing prices in the state, local politicians in Silicon Valley must bear the most responsibility. Housing is a local problem, but the high housing costs have wide and profound effects beyond each location, so we can no longer treat them as a local problem. We need to have a national discussion to focus our attention to the problem. We cannot let local politicians continue to hide behind the shield of "local issue" and let them get away with manipulations and corruption. We need to call voters' attention to the problem and expose politicians' manipulation of housing development. Once the cause of the problem is clear and we know who are responsible for the problem, then we can hit the nail at its head to solve the problem. Otherwise, we only beat around the bush without solving the actual problem.

4.2 High Housing Cost Damages the Vitality of the Economy

Austin is the state capital of Texas with a vibrant high-tech industry and a huge talent pool of high-tech employees. Yet the housing prices are very affordable by California standards. Apple announced in late

2018 that it planned to build a new $1 billion campus in Austin. The new campus would span 133 acres and house an initial 5,000 employees, with the potential to expand to 15,000 staff. Austin is also at the center of the three largest cities in Texas, the triangle of Dallas; Houston and San Antonio where almost all the good universities in Texas are located. With these advantages, Austin's local politicians could easily push housing prices much higher, perhaps closer to Silicon Valley's level. In 2018, the median house price in Austin was only $361,200, a fraction of the price of a comparable house in Silicon Valley.

A similar house in Silicon Valley would be 4 times to a dozen times more expensive depending on the location. A start-up with limited capital cannot afford to hire anyone in Silicon Valley. We will never know how many budding entrepreneurs never get to flourish because of the high housing cost in Silicon Valley. By some estimates, in 2018, Silicon Valley's GDP lost 500 billion dollars.

In the early December 2020, within about 10 days, three well known tech companies announced either moving their headquarters to Texas from Silicon Valley or building new factory in Texas.

On December 1, 2020, the business-focused tech firm Hewlett Packard Enterprise announced it would be moving its headquarters to Houston, Texas. Its predecessor, Hewlett-Packard, was created out of a garage in Palo Alto in 1938, a place which now features a landmark as the "birthplace of Silicon Valley". The company was building the new headquarter in Huston.

Tesla's Elon Musk announced on December 9, 2020 that he was leaving Silicon Valley for Texas, and predicted the tech center could lose its influence. The billionaire entrepreneur declared that California had "too much influence in the world" but that its power was waning. His company, valued at $500bn, had its headquarters in California, but would build a new factory in Austin.

Business software and services company Oracle was changing its corporate headquarters from the Silicon Valley area to Austin, Texas, to provide its workers "with more flexibility about where and how they will work," the company said on December 11, 2020. Depending on their role, this meant that many of their employees could choose their office location as well as continued to work from home part time or all the time, Oracle said in a statement. The company opened a large corporate campus in Austin in 2018, but it reportedly doesn't have any plans to move staff from its existing headquarters in Redwood City, California, to Austin.

A healthy country must have a blend of various housing supplies for all citizens' needs. A country cannot only provide housing for the top 50% of the workforce. By the same token, a small village cannot keep housing prices so high that one half its workforce cannot afford to live in the village. In the US, some politicians try to promote the ridiculous idea that similar housing development must be next to each other. They call this the harmony of the neighborhood. Can a king demand that his palace to be among other kings' palaces? A king may want his gardener to live in the servants' quarter in the palace, or, at least, live right next to the palace. The king cannot expect his gardener to commute one hour to work. Yet, we see in Silicon Valley, gardeners working in Silicon Valley often live an hour away. In fact, even in San Luis Obispo, I haven't found a licensed landscaper who lives in the city. There are examples of multi-million dollars mansion, middle class family housing and affordable rentals coexisting in the same city block. Perhaps we need to properly define what is meant by "harmony". Harmony doesn't mean homogeneity, but diversity.

It is great that Silicon Valley is a world leader in high-tech innovation and the cradle of high-tech startups. But the area cannot just provide housing for CEOs of Unicorns or just for software engineers. To have a vibrant economy, we also need low-wage workers like short-order cooks, busboys, parking lot attendants, sales clerks, school teachers, cashiers, bus drivers, etc. They need to live in the communities where they work. To exclude any of them from where they work is to create many problems we have today. We can never solve these problems if we don't deal with the causes of the problems.

4.3 The Rise of Socialism

Politically, the high housing price is the major cause of the rise of socialism in the US. On June 12, 1987, President Ronald Reagan said at the Brandenburg Gate in Berlin: "Mr. Gorbachev! Tear down this wall!" The Berlin Wall fell on November 9, 1989. On December 26, 1991, the Soviet Union collapsed. It should be the end of Socialism. But in less than 30 years, in 2019, polls in the US showed that most young people preferred socialism over capitalism. What went wrong? How could this happen? A generation ago, no respectable politician would claim to be a socialist. The Soviet Union had just collapsed, and any politician who claimed to be a socialist would be committing political suicide. Conservatism promotes self-motivation instead of government handouts. How can a conservative convince a worker to be self-reliant, if the person needs to spend 50% of their income to rent a room? We are not just talking about minimum wage workers. In San Francisco, the monthly rent of a room was at least $1500 in late 2010s. It takes a lot of workers 100 hours of gross income every month to afford the rent alone. There are a lot of low wage earners in San Francisco who cannot afford to live in San Francisco.

The unprecedented high housing costs pose the gravest threat to the US today. The housing problem is a local issue, so it doesn't get the attention it deserves. The problem appears to be limited to California and a few spots on the West Coast and Eastern seaboard. But there is a saying: "As California goes, so goes the Nation."

When people have no hope of realizing their American dream, they usually turn to the radical left, Socialism, for help. In fact, Bernie Sanders understands local politics and housing problems probably better than anyone else in the US. As the Mayor of Burlington, in 1983, with the support of local Republicans and business leaders, he created the Community and Economic Development Office (CEDO) to carry out his vision for more affordable housing, more locally owned small businesses, greater community engagement in planning, and job development. He knows the importance of affordable housing and how to get it. Yet when he ran for President in the Democratic Primary in 2016 and 2020, he didn't talk about high housing costs. He knew high housing prices were the most serious problem in the country, but he also knew it was a local issue, and he could not propose free housing for all. He knew if he won the Democrat Nomination, he would need local Democratic politicians' support. He knew it would not be easy to explain why housing costs were so high in some states. He deliberately avoided the problem, because he knew that whoever discussed the problem honestly would offend a lot of local politicians. So, he chose a rather simple slogan: "Universal health care, free college education and get jobs back from China and Mexico!" He was smart, but not very honest.

In the past, social and economic mobility allowed the poor to have a fair chance to join the middle class and to realize the American dream. The poor did envy the rich, but they did not resent the rich. Now, for a large part of the US population, the American dream has turned into a nightmare. For those who have no prospect of shaking off poverty, their envy of the rich becomes resentment, and their resentment may turn into hatred. This is a symptom for possible revolt or even revolution; the situation is not politically sustainable. How do we solve the problem? Certainly, it is not the Socialistic way. The leading Socialist presidential hopeful, Bernie Sanders, didn't even identify the true problem: the high housing cost. How could he come up with the right solution?

Socialists know perfectly well that high housing costs give them a chance to prevail in the American political arena. Without the problem of housing shortages and high housing prices, the Socialists have no future in the US politics. The high housing cost is the wave that lifted socialism to prominence in the US political scene. They expect to ride the tide to take over the Democratic Party and to win the National Elections.

Young people are the future of every country. Every individual who is willing to work hard should have a bright future. We cannot expect everyone to be a genius. Nothing can stop genius or extremely smart individuals from succeeding. I always remember my humble beginnings in the US. I just worked long hours, 50-60 hours a week at a low wage job with no overtime pay. In a little over a year, I saved enough to go to graduate school. Today, can anyone do the same as I did about 55 years ago? Probably not. If a full-time job pays minimum wage, the person would be lucky to pay no more than one half of the income for a room. So how could anyone work part time and finish college without other help? It is true that most people can apply for student loans, and this solves the problem for some students. For those who drop out of college with a big student loan debt, student loans only make the situation worse. What about those who don't qualify for student loans? Should they deserve a chance?

Now, what is socialism? In a nutshell, it means that consumers have very limited choices and producers have to follow a planner's order. This sounds a lot like how local officials control of housing developments in California. Local officials decide how big a bedroom needs to be, how much space around a toilet etc. Local officials also decide how many individuals may occupy a unit and the maximum number of individuals that may share a bathroom. In California, local officials' meddling and manipulation on housing are the same as Socialistic engineering. Their meddling and manipulation lead to the rise of Socialism among young Americans. Local officials can arbitrarily decide where to build housing units and how many units they allow on a lot. California's housing developments are much closer to socialism than to capitalism! However, California is a big state and local officials are not all the same. In the San Joaquin Valley, housing prices are rather affordable.

Trump won the presidency in 2016, but he lost the popular vote by 2 million. In the past, Nixon and Reagan, both Republicans, started in California and eventually became US presidents. Now it is no longer possible for any Republicans to win statewide elections in California. In the last couple of elections, Republicans could not even field any candidates on the ballots for several statewide contests. Does it surprise anyone? When housing price went up in California, the State turned BLUE. The logic is simple. When housing prices went up, a lot of the people who worked and lived in California could not afford the housing in California. They were poor and became desperate. They turned to the far left of the Democratic Party. Housing shortages caused the problem, but Bernie Sanders and other Socialists are smart not to mention the housing problem much. They dare not offer free housing for the poor. Instead, he advocated universal health care and free college education for the poor. These are most likely the two largest expenses for young people after the housing cost. Young people turned to them in droves.

There are other states with rather high housing cost. Namely, Hawaii, New York, Massachusetts, Connecticut, Washington State and Washington DC. They are all BLUE states and district! In the past, when Republicans like Nixon and Reagan won national elections, they often won landslides in the Electoral College. Trump barely won the Electoral vote but lost the popular vote to Hillary Clinton. When George W. Bush beat Al Gore, the results were the same. As the trend continues, in less than a generation perhaps, Republicans can no longer win national elections anymore. When that happens, we will destroy the two-party system of the Federal Government. The survival of the Country will be in danger!

So, high housing cost is an efficient machine manufacturing poverty and destroying the upward mobility of low wage earners. Also, it has already changed the political landscape of the US and it has the potential to undermine the two-party system that has served the nation well so far.

4.4 Homelessness

On January 29, 2019, California Assemblyman Marc Berman proposed AB (Assembly Bill) 302 requiring California's Community Colleges to open parking lots to homeless students so they can park their cars there at night. The Bill also required that they would open restrooms in gymnasiums. By estimate, over 20% of the 2 million community college students in California were homeless at least part of the time in the last 12 months. AB 302 is a step in the right direction. We should try to help those who deserve a chance to get ahead and to focus on a serious housing crisis in California and in the country.

Like most politicians, Mr. Marc Berman started his political career from local office. Before he was elected Assemblyman, he was a City Councilman in Palo Alto. The city has some of the highest housing prices, even by Silicon Valley's standard. As a local politician, he should know exactly what causes the high housing prices in California, especially in Palo Alto. He recognizes that high housing prices are a very serious problem. He also recognizes that the high housing prices cause many other problems in California, including pollution and homelessness. He correctly points out that high housing cost in Palo Alto forces many workers in Palo Alto to live far away. Long commutes result in long driving, and thus a lot of pollution.

When Mr. Berman talks about the problem of single-family dwellings on spacious lots, he points out that these housing developments force residents to drive a great deal and make public transportation impractical. He fails to point out that many single-family dwellings on large lots are also the sources of pollution by themselves. Mr. Berman also fails to point out that the large number of single-family dwellings is one of the major causes of high housing prices in California. He didn't mention that local officials are responsible for the large number of single-family dwellings. It was smart for him not to elaborate on the cause of high housing prices. If he did, he had to answer: "Why didn't you do something when you served in City Council?" It would not be great for his political future, as he would offend his former colleagues. The City of Palo Alto is his political base, and he cannot afford to lose it.

Here is the dilemma for Mr. Berman and many other state politicians like him. They started their political career from the local level. When they were at the local level, they probably contributed to the high housing prices by pushing for housing developments dominated by single-family detached houses. Now they are above the local level and realize the high housing price is a serious problem that they must deal with at the state level. But they don't want to lose their political bases or offend their former colleagues. Therefore, Mr. Marc Berman didn't talk about the cause of high housing prices in California. However, if he doesn't get to the fundamental cause of a serious problem, how could he solve the problem?

What should you do if you are enjoying a sauna and it gets too hot? It is a no brainier; you need to find out why! You remove the heat source, so you don't get burned. If you don't care about the cause of the over-heating, you could just open a small window and fan the room to bring in cool air to stay comfortable. You need to fan furiously, but the fan may not be enough. If the heat source persists, the temperature may keep rising, so opening a small window and fanning would be futile for you. It is admirable of Assemblyman Berman to sponsor AB302 to help homeless Community College students, but what happens to them a year or two later?

Suppose that a student finishes their Community College education with good grades and transfers to a CSU (California State University) or UC (University of California) campus to continue. Even though CSUs and UCs have on-campus dormitories for students, these housings are for freshmen and sophomores only. Besides, on campus housing is never cheap in California. Should we propose a similar bill to make CSUs and UCs do the same? Two years later, when the student finishes college education and lands a job in Silicon Valley, this person will still not be able to afford the housing in Silicon Valley. Should we have similar laws to require employers to allow homeless employees to park their cars in company parking lots overnight and use the restrooms in the offices? There is no end to the problem if we don't get to the cause.

We may characterize AB302 as a Band-Aid solution. But first aid is always an integral part of a solution. Unlike most other politicians, Mr. Berman confronted the problem without thinking about votes all the time. It is fairly obvious that the purpose of AB302 is not to get more votes for himself, as his district is one of the richest ones in the Country. He didn't need to care about homeless students to be re-elected. California's government has created other state-level requirements including the housing element, the Regional Housing Needs Assessment (RHNA), the affordable housing density bonus, etc. But the fact that high housing prices continue in California speaks loud and clear. These measures are toothless.

Now there is hope. The problem is so serious that the Democrats in power at the State Capital can no longer sweep the problem under the rug. These Democrats know perfectly well how they defeated Republicans in the state. The rising housing prices make low-wage workers feel hopeless. The high housing costs condemn a sizeable group of workers to the status of permanent poverty. More poor people in the state, more votes for Democrats. This is also why Democrats in California are for open borders. Open borders bring in a lot of unskilled workers. Even though these unskilled workers cannot vote, they keep wages low for some workers who are eligible to vote. Again, more votes for Democrats.

Some Democrats in California want affordable housing now. Why do they want it now? First, the high housing costs in California are not sustainable. Neighboring states would love to have some of California's businesses move to their states. Second, if the housing crisis persists, the left wing, the socialists, will take over the Democratic Party in California. The top Democratic politicians don't want to follow the footsteps of the defeated Republicans in the state.

When a person becomes homeless, a productive individual becomes a burden to society. In the 1980s, I saw a person with a moderate income became homeless. He was a computer programmer working in San Diego, making about $1500 a month. The rent for a 2-bedroom apartment in the area was about $500 a month. If he had managed his money well by renting an apartment with a roommate, he could have had a comfortable life and even saved a little for the rainy days. Instead, he ate in restaurants and lived in a motel I owned with my relative. With monthly car payments, he lived from paycheck to paycheck. The trouble with computer programming is that the field transforms quickly and a person working in the field has to stay up to date. He apparently had no savings, so once he lost his job, he became homeless. I saw him going around neighboring motels searching for bottles and cans in trash bins. At the time, soda cans and beer bottles had only redemption value of one penny. He probably needed to collect at least 500 bottles or cans to feed himself. He likely could not find time to study to keep himself up to date in his field. Once a person is homeless, it is difficult for the person to be presentable for a job interview. I asked him when he had a job, why didn't he rent an apartment and cook for himself? He said that he could never save enough to pay the deposit and first and last month rent for an apartment. Now, the State of California has a program to help these people to move into rental housings. But the problem is so severe and wide spread, there will never be enough funding for this program. If there is not enough money for everyone, then families with children have the priority. So, even if the program existed in the 80s, the computer programmer was still out of luck. So high housing cost, not only destroy low-wage worker's upward mobility but also make some workers unemployable. Since high housing costs can turn productive workers into a burden of the society, we have to solve the problem.

4.5 Energy Waste in Housing

Wasteful energy usage is one problem of housing developments in US. With 5% of the world population, the US uses about 20% of the world's annual production of petroleum products. On average, every American uses about 5 times more energy than the rest of the world population. Housing uses about 7–8% of the total energy consumption in the US. However, this doesn't account for one half of the real energy wasted due to the housing patterns in the US. Because of the large number of single-family dwellings everywhere from rural areas to suburbs to metropolitan areas, the distances between our homes and the places where we need to go increase to the point that we almost always drive. Except in some rare situations, we usually cannot walk to work, cannot walk to a store to buy a loaf of bread, cannot walk to a restaurant to have lunch and kids usually cannot walk to school. Because we drive a lot, there are many huge parking lots. These parking lots further increase the distance between our houses and where we want to go. When we drive a great deal, we use a large amount of fuel for our cars. A very large portion of our driving is because of the large number of single-family homes.

Local politicians promote single-family dwellings that lead to wasteful energy consumption. Perhaps they may feel guilty about what they did, or they try to distract. Usually, they are the first ones to jump on the bandwagon of energy saving. If they are enthusiastic about energy efficiency in housing, recycling and public transportation, perhaps the public will not notice that they are the ones responsible for most of the waste.

Let us take the issues one by one. We will start from energy efficiency in housing developments. It is a known fact that the total population size in the US has been increasing year after year while the typical household size has been decreasing. Thus, it makes sense for the median dwelling size to decrease. Amazingly, the trend went the other way. Roughly, from 1960 to 2010, or in one half of a century, the median size of a house almost doubled in the US. How could this happen? Part of the reason is the increase in the standard of living. When a country becomes more affluent, people want better housing units. But this is not the only reason. Local politicians' meddling account for a large part of the increase in dwelling sizes.

I have a firsthand experience about the contrast in energy consumption of a large housing unit versus a small housing unit. For about twenty years in the 1980s and 1990s, I owned and managed a rather unusual rental property in Morro Bay, a small coastal town near San Luis Obispo. It was a 9-unit structure with a two-bedroom house, about 800 square feet of living space, at one end and 8 small apartments attached to the house. The 8 units consisted of 4 studios about 150 square feet each, 3 one-bedroom apartments about 200 square feet each and a two-bedroom apartment about 300 square feet, so the total square footage was about 2300. The house looked just like any old house, but the rest of the structure appeared to be built with material salvaged from a dump. Some exterior walls were shiplap that looked very much like recovered from a shipwreck. The ceiling of the 8 small units were no more than 7' high. Old newspaper was stuffed in walls and used as insulation. Several holes in walls were patched with various materials including a bath tub mat and a steel oven pan. Old timers in the neighborhood said that the place was a small motel. During WWII, it was a training camp for local colored recruits.

These units didn't have individual utility meters, so they were rentals with all utilities paid and the rents were cheap and affordable. Morro Bay had a lot of low-wage workers in fishing and hospitality sectors, the two major industries of the small city. These units were probably the most affordable housing units in the city, so they were always fully occupied. Because the gas line and most gas appliances were old, I insisted that tenants leave their windows open slightly to prevent possible carbon-monoxide poisoning if they used the gas ranges or gas wall heaters. The 9 units always accommodated about 14-20 individuals during my management and their rent included all utilities. None of the units had any real insulation and none of the occupants had any incentive to conserve on utility usage. We would think the gas bill for this rental property had to be extremely high compared to a new housing unit meeting all code requirements for energy efficiency. My family lived in one fairly new unit. In 1978, it was brand new when my family moved into the house with 5 bedrooms, 3 bathrooms and about 3000 square feet of living space. It was very comfortable for my family of 5. By the late 90s, my mother-in-law passed away and my two sons grew up and went to colleges out of town, only my wife and I live in the house. We were very conscious about energy conservation. I used a programmable thermostat for the forced-air heater. At night it was set at low 60s, in the early morning at high 60s and I turned it off during the day. I expected that a dozen renters in a crummy structure without any insulation would use a lot more natural gas during the winter than two owners who occupied a new dwelling. However, the gas usage of the 9-unit rental was never more than the gas usage at my house in the winter. I tried hard to understand why! Most likely, the gas room heating uses the most amount of natural gas in winter for a housing unit and the volume of air space to be heated is at least as important as the insulation for the house. The living room and the three large bedrooms upstairs in my house had cathedral ceilings. Because warm air always rises, cathedral ceilings waste a lot of gas for heating. Now let us calculate the air spaces for the two structures:

The Nine-unit rental:
House: 800 sq ft x 8' = 3600 cubic ft air volume
The other 8 units: 1500 sq ft x 7' = 10,500 cubic ft air volume
Total: 14,100 cubic ft air volume
My house:
3000 sq ft x 13' = 39,000 cubic ft air volume

The air volume to be heated in my house was over 2.5 times larger. This is why the property of 9 units never used more natural gas than my house did in winter.

Suppose that the 9 units were only occupied by 14 tenants, and each person had about 1000 cubic ft heated air volume. We spend at least one third of our time in a bed. How much room does a bed need? We need only 3'x7' = 21 sq ft for a twin bed and 5'x7' = 35 sq ft for a double bed. Including the space below and above a bed, the air space for a bed is at most 37 sq ft x 8' = 297 cubic ft. My wife and I needed less than 300 cubic ft heated air volume to stay comfortable at night. Yet, building code requires 130 times more than necessary air volume to be heated (39,000/300 = 130). Does it make sense to have such building code? I have had thousands of tenants for my rental units over the years. If they pay their own utility bills for heating, most of them don't use heaters at all. Along coastal area between Los Angeles and San Francisco, it is rarely cold enough to get frost. It is very easy for me to know if a renter used a heater or not. If the walls and ceiling of a bathroom have mildew, it is a sign that the heater is never turned on. This is simple, a heater is needed the most when a person strips down to take a shower in the Winter. If the heater is off, the walls are cold. The person feels the cold too, so the person turns on their shower water as hot as tolerable. Hot water gives out a lot of streams, this steam condenses on the cold wall and ceiling, and mildew grows where this moisture is.

For a housing development to be energy efficient, the size of the units matters. If the units are excessively large, adding a lot of insulation will not do much good. If housing prices are not affordable, one thing that can help ease the problem is to reduce the unit size. This is the free market solution too. If something is too expensive, a consumer should have the right to consume less. Local politicians should not have the power to prohibit room sharing and to force residents to live in large units.

Since the City of Morro Bay needed small affordable housing units, yet there were few of such units available. Therefore, those substandard housing units under my management rarely had more than a couple days' vacancies during any turn-overs. If you think the City of Morro Bay would encourage me to operate these units that the city badly needed, it would surprise you. Since day one of these units during my management, the city tried to shut it down. I just didn't give the city any excuses to do it. Every time the City Fire Dept gave me a list of mandatory improvements or corrections, I never argued or questioned why the fire department didn't require the previous owner to make any of these improvements. This was the only property that I managed and received multiple letters of appreciation from neighbors and occupants. One family of 5, a young couple and 3 children lived there in the two-bedroom apartment for a few years. The unit had only 300 square ft living space, or 60 sq ft per person for the family of 5. Each bedroom is barely large enough for a bed. I believe that the couple occupied the bigger bedroom, and their three girls shared the smaller bedroom with two bunk beds. When they bought a house in the nearby town, they moved out and sent a thank-you letter to me for allowing them to live there. During these years, the couple paid about 1/3 of the rent of a normal 2-bedroom apartment and the saving added up to the amount of the down payment for their house. Yes! It took a lot of guts to squeeze a family of 5 into a tiny place. But there was nothing wrong with the place, I made sure it was safe for them. The prospect of a better future, perhaps, allowed them to endure the hardship temporarily.

What was the other option for the family? The family could have rented a regular 2 or 3-bedroom apartment. It would have been rather comfortable for the family to live in a regular apartment, but they would have been paying 3 or 4 times more rent than they did. They would not have been able to save anything to realize their American dream. To the family, the rent was cheap and this was about the only way they could save money for the down-payment on their future home. Some landlords would not let them, a family of five, rent a regular two-bedroom apartment because of possible over-crowding. I checked my rental records; their rent was really not cheap at all! They actually paid a premium for this small unit. The per square foot rent of the small unit was not lower than the regular rent, because the rent included all utilities. Now suppose local politicians and bureaucrats forced them to rent a three-bedroom apartment that met all zoning requirements and building codes in the name of decent housing and quality of life, do you think the family would thank the local officials for their "caring"? Or the "caring" was really terror in disguise, local officials' "caring" wanted turn the family's American Dream into American Nightmare. Are these "caring" officials much better than a bunch of monsters?

This is not the end of the story. In early 2020, before COVID-19 lockdown, I was shopping at the local COSTCO store. A lady stopped and said: "Hi! Mr. Wu, how are you?" I didn't recognize the lady and didn't know how to reply. She realized that I didn't recognize her, so she introduced herself: "My family rented the 2-bedroom apt. in Morro Bay from you. I answered: "Yes! How are you? How is Romeo?" Romeo was her husband's name. I had thousands of former tenants but only one Romeo, and he was the one who wrote a "Thank You" letter to me after they moved out. Her name was not Juliet, I never remembered her name. She said: "He is somewhere around here." While we were talking, Romeo showed up. He recognized me too. They asked if I still live in the house where they used to bring their monthly rent to me. I told them I built a new house for my family after I retired from my teaching job and the new house was only about two hundred yards from the old house. I asked them about their three little girls, they said the girls were all grown up and married. They had a total of 6 grandchildren. I had last seen them about a quarter of a century ago, it was amazing that they still remembered me. When they rented the apartment from me, they were enduring a hardship. Many would like to forget about it and everything associated with it, especially the loathsome slumlord. I appreciated that they didn't consider me a disgusting slumlord, but a friend. Since I mentioned them in the book, I got their address. After the book is published, I would like to send them a copy.

I was invited to join a Nextdoor group on the internet two or three years ago. Neighbors in the group may post anything within its rules for others to read, to discuss and to respond. My book featured the City of San Luis Obispo's transformation from a place with very affordable housing to the city with the least affording housing in the US. I thought it was appropriate to post a few excerpts from the manuscript for my neighbors to read as a free preview. Since I discuss the causes and the consequences of the housing crisis, I knew many would be offended. As expected, I got some jeers to my postings, but luckily, I got more cheers than jeers. I called those who profited from high housing costs "the housing establishment" or more appropriately "the housing Mafia" including but not limited to politicians and voters advocating for "slow growth" in housing developments.

When one neighbor responded to my posting by asking: "How did you guys manage? I make about $100,000 a year, but I cannot afford to buy a house I like!" Many answered the inquiry and made suggestions. I offered an answer too. I started out saying: "May I offer an example how a couple in the 90s earning minimum wages or close to with a family of 5 managed to buy a house near San Luis Obispo?" Then I described briefly the property in Morro Bay and how the couple rented an apartment from me. They paid only one third to one fourth of the going rate for a usual apartment and saved enough to move into their own house in a few years. I expected officials in Morro Bay would be offended by my posting, but I didn't expect my neighbors in San Luis Obispo would be too. But apparently, the invisible hands of the Housing Mafia are everywhere. Most local housing officials simply don't want to see the fact that a "substandard" housing unit may be good for someone. If they let anyone read the example that I posted, their "noble" efforts to provide only decent housings those meet all the zoning and code requirements would be only counterproductive. I thought many of my neighbors would be interested in my example. But unfortunately, few got a chance to read it. The Nextdoor "Leads" couldn't come up with any even far-fetched reasons to censor my posting, but they had many tricks in their tool bag. If a posting is more than a few sentences long, the posting normally shows only the first two to three lines and ends with a "*see more*" sign. For my posting, "Leads" simply deleted my posting except the first two lines, but they left the "*see more*" at the end of the first two lines. If anyone clicked at "*see more*", nothing would show up! They probably thought my posting was offensive to someone, but they had no justifiable reason to censor it. They used the cheap trick to fool readers and wanted neighbors to think this old man couldn't do anything right.

As housing costs increase in California, many struggling families simply cannot afford to live in large housing units. Yet politicians still restrict any development of small housing units in the name of "quality of life". We feel more comfortable living in a large housing unit than in a small unit. It all comes down to the cost. If we can afford the cost, we can choose to live in a comfortable unit. If it costs an arm and a leg to live in a large unit, we may not want to live in a large unit. If we have to mortgage our future for just a comfortable living-quarter, we may not feel it is worth it. It is ridiculous and cruel for local politicians to deny families and individuals the option to live in a small housing unit in the name of "quality of life". So, these families and individuals will struggle the rest of their lives to pay high rent, and forever be the slaves of the so called "quality of life". Large living quarters may not represent "quality of life" to a struggling family at all, if the family has to spend one-half of their income for housing cost. Instead, large living quarters destroy the chance of upward mobility of the family, thus, destroy the life of the family.

Right after I purchased the property in Morro Bay, I noticed that the roof leaked badly. That was the first thing I fixed. I also found a lot of problems on the natural gas line, several joints were so corroded that the tubing and connectors were barely touching each other. Some concrete shower pans were cracked, so water just leaked into the ground instead of going into the drain. If shower water could leak into the ground, then bugs and rats could get into living space too. I also found a lot of other problems but found no insulation anywhere on the property. The Morro Bay City Fire Dept made an annual inspection of the property in Spring, every time the inspector gave me a rather long, but not excessive, list of defects to be corrected. I always fixed everything on the list promptly. I could not help but wonder what happened before I purchased it, did the Fire Dept ever conduct a similar annual inspection at all? Why were there so many problems waiting for me to take care? But the City Council still thought the Fire Dept was not doing enough to shut the place down. The piece of land was zoned for three single-family houses, yet the three lots had 9 multifamily units. It was non-conforming land–use.

Around early 1990s, the Police Dept of City of Morro Bay hired a building code enforcement officer. The duty of this officer was to find any excuses to shut down non-conforming land-use as fast as possible.

Around 1995, the city gave me a notice to shut it down. But I encouraged all the occupants to appeal directly to the Mayor. Almost all tenants were employed in the city. If the place was shut down, they might have to leave the area. The mayor of the city intervened. The place was spared. Apparently, the Fire Dept inspections were limited to fire hazards and the code enforcement office in the police department didn't have enough expertise to enforce building code. Around the year 2000, the building department inspectors collaborated with the code enforcement officer in the Police Dept. Finally, the Building Dept inspectors used an illegal tactic to close the 9-unit rental. The inspectors couldn't find any legitimate reasons to close down the place. They insisted on checking possible gas line leaks by using new construction's standard, by pumping the pressure to 30 lbs per square inch in the gas line and waiting for 30 minutes to see if the pressure would drop. This test violated their own rules, because this was not a new construction. The normal gas line pressure is only 3-4 lbs per square inch. For new constructions this is normal testing procedure, when every outlet is capped before any gas appliance is connected. For an existing dwelling, this is not the proper way to test the gas line, because many appliances are connected. Each gas appliance has a shut-off valve, but all gas valves are designed to stop gas flow with a pressure only 3-4 lbs instead of 30 lbs per square inch in the line. The Building Dept Inspectors of Morro Bay didn't think the manager of a run-down small apartment complex would know the difference. I told them what they did was illegal and warned them that I would expose their violation. So, they forced me to demolish the structure quickly to get rid of any evidence I might use against them.

If a housing unit is occupied, one never needs to pressure test the gas line for leaks. One's nose is a good gas detector. If there is a bad leak, anyone's nose can easily detect it. There are dozens of detectors available one can use to detect the smallest leak that one's nose may miss. When I bought this complex, there were several copper gas lines in some of the units. Nature gas was corrosive to copper, I quickly replaced them with aluminum ones. This is what institutional racism looks like. The previous owner, a Caucasian lady had no trouble to operate these rental units as some of the copper lines were barely touching the fittings. Yet after I, an ethnic minority, made numerous improvements, the City wanted demolish this complex using far-fetched excuses and illegal tactics. Usually bureaucrats take orders from elected politicians. But some bureaucrats are worse than the elected officials. Elected officials come and go, a racist bureaucrat can last for decades.

This is just a typical tactic that local government officials may use to protect their turf. If they believed that small housing units would harm their benefit, they will get rid of these units any way they can, legal or not. They could not stand a living example that small housing units with numerous code violations were actually good for some occupants. If they let any of these units to exist, it is a proof that their jobs are worse than useless. What they do are counterproductive. These units were demolished on Sept. 10, 2001. It was exactly one day before the fateful day of 9/11, so I will never forget the date. I threatened to sue the city for Building Dept. inspectors' illegal action. However, this property turned out to be an excellent investment, because the three lots with ocean views were worth a great deal by then. So I didn't sue the city. But I read a newspaper report that City of Morro Bay hired a part time city attorney soon after the incident, perhaps in anticipation of my lawsuit. A couple years later, I heard the city government of Morro Bay had trouble balancing its budget. The City of Morro Bay probably got what it deserved. I didn't take it to court, but maybe someone else did.

I have another first hand experience about energy waste in a single-family housing. I didn't know how much energy a single-family house wasted until I bought a condo in South San Francisco near International Airport. The condo complex consists of six buildings each six-stories tall, the lowest two levels are garages and top 4 levels are housing units. After 2008 Sub-Prime Financial Crisis, the housing prices in Bay Area dropped about 40-50%. In 2010, I bought a unit on the second level of the housing complex while housing prices in the Bay Area were about to bottom out. The building was brand new and its insulation met the building code requirement. After the first winter, I noticed that I had never turned on the heater, yet the room temperature was always in the rather comfortable low-70s. My downstairs neighbors probably turned on their heater setting fairly high all winter long. I didn't need to turn on my own heater, because I was using recycled heat from my downstairs neighbors. Not only I didn't need to turn on my heater, but also my upstairs neighbors might not need to turn on their heaters. We recycle paper, plastic, glass, metals etc to save energy. We believe we use less energy to re-cycle a material than to manufacture the same material from scratch. Yet, when we build a lot of single-family houses, we just let heat escape through roofs, dissipating into the atmosphere and contributing to global warming. When we build low rise or high rise housing dwellings, we could recycle the energy for room heating again and again. The saving was nearly 100% every time, so I thought.

Out of curiosity, I contacted my downstairs neighbor. He said that he always set his thermostat at 68 degrees as recommended by EPA, the Federal Environmental Protection Agency. I was surprised that he didn't set his at middle 70s. How could my room temperature end up a few degrees warmer than his setting? I thought about it. Then it made perfect sense. The thermostat is about 4 feet from the floor and 5 feet from the ceiling, and the heat grill is about 8' from the floor. Hot air always rises. In order to keep the thermostat at 68 degrees, the air at the ceiling would be a few degrees warmer. Regardless of whatever the building code requirement for ceiling insulation may be, the heater in my downstairs neighbors' condo heated my condo more than his own. So the heat recycled is not just 100%, it is more than 100%! This tells us how single-family houses are in wasteful energy use, especially those with cathedral ceilings.

Unfortunately, this is not the end of energy waste in housing. Even recycling and public transportation contribute to energy waste due to too many single-family houses in California. Because of large building lots, a garbage truck sometimes needs to go 100', instead of 30', 40' or 50' to empty a recycle can. A garbage truck is heavy, it doesn't have good gas mileage. We cannot even be sure that the energy saving from recycling is enough to cover the energy needs for recycle. In order to recycle, we need to use a lot of energy! We need to manufacture cans and the plastic bags, to move the truck around sparsely populated residential areas, to lift the cans to empty them, to sort the recycled material, to package the material, to transport the material and, finally to recover the material. Recycling has only one obvious benefit, there is less material going into a landfill. But energy saving from recycling is questionable. The most efficient type of recycling is the reuse of heat in multistory housing structures in winter. But local governments in California like to ignore the advantages of multistory housing developments. Instead, they just promote worthless recycling to make themselves look good. Who pays for the wasteful ways of their self-promotion? All the rate-paying customers of the garbage company.

Similarly, almost all public transportation in California is a waste of tax dollars. Every city in California, little, large or in between, has public transportation. Because of the prevailing low-density housing development, public transportation requires heavy government subsidy to survive. Except a couple of metropolitans, most public transportation in California is a bottomless pit for public subsidies. It should replace many private automobiles. But because of low ridership, it becomes a big environmental hazard. Except during rush hours, most big buses with a driver and maybe one or two passengers in small towns wind through sparsely populated residential area trying to pick up a couple more passengers. It is a useless scheme and self-defeating. When a bus winds through a residential area, it takes longer for passengers to get to the destination. The longer it takes, the less frequently the bus may run, the less frequently the bus can run, the longer the average waiting time. The longer to waiting time, the fewer the users. Don't you think the subsides could be better used fiscally and environmentally for residents to use Uber or Lyft instead of city buses.

4.6 Distorted Investment, Wasteful Consumption in Housing

Housing is part of our consumption. When local politicians made housing development harder and harder by creating a lot of red tape, housing prices went up rapidly. When housing prices went up much faster than the inflation rate, all homeowners reaped a windfall. For a lot of homeowners, the largest part of their life savings is in the equity of their houses.

To most homeowners, buying a house is no longer just a consumption. The bigger and better house a homeowner buys, the more equity and bigger the windfall the homeowner will get. When a bird walks like a duck and sounds like a duck, it is a duck! When we put money into something, we can see it growing in value year after year, so it looks like an investment. When we sell it, we can be sure to get a lot more than what we put in, so it performs like an investment. It is an investment! Not only is it an investment, for most homeowners, it is a better investment than any other investments they could ever put their money into. When a homeowner sells their primary residence, one half of a million dollars of capital gain is exempted from income taxes for a married couple and a quarter million for an individual. It is more profitable and safer than other investments. If you buy stock on the margin, there may be margin calls. That is, as stock prices drop, you may be forced to put more cash into the stocks. Say you bought a share of X Stock for $100; you put in only $20. The broker loaned you the rest. If the stock price dropped to $80, you would need to cough up more cash to protect your share. Otherwise your share would be sold to pay for the broker's loan. Nothing like that would ever happen to homeowners. If the house value dropped down and the homeowners' equity was wiped out, the bank or other mortgage lender could never force the homeowner to put in more cash into the house. During the financial crisis after 2008, housing prices dropped up to 50% in some places. No mortgage lender could force a homeowner to put more cash into the house and the federal government even came up with HARP (Home Affordable Refinance Program) to help those recent buyers who lost equity on their houses.

How did the local officials push housing prices up far above inflation? At first, it seemed innocent enough. A house would last for decades, so city officials just encouraged builders and homeowners to make houses look nice. Building code could force thicker insulation on new houses and it made perfect sense for energy conservation. Also, local officials required better structure for better earthquake resistance, and better roofing material for better fire resistance. As all these sensible improvements were added, bureaucrats also snuck in a few rather senseless requirements, and house prices went up way above inflation.

I mentioned my personal experience in the city about this change. Let me repeat briefly to show the increase in housing price in town. In 1972 I bought my first house for $23,000 and sold it in 1978 for $80,000. I bought my second house a year later for in 1973 $31,000 from the owner who bought the house a year ago for only $22,000. In 1978, I moved into a new house that was more than double the size of my first house. I paid $100,000 for the new house in 1978 and I sold it in 2002 for $540,000. These examples illustrate how lucrative the investment in housing could be. Of course, every homeowner in town reaped the same windfall in their houses. I just profited more than most of them, because I owned more than 50 housing units by early 80s.

As housing values rose, homeowners and local politicians reached a silent pact. In the name of "quality of life," politicians added more and more restrictions and red tape on housing developments. Homeowners supported these politicians in anticipation of higher housing prices and windfall for their "investments." But they claimed that they were for "slow growth" to prevent "urban sprawl" or "to preserve rural lifestyle and to prevent damage to environment." This is a powerful alliance that few dared to go against. Local politicians are a diverse group. Some push the housing price to high levels like the ones in California, while others didn't, like the ones in Texas. Even within the State of California, housing prices are different. San Luis Obispo and Santa Maria are very similar cities about 30 miles apart. Both are close to the coast but not on the coast. Fifty years ago, the two cities had about the same population, around 30,000, and about the same housing prices. Now, 50 years later, Santa Maria has triple the population and one half of the median house price as those of San Luis Obispo. Some claim that when politicians restrict housing developments, there may be a trace of racism in their decisions. They use restrictions to push up housing prices to keep low income ethnic minorities out. It is always difficult to prove the intention or motivation of a politician's decision. But the fact may speak for itself. San Luis Obispo doesn't have any concentration of ethnic minorities, but Santa Maria has a big Chicano population.

Once housing price increase exceeds inflation rate, it is the beginning of a vicious cycle. After World War II, there was a sudden increase in housing demand for returning GIs. The US's industrial power had no trouble changing from the Arsenal of Democracy to production for peaceful times. Regardless of a spike in housing demand, nobody dared to rip off returning GIs for their needs of new housing. The free marketplace worked exceedingly well to provide affordable housing for the heroes everywhere in the US. Housing prices did go up, but they mainly just kept up with inflation. When a middle-class family moved into a house and took out a 30-year mortgage, the family often stayed put. If the family size didn't increase drastically, there was no reason or incentive for the family to move into bigger houses.

During the first few years of a new mortgage, the monthly mortgage payments cover mostly the interest, so very little of the monthly payment goes into the principal. The owner's equity in the house increases slowly at first. To move into a much bigger or better house is an expensive proposition. To sell the old house, the realtors normally charge 6% of the sales price. To get a new mortgage, the borrower normally pays a 1 to 1 & ½% of fee up front. To move into another house, the family's equity in the old house may be wiped out by the realtors' fees and lender's charge. In this situation, the family is prudent to stay in the house until they pay off the mortgage. Then the equity of the house is worth about two to three years of annual salary and it is still a sizable saving for the family.

Let us look at the owner who sold me the second house I ever owned. He made about 350% profit in a year for his investment. If the house was his primary residence, then he needed to buy a replacement house. What kind of house should he buy?

First, he made a killing on the house, so he could afford to buy a bigger and better house. He might not need one, but could he find a better and more lucrative "investment"? If buying a house was the best "investment", it made sense to buy a better and bigger house. A better house would be a better investment and a bigger house would be a bigger investment. You didn't need to be a genius to figure out why California's housing prices took off in the 1970s. Whatever were the reasons, they were not aberrations. Once the price took off, it was like a snow-ball starting to roll downhill. It was hard to stop, and it got bigger and bigger. It was really a vicious cycle. Bigger houses led to higher prices and higher prices led to bigger "investment".

Usually, for a small investor, before the person can invest in anything, the person needs to save part of their disposable income; instead of using the money for necessities or indulgence, the persons must put off the spending for a later day. The profit of the investment is a reward for the person's willingness to take on the risk and the sacrifice for instant gratification in exchange for future enjoyment. But "investment" in a house differs from the normal investment for a small investor. It doesn't have the usual risk of other investment, because local politicians will make sure that there will be no sudden increase in housing supply and, thus, very little chance the house would not appreciate in value. Investment in housings give homeowners instant enjoyment of a spacious house and the prestige of owning a great house.

When there was a demand for larger and better houses on larger lots, local politicians were more than willing to provide. It was their idea in the first place, and now, they got local homeowners on board. This was a powerful coalition. It had names like "Citizens for slow growth!" or "Coalition for quality of life!" These groups had very convincing slogans: "Maintain small town character!", "Alliance for neighborhood harmony" or "More parks and open space!" The slogan: "Maintain small town characters!" means no housing development can be taller than two stories. "Maintain neighborhood harmony" means no apartment or condominium buildings can be next to any existing single-family houses. "More park and open space!" mean no housing development at all and let my house double in value in the next few years.

As new housing development provided bigger and better houses on more spacious lots, prices had no place to go but up. If anyone proposed a multi-family housing development anywhere, the neighboring homeowners would cry fault. They attended public hearings in droves: "Not in my backyard! (NIMBY)" or "This project destroys the harmony of the neighborhood!"

Who were the victims of the high housing prices? The ones who wanted to buy but could not afford to. Since they could not afford to move to an area, they could not vote. Another group of victims were those who spent large parts of their income just to pay rent. They were busy working, probably overtime, so they didn't have time to go to public hearings. They were silent, but they were not the majority, so local politicians paid little attention to them.

What might be wrong with the best "investment"? Suppose that a family bought a bigger and better house, not because the family needed the house, but because it was a good "investment." First, the family is buying something that is not very useful to them, so it is a waste. All levels of government more or less encourage this kind of waste. Federal government tax code allowed unlimited mortgage interest on itemized deduction until President Donald Trump put a limit on it in 2017. All state governments still allow unlimited itemized deductions for mortgage interest. Local governments, especially California's local governments, cater to buyers who look at houses as investments instead of life's necessity, while ignoring the needs of affordable housing for low-income workers. Housing is a consumption, and it is necessary just like water and electricity. If it is a necessity, we should encourage individuals to use a moderate amount, or maybe just enough to support a comfortable life, so there will be enough to go around. When individuals considered homeownership as an investment, they believed the more the better. What happened was an extravagant amount of waste. Usually, state and local governments give homeowners partial exemption on Property Tax. This is a clear discrimination against renters. Homeowners are in much better financial positions than renters are. Governments play the reverse role of Robin Hood by robbing the poor and giving to the rich. In fact, instead of exemption for owner occupied housing units, the property tax, like income tax, should be progressive. As the value of a house gets higher, the property tax rate should be higher too. This is just like how a utility consumer using low amounts will pay low-lifeline rate. When a user wastes, the rate should increase progressively.

The allure of a big profit for homeowners is tempting. Unfortunately, the harvest is far away, but the cost to maintain the investment is immediate. Let us look at some of them:

1. We already discussed high utility bills for big houses. They pay part of the utility bill because the house is bigger than necessary;
2. The cost of monthly mortgage payments: If homeowners only buy what they need, the mortgage payment will be lower. The loan-initiation fee will be lower;
3. Property Tax: Because the houses are much bigger than needed, homeowners pay higher taxes year after year;
4. Bigger houses need more insurance, so premiums increase proportionally to the value of the house.
5. Bigger houses need more maintenance, so homeowners pay more to protect the "investment". These costs include maid services, exterminator services to keep pests under control, plumbing, electrical repair, exterior and interior painting, fence repair, etc.;
6. Usually, a large house comes with a spacious yard. The fancy house needs a fancy garden to match. The cost of gardeners' services adds up fast;
7. When housing cost increases in an area, the price of everything else increases too. The cost of living also increases, including grocery bills, restaurant checks, entertainment, auto expenses, clothing, etc. In San Francisco, some restaurants not only recommend 15–25% for gratuities but also add 4 or 5% for workers' health insurance on the checks.

8. When a family buys a big house, they may rarely use some rooms or areas. But the room and area still need proper furniture and decoration. All floor needs proper coverings, windows need blinds and shades whether they use them or not;

9. Last but not least, because houses are big and on spacious lots, public transportation is inefficient and private automobiles are necessary. Almost always automobile expense is the second largest expense on a family budget. Most people may not even realize that large houses on big lots result in large automobile expenses.

The extra expenses could have been a family's real savings, but now all become an investment in the house and are tied up. Of course, if house values increase as the owners expect, the owners can take the money out by refinancing. The trouble is, it is supposed to be the owners' money. Yet, if the owners want to use it, they have to pay interest. In this respect, the investment may not be that great.

In some high housing cost areas, homeowners may have a hefty nest egg in their houses. Yet, the homeowners have to wait for a long time before they can use the money. Often the owners have to sell the houses and move away to a place where housing prices are low. This happens in Silicon Valley. People spent their lifetimes growing up and working in the area. But after they retire, it makes little sense for them to live in an expensive house any more. About one third of the residents who moved out of the state moved to Texas where housing prices are very reasonable.

Suppose a couple in Silicon Valley have retired. Their children grew up in the Valley, have finished college and would like to return to the Valley to work and to stay close to their parents. Unfortunately, they wouldn't be able to do so. It may not be difficult for them to find jobs in Silicon Valley, but it would impossible for them to find affordable housing. Couldn't their parents help them? Sure, but in order for the parents to take money out of their house, they would have to sell their house and move to Texas or, maybe closer, to Nevada. This means that parents and offspring could not live close. The investment in the house has been great for the parents but not good for the family, and especially terrible for the next generation. Isn't it better if housing prices just keep up with inflation and not much more? Everyone lives in a unit that is just right for one's needs. If housing is affordable everywhere, many of the problems we face today would just disappear. There will be no working poor! If a person has a full-time job, the person can live comfortably close to the job. Every worker could build up a saving for the rainy days. Most of the homeless will disappear too. The City of San Francisco doesn't need a budget of hundreds of million of dollars to house or help the homeless. There will always be a few homeless people, but the number is rather manageable. If most workers can live close to their jobs, the morning rush hour will disappear too. The freeway will be free for traffic to move, and air will be clean too. College students can get part-time jobs to support themselves like in the 'good old days.' When they graduate from college, they are not deeply indebted with student loans. Since housing cost is very affordable, the health care may become affordable too. States with high housing costs usually also have high healthcare costs. In the US, there are people who cannot afford to buy enough food to maintain a healthy diet. It is not because food is expensive, but because housing costs too much and many don't have enough left to buy food.

4.7 Not Enough Saving, Not Enough Investment on Infrastructures

2018, the last year the date for GDP (in million) by countries was available:

Table 5: GDP in 2018 for US and China

	United States	China
GDP	$20,494,050	$13,407,398
Population	327,096,265	1,427,647,786
Saving Rate	17.6%	46.7%

Roughly, China' GDP is about 2/3 of that of the US while China's population is 4 times larger. Per capita, an American is about 6 times richer than a Chinese. Yet, on average, an American saves only about 17.6% of their income and a Chinese can save 46.7%. The total saving in the US is 17.6% of $20.495 trillion or around 3.6 trillion. In China, the total saving is 46.7% of $13.4 trillions or $6.26 trillions. The total saving in China is almost double of the savings in the US.

Normally, the rich can save more than the poor. What happens here? I discussed part of the answer in the last Section, where we learned that in the US, many families consider their equity in their houses as part of their savings. Unfortunately, when we look at the country, the savings in housing is not really savings at all. You can use the real savings, or you can invest it in something productive. For example, you can use your savings to buy stock in a company like Amazon, which provides a service, or in a company, like Ford Motor Company, which manufactures a product. You could also buy a government bond which enables the government to improve infrastructure. The money in a house is just consumption. If the owner buys a huge house that the family doesn't need, it still is not an investment. It is just wasteful consumption. But to the owner, if he can get more out of it than what he put in, isn't it an investment? To the individual, yes? It works as an investment. To the country, it is not! As the owner sells the house, the owner needs to find a buyer. The buyer is just a person who takes over another person's extravagant consumption.

Big houses on large lots create a serious problem in the US. The illusion of saving on house leads to a lack of real saving, a lack of nest eggs for the rainy days, a lack of capital formation, and especially not enough investment in infrastructures.

During any unexpected crises, like the Covid-19 virus outbreak in 2020, everyone could see the advantage of high savings. China appeared to handle the crisis firmly and efficiently. Yet, rich countries like the US and Western European countries appeared less decisive to stop the spread of the virus. Communist China wanted to brag about that its authoritarian regime might be better suited to handle a crisis than all the rich democracies could. Then, the case in Taiwan totally crashed the myth before China could spread it. Taiwan has been a solid and vibrant democracy since the new millennium. During the outbreak of the virus in Wuhan, there were three daily commercial flights from Wuhan to Taiwan. Almost all experts predicted that Taiwan would be the first hot spot of the outbreak outside China. But Taiwan never used Draconian decrees or total lockdown to stop the pandemic. As of

April 10, 2020, there were 435 confirmed patients and 15 death among 23 million citizens.

But China had one advantage. When the government ordered a total lockdown, government officials didn't need to worry about how unemployed workers would survive the crisis. Even workers earning only minimum wages never spent one half of take-home pay for housing cost. All workers with a job could build savings to protect themselves for the unexpected. Many workers in the US cannot even afford to live near where they work, let alone to build savings. It is absurd! How could workers in a poor country have savings, but workers in the richer country could not? It appears ridiculous, but it is true. If President Donald Trump and Governor Andrew Cuomo didn't need to worry about the hardship of unemployed workers, they might have acted more decisively to stop the spread of the Covid-19 Pandemic. They could have saved hundreds of thousands of American lives. But we should not blame them for their hesitations, let us blame those who caused the problem of high housing costs that made many American workers spend 50% of their income on housing. So, the high housing cost is not a local problem, the high costs destroy the low-wage workers' ability to save and also weakens the ability of federal and state governments to respond decisively in a crisis.

4.8 Big Houses Led to Big Trade Deficit

Up to the early 1970s, housing prices were still fairly affordable. This was also the time that the increases in the housing prices started to exceed inflation. Up to this point, the US trade deficit was non-existent to negligible, but it was creeping up. By 1992, the pattern of housing price increase was fairly clear. Housing was no longer just a life necessity, and many owners considered the cost of housing to be an investment. The vicious cycle began, bigger and bigger houses led to higher and higher price increases, and vice versa. Bigger and bigger houses represented even more wasteful consumption. In 1992, the US trade deficit was only $39 billion. Yet, in 10 years, it ballooned to more than $400 billion. The consumer price index only increased 28% in the same period. Something very basic in the US economy had changed in these years. Consumers didn't eat much more or spend much more on clothing, but housing costs increased by leaps and bounds. This increase was reflected in the trade deficit. As we looked at the entire country, housing expenses were part of consumption, regardless of how individuals considered it as consumption or investment. We discussed earlier in this Chapter that as the size of houses increased, other consumptions also increased to keep up with the big house. Increasing usage of energy for heating and cooling, of course, as well as driving greater distances were a direct result of the bigger houses.

Since the early 1990s, the US has consistently rung up huge trade deficits. It peaked in 2006 at about $750 billions, right before the real estate bubble burst.

But according to the basic economic theory, a country's trade deficit is not sustainable for long. As a country's trade deficit increases, the country will have trouble paying for its debt. The country's paper money will be worth less on the world market. The economic term is called devaluing a country's currency. It makes the country's goods less expensive to foreigners, so foreigners will buy more. This makes everything in the country more costly, especially those imported goods. If things become more expensive, people will buy less, and imports will decrease. If imports decrease and exports increase, the trade deficit will decrease or will even reverse into a surplus. But, in the US, it didn't work in the usual way.

The trade deficit in the US shows that we spend too much or we live beyond our means. Americans are the richest in the world. How could we live beyond our means? Did we eat too much? Yes! We eat too much. An average American is over-weight. Many of our kids are obese. But food is cheap in the US. The average poor family only spends about one eighth of the family budget on food. This is about the least amount among all rich countries. College education is expensive, but it is only for a few years. One doesn't need a college degree to survive, so college education is not a necessity. Health care is very expensive. But if one stays healthy, then the cost is very limited. Automobiles are very expensive, but used cars are not. Auto insurance is expensive, but it depends on how one drives and how much one drives. For a good driver it is affordable, or at least, manageable. Going to a foreign country for vacation is expensive. You need not go, if you cannot afford. What causes the trade deficit or our over consumption? There is only one thing left - housing! Many of us live in a big house we don't need. I am guilty myself. I live in not just one house but two. I built my primary residence myself, so it didn't cost me much. But it is a big house with 10,000 square foot roof area. It is too big for an old couple. I wish I could convert it into ten units so 20 occupants could live in them comfortably instead of just two. But zoning regulation doesn't allow it. In 2011, I bought a condo in Silicon Valley after the housing bubble burst. To maintain the second home has been costly, but the appreciation in value still gives me a handsome profit besides the luxury of a second home. I hardly use my second home one tenth of the time. My two homes are fully furnished, even though both are under used. Many of the construction materials and furniture in my homes are imported; I am sure my house and second home contribute to the trade deficit of the US. Please don't blame me for my indulgence, I only buy what is available. Of course, local politicians and bureaucrats may claim that they only provide housing for what people want. Now let us ask this question: "What does a minimum wage worker want for housing in San Francisco?" A million-dollar 800 square foot one-bedroom condo? A minimum-wage worker could not afford a million-dollar condo in San Francisco! San Francisco need a lot of minimum wage workers. These workers need small but affordable rooms, we just cannot find any in San Francisco or even within 30 miles of San Francisco. The US's trade deficit will never disappear as long as local politicians continue to shovel big houses down our throats.

Now we look at those foreign countries that ring up a big trade surplus against the US. China is the country responsible for about one half of the US's trade deficit. But China doesn't want the imbalance of trade to change. It wants to maintain a big surplus in the trade with the US. Export drives China's economic engine, without a big surplus from trade with the US, China's GDP growth will grind to a halt. China used trade surplus to buy a large amount of US Treasury Bills, so the Chinese government actually financed the US federal government's deficit spending and propped up the value of the US dollar. If the dollar doesn't devalue, then China can continue its trade surplus with the US. Some Chinese also bring money to the US to buy US companies and real estate.

President Clinton helped China to get into the WTO, World Trade Organization. Many Americans had the illusion that as China joined the world community and became rich, its authoritarian regime would gradually loosen its grip and allow more freedom and rights to the people. Yet China only took advantage of its trading partners and rarely played by the rules. For example, after joining the WTO, other countries expected China to open its financial market to foreign banks. Almost two decades later, foreign banks could only own minority shares until 2018. When foreign banks were finally allowed 51% stakes, China still didn't play fairly. In a recent report on The Economist, a British weekly news magazine, a foreign banker applied for a majority share in a Chinese bank. Instead of formally rejecting the application, the regulators simply refused to acknowledge the receipt of the application. The report didn't show all the details. Perhaps the banker wanted to remain anonymous so he would not offend the Chinese regulators.

With the exception of agricultural products, when a US company tried to sell goods to China, the company would be advised or be compelled to manufacture the product in China. Usually the company needed to find a domestic partner and transferring technology was a must. In August 2019, the first Costco store opened in Shanghai. The store opened for business at 10 AM, not only were there long lines outside the store before it opened but it was also the first time in the company's history that the store had to close at 3 PM. Chinese shoppers almost grabbed every single merchandise in sight, and the store could not restock fast enough. By 3 PM, all shelves were nearly empty, the store had to close for the day. What did it mean? The so-called free market economy in China was not nearly free enough. There were not enough competitions in retail business. Possibly, the central planner of the country wanted to keep retail price of all merchandise high enough so Chinese consumers would not over consume anything. Why? Perhaps the purpose is to keep Chinese consuming less and saving more. Or, the Party's big wigs decided not to import too much agricultural product from the US. The fact is that Costco's low prices shocked Chinese shoppers. Nowhere else in the world had consumers been shocked as much as Chinese shoppers had.

In the US, a lot of local politicians forced big houses on Americans. In China, the Communist regime manipulated their currency to keep the US dollar over valued. Both groups kept the US trade deficit high. Some Chinese expect the stubborn trade deficit will lead to the downfall of the US. Some of them already brag about China's soon-to-be dominance on the world stage. In September 2020, the Pentagon acknowledged the grim fact that China's Navy became the world largest in number of warships. It might not mean much if a small patrol boat or a Nimitz-class aircraft carrier counted as one. But there is another number, the total tonnage of warships launched by the Chinese Navy between 2015 and 2019 exceeded that of America over the same period by almost half (Source: Janes).

Normally, all governments discourage excessive consumption with luxury tax. Amazingly, US federal tax code, state tax codes and local property tax law all encourage over consumption in housing. To encourage homeownership, local property tax always allowed some exemption for owner-occupied housing units. If the value of a house is moderate, it is appropriate to give the owner partial exemption of property tax. If an owner can afford a multi-million-dollar house, obviously, the owner doesn't need the exemption. It makes sense to void this exemption. Federal tax code had no limit on the deductible property tax or mortgage interest on income tax returns until President Trump finally put a cap of $10,000 on the deduction for state taxes. Plus, homeowners who deduct mortgage interest are limited to the amount they pay on $750,000 worth of debt, down from $1 million. President Trump is the only US President who did anything to promote moderation on housing in recent history. He not only did the right thing in 2018 but also went against his personal interest. His family business is a development of luxurious housing in Manhattan. When he signed the Federal Income Tax Law to put these caps on deductions, he knew that these caps would not help his family business.

To own one's dwelling in the US is "realizing the American dream". In other cultures, there are similar ideas. In some Asian cultures, a piece of real estate is called an "enduring property" and owning a piece of "enduring property" leads to "endurance" or perseverance. As many Asian immigrants are concerned, owning one's home is not just a sign of "realizing the American dream", it is also a demonstration of a superb personal characteristic of will power. In western cultural, there seems to be a similar idea. A house is a piece of "real" estate, implying everything else is not as "real" or somewhat "pretended".

If homeownership represents the realization of the American Dream, then a better house represents a better American Dream. Since we transform housing from a necessity into an investment, the bigger house means a bigger investment. But we should not forget that housing is still basically a shelter, or a necessity. So, moderation should be the norm and excessiveness is harmful, even destructive. Yet those who indulge themselves in extravagant and wasteful consumption are not discouraged or taxed. Instead, they are generously rewarded by all levels of governments. This is wrong and unfair. When a homeless person goes to a second-hand store to buy a used sleeping bag, the person needs to pay a sales tax. Yet when a billionaire spends multimillion dollars on a 20,000 square foot house, the billionaire gets tax benefit and exemptions. This is not just unfair, it is immoral. One may ignore a little unfairness to a homeless person, but the misconception on housing may destroy this great nation. No one should ignore the possibility!

Let us look at the so-called super power rivalry between the two largest economies in the world, the US and China. To call China a super power is a little far-fetched and exaggerated. China is still a developing country and one of a few countries with an aging population before the country becomes rich. In just about every aspect of the economy, China is not in a position to compete against the US. The US has a rather free marketplace economy, except the housing sector.

China has opened its economy slightly and allowed some entrepreneurs to flourish, but central planning and state-owned enterprises have always been part of China's economy. The evidence of mis-allocation of resources by socialists' planners is plainly visible from many ghost cities. They are not old abandoned cities, but brand-new cities with no occupants. Even casual foreign tourists couldn't help to notice many half-finished high-rise buildings or unoccupied buildings. After I retired from teaching job more than 20 years ago, my wife and I travelled often and joined various tour groups, ocean and river cruises. One question my fellow tourists or shipmates asked me often was: "Why are there so many half-finished or empty buildings in China?" My answer was always: "Central planning and cronyism!"

A story appeared in the February 2019 issue of National Geographic magazine: "Entrepreneurial immigrants have always contributed to U.S. economic growth: First-or-second-generation Americans were instrumental in founding 44 of the top 100 Fortune 500 companies listed in 2018. The companies range from innovators such as Apple and Amazon to financial blue chips like AT&T and Procter & Gamble. The free-market economy provided opportunities—for immigrants and non-immigrants alike—to create companies delivering new services, products, and visions of the future."

America is the land of opportunity. The US Constitution guarantees religious freedom and freedom of speech for everyone. The Chinese Constitution guaranties absolute power for Communist Party bosses. We enjoy basic human rights. In China, the bosses of the Communist party have absolute power to control every aspect of human lives of all residents. Given the choice between the two countries, who in his or her right mind would live, work and raise a family in China. So, counting "entrepreneurial immigrants," it is US 44 vs China 0.

About 15 years ago, many Chinese thought China could easily overtake the US and became the world largest economy. Even if it turned out to be true, it wouldn't be a huge accomplishment. With over 4 times population of the US, being number one economy in the world, China's per capita GDP only reached one fourth of that of the US. The four Little Dragons of Asia reached the "milestone" a long time ago with no big fanfare. But almost all economists know that as the economy of a developing country takes off, GDP can grow rather rapidly at first. Then it always slows down. China is no exception. Also, all rich counties except a few Arabic oil exporters are democracies. Again, China cannot be an exception. Power corrupts! Absolute power, corrupts absolutely. Communist Party bosses have absolute power, and the regime is absolutely corrupt. People living under a corrupt government can never fully develop their potential and any country with corrupt government can never have a fully developed economy.

But China has a big help inside the US. If local politicians keep pushing single-family housing developments and making housing expenses superb investments for home buyers, then the real saving in the US will never catch up with China's. With the vast amount of saving and especially the surplus from trading with the US, China will expand its influence around the world. Money talks and a lot of countries will listen to China. This is the Chinese strategy to dominate the world. It is rather an ironic development. The City of Los Angeles enacted the first zoning regulation to keep laundry business, mostly ran by Chinese, away from white residential areas. Quickly, this practice spread to the whole state and beyond. San Francisco and surrounding Bay Area have about the most stringent zoning regulations in the world, yet the region has a vibrant Chinese community. The zoning regulations not only fail to restrict Chinese but also may help Communist bosses in China to dominate the world.

4.9 Environmental Disasters in Addition to Energy Waste (Paving Footprint Per Person)

In California, politicians use the "Environmental Impact Report" to slow down housing developments. They also promote single-family houses that waste a lot of energy. Just about every local bureaucrat and elected official appear to care about environment. Since they require environmental impact study for each housing development, they obviously scrutinize every report thoroughly and make sure that every development meets the highest standard to protect the environment. So, other than energy waste, housing developments must be environmentally sound. Unfortunately, this is far from the reality! The so called "Environmental Impact Report" is mostly just for a show. Local politicians usually just want to pay lip service for environment. In fact, California's housing developments are disastrous to the environment.

Let us take a 3-acre lot as an example. Suppose we keep the lot vacant, then the lot generates no noise, no pollution and no traffic. Not a single person lives there. It requires no public services, unless, perhaps, a wild fire starts there. There is not a single square foot of paving or roofing, it doesn't put any burden on the storm drain. So, the environmental impact is almost zero. Now suppose we put a house on the lot. There will be a little noise, pollution and a couple cars may enter or exit the lot a few times a day. The impact on the environment is no longer zero but still negligible. Similarly, the house requires some public services, but its impact is still negligible. However, if there is a house, there must be a roof, say 3000 square feet. The house needs access road, driveway, sidewalks and patio area. The road, driveway etc are covered by bricks, asphalt or concrete. Let us give them reasonable numbers. We assume the lot has a frontage of 200' along the road. The road needs to be at least 20' wide. Assuming there are building lots on both sides of the road, so the lot requires 10' x 200' or 2000 square feet of asphalt paving, that is, one half of the road along the frontage. Let us allow a 16' x 50' driveway for the house or 800 square feet of concrete or asphalt paving area. Finally, we add 500 square foot brick covered area for sidewalk and patio. Add up all covered areas, the total is 6300 square feet. A typical family or household has three individuals, so this housing unit requires 2100 square feet of covered areas for each occupant. This is not a negligible number any more. During a storm, rain falling on the 6300 square foot covered area will quickly rush to the storm drain and reach creeks or streams in no time. Instead of replenishing underground water, the flow from the covered area contributes to the flood down stream. Usually the covered area has no vegetation. Sunshine reflects into the atmosphere, so the covered area contributes to global warming. We summarize the covered areas:

> Street or road: 10' x 200' = 2,000 sq. ft.;
> Roofing area: 3,000 sq. ft.;
> Driveways: 16' x 50' = 800 sq. ft.
> Sidewalk = 500 sq. ft.
> Total covered area: =6,300 sq. ft.
> Covered area per occupant = 6,300 sq. ft./3 = 2,100 sq. ft.

Now suppose we put 100 2-bedroom apartments on the 3 acres lot. Instead of 3 occupants in a house, we have 300 occupants in an apartment building or condominium complex. Inevitably, the complex will generate some noise, pollution, and traffic. The complex will require some services from local government. The total roofing area and paved area will be far bigger than 6300 square feet for a single-family house only. The 20' wide road will not be wide enough for this development. We need to calculate covered roof area, street, driveways, parking lot, sidewalk, patios, playground, etc for this kind of high-density housing developments. The street needs to be at least 70' wide.

> Street: 200' x 35' = 70,000 sq. ft.;
> Roofing area: 26,500 sq. ft.;
> Out-door parking spaces and driveways: 30,000 sq. ft.
> Main driveway: 30' x 1200' = 36,000 sq. ft.
> Sidewalk 5' x 1200' = 6,000 sq. ft.
> Play ground and patios: 3500 sq. ft.
> Total covered area: = 145,000 sq. ft.

Covered area per occupant = 145,000 sq. ft. / 300 = 483 sq. ft.

This calculation is based on a 4-story structure with 2 levels of underground parking garages. It is a 100-unit apartment, and each unit has 1000 sq. ft. living space. The complex has a 6000 sq. ft. common area for office, gym, meeting room, etc. The total living area for this complex is 106,000 sq. ft. Divide this total living area by 4, the number of stories, the result is 26,500 sq. ft., the roofing area. Each unit has two parking spaces, either in the garage or out door, and several additional parking spaces for handicapped, loading, etc. In this development, each occupant requires only 483 sq. ft. of covered area versus 2100 sq. ft. of covered area in a single-family detached house.

Let us compare the advantages and disadvantages of the two developments: one house vs a 100-unit apartment or condominium. The advantages of the single house development are limited to the locality. Instead of allowing 300 occupants, a single house typically accommodates only 3. Any adverse impacts, noise, pollution, traffic, or demand for public services etc, on this location is hardly noticeable. But where do the rest of 297 individuals live? If every local government wants the same housing developments, we will need another 297 acres to accommodate another 99 houses for 297 occupants. This is very close to what is happening in California. There are a lot of single-family dwellings, and housing prices are out of reach for many residents, including middle-class families. Local politicians get the most benefit from these housing developments. They get a continuous flow of campaign contributions from landowners, developers and others who have a vested interest in high housing prices. I may be one with a vested interest in high housing price, because I already own my house. Any price increases above inflation in the house I own is pure profit to me. I also own a second home near San Francisco, I don't mind housing prices going up sky high in Silicon Valley for a very selfish reason. But I can never forget how my life got started here. I like to see everyone willing to work hard to succeed.

When we look at the environmental impact of a housing development, we cannot just consider the impact at the particular location. At any location, a 3-acre lot with only one dwelling has less impact than the same lot with 100 dwellings. If every locality wants minimum impact, then all these minimum impacts add up to a disaster.

Because paving area per person goes up. As a country or a state, we have a certain population. Every one needs and is entitled a shelter. We want paving area per person to be close to a minimum while we provide the necessary shelter at reasonable cost. This why we cannot let land-use be just a local issue, because politicians in California have greatly abused their power and created a housing crisis for the state and beyond.

Usually, when a person buys a big house on a big lot, it is a huge "investment" for the person. To protect the investment, the person cannot leave the rest of the lot like a wasteland. So, the person must have the yard properly landscaped. A lawn will look nice, but it takes a lot water, fertilizer, pesticide and herbicide to maintain the lawn. When these chemicals are washed away during storms, they pollute streams, lakes and rivers. These houses are pictorial perfect. The road and streets are quiet and pretty. The neighborhood looks like a big botanical garden. What is the environmental price that we have to pay? Ground water level becomes lower and lower. We have to dig wells deeper and deeper to pump out water to irrigate a lot of family gardens. Some polluted rivers and lakes directly result from these beautiful gardens.

EPA, Environmental Protection Agency, October 2006 report stated that the average American of four used 400 gallons of water per day, and about 30% of that was devoted to outdoor use. More than half of that water was used for watering lawn and garden. Or, over 15% of residential water use was for landscape. In the same report, nationwide, it was estimated that 9 billion gallons of water per day was for residential landscape-irrigation and about one half of the water was wasted. In California, especially in Southern California, because of desert like weather, the average usage is considerably higher. Any lawn in Southern California is one lawn too many. Most water used in landscape-irrigation is clean potable water. Any single-family house on a large lot represents wasteful consumption and contributes to global warming, depletion of groundwater and flooding.

CHAPTER 5

▬

Solutions to the Housing Crisis

5.1 Introduction

In the early 60s, the housing prices in the US were about the same everywhere in the country. The only state that stood out was Hawaii with a median price ($20,900) about 1/3 higher than the next tier of states (New Jersey, $15,600; New York, $15,300). California's median price ($15,100) was actually lower than that of Nevada ($15,200). The variation was not huge. The difference between the most and the least expensive state was less than 300%. The least expensive one was $7500 in West Virginia. It makes sense that housing in Hawaii would be so expensive. It is in the middle of the Pacific Ocean, far from US Mainland, and it has to import almost all building materials. Inevitably, the construction cost of a house in Hawaii is always higher than other states. The island with the most population is not a big island. Because there is very limited land for housing development and high construction costs, Hawaii has the highest housing prices. By late 2010, California's median price ($600,000) was inching up close to Hawaii's ($620,000) and 2.5 times higher than Nevada's ($237,000).

California's mild temperature attracted many immigrants from other states and from foreign countries, but population increase in

California doesn't explain the high housing price at all. California's population increased about 100% from 1960 to present time. Nevada's population increased over 1000% in the same period. The two states, California and Nevada had virtually the same median house price in 1960, but now California's median house price is 2.5 times higher than Nevada's. More stringent building codes don't explain California's explosive housing price either, because all states abide by similar codes. Neither bigger houses nor bigger lots explain California's high price, because most states have similar increases in house size and lot size over the years. The only explanation left is local politicians' manipulation in California.

Let us consider the potential outcome if a person, possibly a local public school teacher, bought a house in Silicon Valley a long time ago when the price of a house in Silicon Valley was not much different from a similar house in Nevada. Let's say this person retires from the teaching job and sells the house for 3 million dollars; then the person can move to Las Vegas and gets a better house for $300,000. Even if the person has no other savings at all, the person can retire comfortably on Social Security, the Pension and the profit of a couple of million dollars from the old house. This person should definitely thank the manipulations of local politicians for the windfall. However, these are only the few lucky ones. The vast majority of home owners are not this lucky.

In Silicon Valley, a moderate house may be 3- 4 million dollars. Very few owners bought their houses when the prices were 300,000 to 400,000. Most owners bought their houses for a million dollars or two. Yes! They have all made money on their houses, but how much is the real gain? We cannot just look at the appreciation of the value of the house as the real gain. It is true that local politicians cannot manipulate housing development without the approval of voters. Yet, voters cannot always get what they want. Homeowners are usually in the majority everywhere. They don't mind a tight housing supply, because they like housing price going up a little. But some homeowners don't want housing prices going up too much. The higher the price, the more windfall homeowners will get. But the windfall may be 10, 20 or 30 years away and increase in the cost of living happens immediately. So how much to push up the housing prices is still mainly a local politicians' decision. As California's housing prices explode, they should bear the most of the responsibilities, not the homeowners.

There was a time when the City of San Luis Obispo limited real estate developments so much that almost all large housing and commercial developments stopped. Not only was there a housing shortage, a lot of popular big chain stores and restaurants could not find a foothold in the city. For a lengthy period, there was no Costco, Home Depot, Staples, Target, K-Mart, Wal-Mart, etc. For several years, I saw my neighbors and colleagues more often in a Costco Store or Home Depot in Santa Maria, a city 30 miles away, than in my neighborhood and workplace. Eventually, local politicians realized that residents of San Luis Obispo paid a lot of sale taxes in Santa Maria that is in Santa Barbara county. Finally, the city of San Luis Obispo loosened up a little. Costco, Home Depot and Target operated in the city, only after the city lost an enormous amount of sales tax to Santa Maria and residents wasted a lot of fossil fuel driving to Santa Maria to shop.

To solve the housing problem, it is crucial to understand the basic cause. Politicians are smart, so they find ways to distract voters. For example, in 2018, California voters rejected Proposition 10, Local Rent Control Initiative overwhelmingly (7,251,443 59.43% for NO and 4,949,543 40.57% for YES). Yet, right after the election, California legislature led by Assemblyman Chiu (Democrat San Francisco), in 2019, proposed new rent control bills and quickly passed AB1482 and Governor Newsom immediately signed it into law. We don't need rent control if rent is reasonable. If rent is too high, we know there are not enough rental units to go around. How could rent control ease the problem of the housing shortages? Economic theory and common sense tell us the same thing: rent control discourages investments in rental housing, and in the long run reduces supply. A small group of renters may enjoy lower rent. But the artificially cheap price of anything always leads to waste. Artificially low rent ends up reducing rental supply, so instead of softening the blow of rental shortages, rent control intensifies the harm and makes the problem worse for most renters. Rent control always benefits a few and makes the problem worse for other renters. Those politicians who propose rent control think voters are not smart enough to understand this. They think they can fool us all.

The Sierra Club, a club of environmentalists, correctly identifies the housing crisis in California also to be an environmental crisis. One solution that the Club proposes is more funding for affordable housing. A lot of politicians also pay lip service to affordable housing. The trouble is, all housing units should be affordable, except some multi-millionaires and billionaires want their palaces. There will never be enough funding for affordable housing, if we don't get rid of the cause. When a few artificially low-priced housing units are available for low-income individuals to purchase, the rules can never be fair to all low-income individuals. Only a few lucky ones can get the benefit and the rest are just not lucky enough. All the legislation and funding for affordable housing cannot solve California's housing crisis, just as the lottery cannot solve the nation's poverty problem.

Local politicians are the cause of California's crisis, this is where the solutions are. We could never take the control completely out of their hands, we just cannot let them have control without rules, transparency, justifications, or scrutiny. In most localities in California, the free market function in housing is completely destroyed. To solve the housing crisis, we must restore some of the free market mechanism in the housing market, there is no other way. The key is to separate campaign contribution and real estate development. We can do this only through campaign finance reform.

The housing crisis in California needs quick relief to avoid explosive consequences. During the wide-spread protests after the killing of George Floyd in Minneapolis, San Francisco suffered severe damages in the downtown business district due to riots and looting. The protest should be against police brutality or the use of excessive force, but what was police brutality in San Francisco? The key word is "excessive" use of force. Being an ethnic minority, I think I know a thing or two about police bias. I have experienced more than my fair share of encounters with various police from San Diego to San Francisco. A lot of people call me a fighter. Sometimes, I call myself a fighter too. But I never fight police with physical force and police never gets a chance to use "excessive" force on me. I had my finger prints taken at San Luis Obispo Police Department, but it was for my application for the US Citizenship. If any police wants to handcuff me, I will extend my wrists and cooperate willingly. But, for sure, I will sue police for false arrest. I may drive over speed limit or don't stop fully at a stop sign. But I never commit crime that deserves an arrest by any law enforcement agency. San Francisco's police officers are not known to use excessive force often. They are rather at the opposite end, excessively tolerant to homeless people and minor crimes against properties. If San Francisco's police force has avoided using excessive force and show restraints on the homeless, you would think San Francisco could have escaped nation-wide protest and looting. High housing costs in SF create hardship, frustration and desperation among all low-wage workers. They will vent their frustration whenever they can. In 2020, the US experienced the widest spread of protest and looting in history. San Luis Obispo had its first looting I have ever seen on May 31, 2020. San Luis Obispo is known to have the least affordable housing price in the US. There are many low wage workers who can not or barely afford to live in the city. They are frustrated and desperate. When a community has many frustrated and desperate residents, it is not a healthy or a safe community. Just in the middle of a prolonged protest, I experienced an incident that might shed some light on the racism in the US.

I own a rental property exactly one block north of the San Luis Obispo City Police Department. It is a "T" shaped lot with a duplex on each side. On the one side of the T is a corner lot with a house and granny's unit owned by a retired police officer. The house was rented to a few young black males and the granny's unit was vacant. I paid for two 96-gallon garbage cans emptied weekly. In early July, 2020, one of the two cans disappeared from my property. San Luis Obispo is a college town. June and July are usually the time for rental units' turnover. This was the time when occupants got rid of cumulated junk before moving out, so the missing garbage can resulted in a big mess of scattered trash. On the date of the next garbage collection, I noticed that those young black men used the missing garbage can to get rid of their trash. I called the Garbage Company to check if my neighbor paid for a 96 gallon can or not, he only paid for a small can. So, I confronted those young men. Normally, a simple apology was proper and enough. But not only they didn't apologize, instead, they sneered at me. I told them that it was against law to steal a garbage can from others. The BLM (Black Lives Matter) protest was in full swing across the US, "Defund the Police" just became part of the protest. Perhaps they thought being black and renting from an ex-cop gave them special privilege. Normally

I would contact my neighbor first, but I didn't have his number with me. So, I called Police Department to report the theft, I specifically mentioned the landlord's name. The dispatcher who answered my call immediately recognized the name and promised an investigation. A couple hours later, I received a call from a police officer saying that he had warned those offenders and they promised that it would never happen again. So obviously these offenders got away with stealing my garbage can and left a big mess for me to clean up. During my life time, only one policeman in San Luis Obispo wanted to arrest me for serving a legal notice to a Caucasian woman. She called 911. When a Caucasian woman calls police complaining against a minority male, usually Caucasian policemen respond very fast. I actually thanked the policeman for his fast response, because his presence proved that I had given the legal paper to the woman. I wondered what lie did the woman tell to get a quick response from police. After I explained the situation to the policeman, he still claimed that he had a proper cause to arrest me. I asked him what was the charge. He said I struck her with a piece of paper. I swear I am telling the truth! I told him that if there was such offence in the book, he should arrest me. Otherwise he would become a laughing stock. He stopped and left. I didn't forget this incident. Obviously, police don't treat different groups equally. I have experienced numerous occasions when white police officers let white offenders off the hooks. Now I experienced the first case when a white cop lets black offenders off the hook too. Perhaps the owner of the property where the offender lived being a retired officer was a factor or the BLM protest played a role too. In fact, when "Defund the Police" became part of the protest, I showed my support for the local police by responding to their request for donation. To me, a less than perfect police force is much better than a totally lawless mob. After the protest, the pecking order appears to be White, Black and down to Asian. I just don't know where to place the Chicanos and Muslims. I am very sure I could not get away with any offence like stealing neighbors' garbage cans and, at least I would be required to clean up the mess. Also, I would be prosecuted to the fullest of the law. Former DA Shea, before he dismissed a case against me, asked San Luis Obispo Police Department if I used "foul language" against anyone. I said in my letter to him that if he charged me for the crime of using foul language, it would have been a first in the county. Fortunately for me, his fishing came up empty! I was a college professor during most of my working life, obviously, using foul language was not my usual habit.

Since I talked about the T shape property, it might be proper to use it to illustrate how bureaucrats can make arbitrary decisions without any consideration of rules or fairness. One of the reasons that I still own this property is to preserve the evidence about bureaucrats' total control on land-use. Please allow me explain what does it mean by "total control". Bureaucrats can use every zoning and code requirement to harass anyone they don't like. Yet, they are free to ignore any of their own rule. The "T" shaped lot is very narrow, only 50 foot wide. The overall size of the T is 150 x 150. The top strip is 150' wide and 50' high. The bottom strip is 50' wide and 100' high. So, the two lots on the two sides of the T are each 50' x 100'. On the retired cop side, the granny's quarter was only 1' from the property line, even though Zoning Ordinance requires a 5' setback. When I applied for a building permit about 45 years ago, I tried to request a 4.5' setback. I couldn't even get a hearing with the Planning Commission, the Building Department shut me off saying: "A rule is a rule is a rule." A few years ago, the owner of the other side of the T applied for a building permit for a new granny's quarter. The owner talked to me if he could reduce the set back to 4.5'. I had no objection. Of course, the Building Department accepted his application and got a hearing at the Planning Commission meeting. I attended the hearing and the Planning Commission quickly approved the application. I had no objection to a 4.5' setback, but I did object to the Planning Commissions justification that the two-story high new unit was only facing neighbor's (that is my property) parking lot. This was false. An entrance door of my duplex was closer than any of the parking spaces to the new landing of the granny's quarter. I was not even allowed to point out Planning Commissioners' factual error.

This property also preserves another evidence that the enforcement of zoning and codes are very arbitrary and selective. Some codes don't make a lot of sense anyway. The three lots at the bottom of the "T" slope from one side to the other, the corner lot has the lowest elevation. Building codes require drainage toward the street. That is, the lot with higher elevation, may not drain water to neighboring lot. This requirement is not essential anyway, because the annual rainfall in this part of California is about 25" and often we get less than 10". As my neighbor built his granny unit, he built a retaining wall with drainage holes toward my property. Since he didn't ask for permission, I just plugged them up. Then he asked city building department official to call me to unplug them, I refused. Then the official said he was asking a favor from me. Of course, I never expect any favor from the building department. I said to him that the owner of the granny unit promised me to build a screen around the upstairs landing, but he didn't keep his promise. If he built the screen as he promised, I would unplug the drainage holes. Then two years ago I turned in an application to Building Department to add insulation to a cinder-block wall and a few minor improvements for a building, the official at the counter refused to accept my application because two different paper sizes of my documents.

How dare I offend City officials? My age is a factor. I am in my mid 80s now. I still own rental properties, but they are not my livelihood. I can live comfortably on my pension and Social Security benefits alone. But this incident demonstrated the reason why are there so many zoning ordinances and building codes. These rules and regulations give local officials absolute power, they can choose to enforce them any way they like. Nobody dares to hold any of them responsible for anything. Early in 2020, the retired cop, my neighbor on the lower side, built a new drainage from the back of the granny unit. He didn't direct the drainage to the street, instead, it drained to the driveway of my property. I often feel I am a second class citizen, because I rarely get fair treatment from local officials. My tenants become second class tenants because they rent from a second-class landlord. Even my properties are second class properties, they become the drainage of neighboring properties.

5.2 Quick Relief for Homelessness

No local government or community would like to host a ghetto or slum. Most local governments are capable of stopping the formation of a ghetto or slum in their communities, but they are incapable or not willing to provide decent and affordable housing for all. The result is that there are close to half a million of homeless people in the US according to a 2019 US Department of Housing and Urban Development report. If anyone in the US spends one half of their take-home pay for housing, it is one person too many. In November 2019, State Government of California tried to raise 2 billion dollars to help the homeless in the state. Two billion dollars sounds like a huge amount of money for the homeless. But compared to the amount that the residents in the state pay for housing, two billion dollars amounts to a few tiny drops in a big bathtub. If we understand the cause of the housing crisis and solve the problem, we don't need the two billion dollars at all. If we don't understand the cause and cannot solve the problem, 20 billion dollars is not nearly enough.

Let's look at how the US solved the problem of famine, the worst scrooge for human survival. Apparently, the US solved the problem completely and thoroughly. With only 2% of her population engaging in agricultural production, the US produces enough food to feed her population with plenty to spare. Whatever the US did in food production, the policy can be the model to solve housing problem. In food production, there was no problem to start with. The government has taken its hands off food production and consumption and only involves itself in safety and health inspections. Local governments do not tell restaurants what to put on their menus, what ingredients to use or how to prepare each order. If a person wants to make a sandwich for lunch, the person is free to do so without approval from anyone. Yes! Local governments are still in control and inspect grocery stores and restaurants regularly.

Federal and state governments don't order farmers what to produce, how to produce, where to produce, or when to produce etc. The federal government checks to make sure whatever farmers have produced will be suitable for human or animal consumption. The Federal government doesn't tell a farmer how much to produce on an acre of land. The more, the better. The federal government never tells consumers what to eat, when to eat, how much to eat, etc. The Department of Agriculture makes dietary suggestions, but it is up to each individual to decide. The federal government also provides food stamps for those who cannot afford to buy enough food to lead a healthy life. The Federal government does an excellent job on food production and distribution; not too much or too little, and the marketplace handles the rest.

Suppose there is a sudden increase in demand for beef in the US. As demand increases, the price of beef will increase. Immediately, domestic supply of beef will increase because ranchers will send more cattle to the slaughterhouses. If domestic supply cannot satisfy the new demand, meat suppliers will try to find foreign supplies from Argentina, Australia, Brazil or Mexico etc. If the increase in demand appears to be rather permanent, American ranchers will raise more cattle. On the demand side, consumers are free to choose. If beef becomes more expensive, the government never orders consumers to eat more beef. Some will eat less and some will switch to sea food, pork or poultry. The balance between demand and supply will be reached and the price of beef will stay reasonable. People will never wait in line for hours to buy a piece of steak. Neither will any workers, even the ones earning only minimum wage, spend half of their take-home paycheck to buy food.

If the housing market has a little free-market mechanism left, how could the housing crisis be solved? Let us take a homeless person for an example. If the homeless person lives in a car, what does the person need the most? We will look at the person's needs in order of urgency.

First, the person needs just a little space to park their car. A space of 10' by 25' is enough for a car and access. Next, the person needs a restroom. Do we need to provide one restroom for every 3 homeless persons like some zoning ordinances require for boarding houses? This kind of senseless rule has no place in any free marketplace. So, let us apply the standard requirements for restaurants or commercial airplanes, maybe one toilet for every 30 parking spaces. Next, they may need one shower stall for every 50 parking spots. Better yet, let the free market decide. If a provider follows the excessive code requirements of one restroom for three parking spaces, this provider will have to charge a lot. The homeless may pay for bare necessities but not excessive luxuries. This vender will be out of business fast. The free marketplace will decide the best price-and-convenience combination quickly. With this minimal facility, we can turn these homeless people into productive workers. Instead of being kicked around, a person can have an inexpensive place to spend the night, to get some sleep and to go to work next morning. Instead of being a burden to society, these people can be self-sufficient and contribute to society.

The problem is where do we put these facilities. Nobody wants them nearby. This is the typical NIMBY, not in my backyard! Most communities don't want this facility. Local government may require law enforcement agencies to order homeless people to move on. This is a common practice to deal with the problem, but it is a waste of resources for both sides. Law enforcement agencies need to deal with more serious problems. Homeless people just want to survive, they have no intention to break any laws. But local communities create a bunch of laws to turn homeless into criminals. So homeless people cannot get enough rest, and they cannot work and become a burden of society. Some may argue against this solution. America is a rich country. How could we allow anyone to live in a car? That is a good point! But unless there is better and less expensive way to help the homeless, let us give this way a try.

When I was a student, I never stayed in a motel while driving long distances. If I was exhausted, I would find a spot near a gas station to park and sleep for a while. When I woke up, I drove to the gas station to get gas and use the restroom. I was not alone. Many told the same story. We need to minimize the hardship for the homeless. It is not a choice between sleeping in a car or living in a decent house. It is a choice between chasing the homeless around or letting them have a little rest. It is a choice between making them un-presentable and unemployable or giving them a chance to be self-sufficient. In 2018, California lawmakers proposed legislation to open community colleges campus at night for homeless students to park their cars. If it is a good idea, why limit to community college campuses? In 2020, the Supreme Court ruled that the homeless might camp in public parks if local communities didn't provide shelters. These actions by the state legislators and the Supreme Court represent a ray of hope to solve the housing crisis. Many cities and towns are Beverly-Hills-wannabes and many coast towns are Newport-Beach-wannabes. These communities promote high-end housing developments and allow little or no affordable housings. As housing prices rise, homeowners reap a windfall and local politicians get re-elected again and again. This seems to be a win-win situation for everyone. Only the rich can afford to live in there, so these places have a solid tax base. Since the rich can take care of themselves, local governments can afford to make these places cute, pretty and more livable.

But the win-win situation is not for long! Every city and town need basic services, such as public schools, law enforcement, hospitals, restaurants, etc. Can elementary school teachers, police officers, nurses, cooks, waitresses, etc afford to live there? If not, maybe they can live nearby! But nobody wants to invite the poor and often ethnic minorities with open arms. We can just look at Silicon Valley as an example, many cannot afford to live where they work. Many become homeless and many live far away.

Where to put this facility is always a problem! We can put the facilities for homeless on wheels around the outskirts of a city, or in parking lot empty at night. Restrooms and shower stalls can be mobile. Hopefully, these empty parking lots would be enough to accommodate all the homeless on wheels. There are very little improvements necessary for this to work. If there is a parking lot, there must be buildings nearby. If there are buildings, there must be water and sewer lines nearby. It requires no more than a 50' trench to bring potable water and sewer line to the parking lot for mobile toilet and shower facilities to operate. This solution is not a permanent one for homelessness. Most of us wouldn't want to live this way for long, but for a homeless person, this solution is a vast improvement over no solution at all. San Francisco has some of the highest housing prices in California and in the country. It is not surprising that it also has many homeless people. There seems to be a high correlation between the number of homeless and the number of crimes against properties. We don't know who committed these crimes, because SF police don't investigate minor crimes against properties. In some neighborhoods in SF, there is a lot of broken glass along sidewalks from broken car windows. Car windows get broken often, but don't call the police in SF. The police will ask: "Do you know who did it?" and "Was anyone hurt?" If the answers are "No!" The police will just hang-up. So high housing prices don't just hurt low-wage workers. Local officials cannot just keep pushing housing price higher and higher. If they have to deal with all the consequences of high housing prices, there is hope to solve the problems.

Figure 18: Homeless camp along Embarcadero
in San Francisco, August 2020

The nice part of this solution for homeless is that rental costs may level off, instead of rising indefinitely. With this alternative, low-wage workers will have some leverage and bargaining power to bring down the rent. This alternative competes against rental units head on. When there is competition, rent may come down across the board. The cost of this solution is very minimal. A charitable organization may step in to help, it may even be profitable for private businesses to offer this service on public parking lots. Because these parking lots are empty at night, why not let us use them? If a city or county's housing affordability falls below a certain mark or if a minimum wage worker cannot afford to live close to where the job is, the State can require the city or county to provide this service. Places like Silicon Valley would definitely have to follow this requirement. This requirement will give local politicians incentive to not push housing prices too high. We may reserve some of these parking lots for local workers. The environmental benefit would be immense and immediate. They don't have to commute a long distance daily, so there would be less congestion on highways and less pollution at each locality. To prohibit this kind of solution is like prohibiting a person to make a simple cheese sandwich for lunch or prohibiting any restaurant to be in business without a Michelin star.

5.3 Tiny House on Wheels

Next, if the housing market is under the rules of the free market, how will it solve the problem of shortage?

In recent years, as house size and lot size expand with prices soaring out of sight, there is a counter-movement of tiny houses on wheels. Apparently, a house on wheels is mobile and has no foundation, so local building code doesn't apply. A tiny one can be 10' by 17' and cost around $17,000. Is it functional? A person needs only 20 square feet of space for a twin bed and two people need only 30 square feet for a double, 10 square feet for a shower, 10 square feet for a stove to cook simple meals, 10 square feet for a small sink to prepare food, 10 square feet for a lavatory, 10 square feet for a toilet, 20 square feet for a desk and chair, 10 square feet for a closet, 20 square feet to set up a table for two to eat, and 40 square feet for a couch to read, watch TV or use a laptop computer. Most tiny house on wheels have an added loft for bed. This will free about 30 square feet for open space. The total adds up to 170. With proper arrangement, all these functions will fit into the house. It just has no room for entertainment. The rule to allow this housing may be the same rule for cities or counties to open public parking lots to homeless living in automobiles. If housing affordability falls below a certain limit, the city or county may not prohibit tiny houses on wheel to park behind any single-family houses. Again, this rule will give city or county officials incentive not to push up housing prices too high. There are actual cases that young couples with one baby can get by with a tiny house. In a few years, they can save enough to move up.

Figure 19: The outside and inside of a tiny-house, October 2019. Tiny House Exhibition in San Luis Obispo, Calif.

Some cities in California already allow a small house on wheels in the backyard behind a single-family house. Since California has a lot of single-family detached houses, this is a quick way to provide affordable new housing units. They need no extensive or expensive new infrastructures. Some communities allow tiny houses on wheels, yet impose senseless restrictions to stop them. Some communities require the owner to occupy either the main house or the tiny house. If what we need is additional units to ease housing shortage, why does owner occupancy matter? Apparently, there are many community-imposed restrictions. However, in 2019, the State of California prohibited any unauthorized restrictions against tiny houses.

To solve the housing problem in California, local politicians need NOT to take their hands-off local land-use decisions completely, they just need to loosen their grip a little. Between homelessness and a one-bedroom apartment with a one-million-dollar price tag, we need a lot more choices. California's voters, instead of hoping for Socialist handouts from government, need to wake up and demand the freedom of choice, not as slaves of the housing establishment.

We may learn a lesson from Hong Kong. As Communists took over Mainland China, many Chinese fled to Hong Kong. The British Colonial Government didn't close the border to stop the flow of refugees. The Colonial Government's humane policy was rewarded generously. The government didn't even need to open a refugee camp to house the new arrivals. But these refugees did not become a burden to Hong Kong; instead, they were valuable assets. There were few fiefs or laborers among the refugees, Mao's Communists claimed to save the working poor from exploitation. So, fiefs and laborers welcomed communists with open arms. Only the enemy of the working class fled. Most refugees were Nationalists, landlords, capitalists, small businessmen, teachers, etc. Some of them were rich, most of them were not. Some of them became entrepreneurs and others supplied cheap labor for the new businesses. Hong Kong didn't have a housing industry that could churn out new housing units quickly. Obviously, there was a severe housing shortage because of the large number of refugees. There was no reliable count of the number of refugees. A friend who grew up in Hong Kong told me that the Colonial Government didn't bother to count the number. If the government did, it would scare many refugees to death. Refugees had no idea why the government wanted to identify them. If the Government ever deported any refugees back to Communist China, it would have been a death sentence to the person.

How did the refugees solve the housing problem? Some of them built make-shift shelters. Hong Kong rarely got freezing, so they needed no insulation. Anyone with a spare room could be a landlord. A spare room was not for just one person or two! The room, furnished with triple or double deck bunker beds, could accommodate 6 or 12 tenants at a time. That was not all. A landlord could rent each bed to three individuals a day. Factories and many shops had 3 shifts. Constructions, industrial productions, maintenance and cleaning went on day and night. A bed was in demand around the clock, there were enough renters to keep most beds occupied all the time. So, the living conditions were horrible for these tenants. But do you want to kick these people out, 36 of them or 3 for each bed, on the street? From these horrible living conditions, refugees helped to transform Hong Kong from a fishing village and trading post to a world-class financial center and industrial powerhouse. Hong Kong's GDP (year 2017) per capita rivaled that of the US [Source, CIA World Factbook, 2020]. In 2019, these refugees' grandchildren and great grandchildren were the ones on the streets to protest against Communist Government in China and demanding democracy. So how horrible was the housing condition in Hong Kong for the refugees? Obviously, the terrible condition didn't hurt them much. How did the Colonial Government solve the problem of housing shortage in Hong Kong? What problem? Colonial Officials only worried about how to maximize land-sale revenue. They let the free-market take care of the housing problem. It was a beautiful solution, a problem solved, and the government didn't need to do a thing! Just as President Ronald Reagan said: "Government is not the solution; it is the problem!"

In 2020, the Covid-19 pandemic started from China. When the government-imposed lockdown, it was thorough. Not even grocery stores and pharmacies could open for business. To supply the necessities to the public, governments allowed online order and home delivery. Suppliers hired many riders with motor bikes to deliver grocery and medicine. In big cities like Wuhan and Shanghai, these riders earned about $1000 a month. It was a good wage by local standards. However, housing in big cities is not cheap, as Shanghai's housing price could rival California's. How could these riders survive? They survived just fine, they could save 80% of their income just by sharing a room, 6 to a room. In a few months, a rider saved a few thousand dollars. If it were in San Francisco, a rider could have earned at least three times more, but none of the riders could afford to live in San Francisco. Either these riders would have lived an hour away or they would have been homeless. If they were homeless, they might not have been employable. If they had lived an hour away, they might have been tired of commuting and could not have been good riders. The high housing cost in San Francisco not only destroys low-wage workers' upward mobility but also limits policy makers' options. San Francisco could never have imposed a total lockdown, even if it were the only effective way to fight the pandemic.

At the height of the pandemic in 2020 Spring, California Governor Newsom was on TV news reports daily. For a few days, the top news was that Governor Newsom tried to secure 12000 motel rooms to house the homeless. He really showed his compassion for the unfortunates. His administration also sued local government for lack of affordable housing, and he signed legislation to force local communities to provide more housing. He also stopped landlords from evicting any tenants during the shelter-at-home time. But how serious was he? Before elected governor, he was Lieutenant Governor. Before elected Lieutenant Governor, he was Mayor of San Francisco. Before elected Mayor, he was a member of the Board of Supervisors. For over 12 years he was part of the power center of San Francisco, in charge of the land-use policy. We need to ask him what did he do to provide affordable housing in San Francisco!

Did Governor Newsom solve the problem of homelessness in San Francisco during the Pandemic in 2020? Of course not! Why should anyone bother to ask? You can call whatever he did anything you like; posturing, political show, lip-services, pretending, etc., but not solutions. If anyone doesn't believe me, just go to San Francisco, look at the homeless camp on sidewalk along Embarcadero Blvd. where CalTran and Muni tracks meet. From April to August, 2020, there were more and more homeless tents almost every day.

5.4 General Rules on Zoning

Zoning is a local issue, so there is no federal law about zoning. States may have some guidelines, but, in California, the state either doesn't enforce the law or the law is toothless. If we compare zoning to criminal cases, it would be as if there were no federal or state criminal codes and all criminal prosecutions are done locally. Thus, district attorneys, the chief law enforcement officer in a county, could arbitrarily decide what cases to prosecute and which ones not to. That is not all: there would be no juries, no trials, nor judges. A district attorney would decide whether a suspect is guilty or not and would also hand out the sentence if DA found the suspect guilty. We can all agree if the district attorney had too much power, justice could rarely prevail.

As for land-use issues, local politicians have absolute power and discretion. They can almost arbitrarily decide if the city may annex a piece of land, and whether the land is for low density or high-density housing development. Isn't this just like a district attorney having the discretion to charge a suspect or not, or what crime to charge the suspect with, without guidance from the criminal code? The local government can decide whether to issue a building permit and when to issue a building permit for a project. So, it should not surprise us that some places in California have a lot of open spaces, but the city nearby has outrageously high house prices.

After I came to the US in 1962, it surprised me to learn that a D.A. had the discretion to charge or not to charge a criminal suspect. My naïve thinking was, as a resident in a country of law, I had no discretion whether to obey the law. In the US, we don't live in a homogeneous society. Racism and racial prejudice are deeply rooted in the society's fabric. For a society to function properly, we have no choice but to follow the rule of law. Any discretion that a D.A. may have is one discretion too many. My naïve instinct turned out to be right 40 years later. My ordeal in San Luis Obispo is the strongest proof.

In 1999, San Luis Obispo County DA Gerard Shea filed a felony charge against me for a crime against one of my tenants, a single mom and a Chicano who was a tenant in an apartment that two friends and I purchased about 20 years ago. Because of the size of the apartment, state law required a resident manager on site, I hired one. But around Christmas 1998, the resident manager was on vacation and out of town. Usually during the holiday season, it was a very quiet time around all the apartments in town. Most college students went home during the Christmas break. I had no one to check-in or check-out around that time. Check-out normally required at least a 30-day notice. But the tenant, Maricela Huerta, a single mom, wanted to break her lease and gave the management an unsigned and undated 4-day notice. The unsigned note had a hand written statement: "If you have any questions call ana borgos 546-93-70." The checkout date was December 20 on the notice and I picked it up at the drop box on December 16, 1998. Any notice that my tenants deposited in the box was considered legally served to the management, so it was checked daily. Then Ms. Huerta called a day before December 20, informing me the time when she wanted to check out. I usually respected my tenants' rights, because I was one of them not long ago. I didn't use any excuses to refuse to meet her because she didn't give the management a 30-day notice. In fact, her 24-hour notice was not legally binding, because it was not in writing but only a phone call.

The next day I met Ms. Huerta at her apartment. She had moved out completely and a Caucasian young woman accompanied her. The Caucasian woman introduced herself as an employee in the Division of Victim Assistance in the Office of the District Attorney of San Luis Obispo County. I believe this woman was "ana borgos" and her name appeared on the undated and unsigned notice and the phone 546-93-70 was under her name. Her name never appeared on any police report. She claimed that the apartment was in run-down condition with many code violations and uninhabitable. She also told me to allow the tenant to break the lease and to refund her full deposit and unused rent immediately. I told her that law required the so-called victim to notify the management in writing if there were any uninhabitable conditions in the apartment and to allow the management reasonable time to correct these conditions. Since she didn't give any notice, she wasn't entitled to receive an immediate refund. Even if she had proper cause to break the lease, she was required by law to give a 30-day notice. I told the woman from the DA's office that the DA was the chief law enforcement officer in the county, yet, he didn't seem to have any respect for the law. I was a teacher during most of my work life. I liked to lecture whenever I had chance.

The woman made a phone call and a police officer (Berg, J 16032 SLOPD) arrived in minutes. I had never seen a police officer in San Luis Obispo respond so fast except responding to calls from someone in the DA's office. In front of any ethnic minorities, police officers often act like a fierce tiger, but in front of an employee from the DA's office, they act like a pussycat. Whenever someone from the DA's office asked a San Luis Obispo Policeman to give me an illegal order, the policeman never refused. The woman from the DA's office and the San Luis Obispo City police officer talked for a while and the police officer told me: "Why don't you just give their money back?" I replied: "If you are ordering me, please put your order in writing!" This was my standard answer in this situation. Since I didn't even hesitate for a second, the officer realized that it was not my first time to say so. He turned around and left. Normally, I would call the police department the next day and talk to the police officer to request a detailed police report. I would remind him he should record the incident truthfully in details. In this situation, no police officers would lie for anyone from the DA's office and no one from the DA's office would like to see a police report showing his or her illegal demand. Always I would get an apology in a few minutes from the person in the DA's office begging me not to request a report but keeping all the money that the person had demanded. The mayor of San Luis Obispo was one of my good friends. I didn't want him feeling embarrassed that a police scandal happened during his watch. Neither would I want to appear to take advantage of my connection to the mayor to interfere with a police investigation. But my lack of action misled the police officer and the DA into believing that they could easily bully and take advantage of me.

Because I refused to make a refund immediately, the two women refused to return the keys. So technically the Chicano woman had not checked out. Since there were no belongings left in the unit and the tenant had cut utility services, electricity and gas to the unit, the tenant had no reason to reenter the apartment. Two days later, I found one of the doors was unlocked and another wide open, so I legally entered the premises to secure it and to protect my property. I had an agreement with the electricity provider, PG&E, to put electricity under my name whenever a resident called to close an account. Prior to entering a unit, I made sure that the utility accounts were under my name.

Apparently, the DA or someone in the DA's office wanted to show off to the Chicano woman who probably was the person's housemaid. I knew about her profession just by examining her application for the housing unit. The woman might have tried to re-enter the apartment after our meeting, but I already changed the lock, and possibly new tenants already occupied the unit. The new tenant signed lease on December 27 and checked in a day later. The DA knew about the electricity account for the apartment, because I told Officer Berg why I entered the premise and changed the lock. But the DA was so angry that he failed to impress his housemaid, he seemed to lose his mind. The DA filed a felony criminal case against me for illegal entry to the apartment. But California law was clear: when a tenant had closed a utility account, the law considered the tenant had checked out. The logic is simple: to end a utility account for a dwelling renders the unit uninhabitable. If a tenant wanted to repair anything in the unit or to clean up the unit, the person should work prior to cutting any necessary utilities. If a tenant might not live or do anything inside, the tenant had no cause to re-enter the unit. If she reentered the apartment and flipped on a light switch, she became a thief stealing electricity from me.

Because the charge against me was so far-fetched and outrageous, I decided to represent myself against the charge. On April 8, 1999, I showed up in court all by myself to be arraigned. Assistant DA Wilson came over to shake my hand. He acted like he was greeting an old friend instead of a criminal suspect whom he would prosecute. He knew the case didn't have a single leg to stand on, but he failed to move to dismiss the case. I was in no hurry, I just wanted to see how ridiculous this process could go on.

On April 20, 1999, I showed up in court again the second time for this case. When Judge Ream called the case, he said this case should be handled in a civil court. Assistant DA Wilson didn't say a single word to object. If I made a motion to dismiss the case, could Judge Ream deny my motion? He would contradict himself. Judge Ream just confirmed what I believed all along that the case against me was totally without merit. I was glad to see that the DA was walking into a trap that he set up for himself and the police officer lied repeatedly on his report. Judge Ream's comment exposed a fundamental flaw of the criminal justice system in the County. Anyone with an elementary school education could tell that DA's case against me was groundless.

I admire Judge Ream's candor. Most other judges would not have said it. Unfortunately, Judge Ream didn't do the right thing to dismiss the case. If he did, he would have saved a tremendous amount of valuable court time. If I were Judge Ream, it would have upset me very much to waste my time. Yet, he allowed the case to continue and waited for former DA Shea to come to his senses. Judge Ream asked Assistant DA Wilson if he wanted to book me. Mr. Wilson answered: "Not at this time." Judge Ream said: "Either you want Mr. Wu to be booked or not, don't say 'not at this time'." Then Mr. Wilson said, "No!"

The most bizarre thing happened in court during my next appearance on May 3, 1999. Instead of Assistant DA Wilson and his usual partner handling the case against me, Assistant DA Sheryl Manley and another assistant DA took over and Judge Picquet was presiding. Ms. Manley immediately asked Judge Picquet to order me to be booked within two days. I wondered how low and how childish Mr. Shea could be. He wanted to add insult to injury. Even though I was representing myself, I had the common sense to object.

I told Judge Picquet the discussion about booking between Judge Ream and Mr. Wilson. Judge Picquet immediately ordered the court clerk to cross out the order and said he would check the court records. Then Judge Picquet wanted to read the DA's offer of a reduced charge. I said: "With due respect, your honor, please don't waste your time. I would accept any reduced charge over my dead body. If the case goes to trial, the DA would make a fool of himself."

On July 20, 1999, right before jury selection, the DA finally dropped the case with prejudice (DA might not file the same charge against me again) and I made the statement: "The DA, in the name of the people, practiced racism and favoritism against me." I explained this case in such detail to show the fraud of local governments in the US.

In 2007, I read a news report that DA Mike Nifong for Durham County, North Carolina was disbarred for his prosecution of three Duke University lacrosse players falsely accused of rape. On June 25, 2007, I wrote to DA Shea demanding a written apology for the bogus charge against me that forced me into the court six times. He had his Deputy DA, Mr. Brown (the second in command) call me, not from his office phone, probably from his wife's cell phone. My phone's caller ID showed a female's name. He said that Mr. Shea told him that the charge against me should never have been filed. I told him I knew it all along; he didn't need to tell me. If this is meant to be an apology, it was not acceptable. It needed to be in writing and signed. Then I would forgive and forget. He refused, so I documented the conversation and mailed a certified letter to Mr. Shea. I told him that this letter gave him a chance to defend himself, if he disagreed with my documentation. He didn't answer my second letter. In fact, if he had apologized in writing, I would not have mentioned the case ever again to anyone. Even if I don't use his case to make a point, I have plenty of other cases I can refer to. I probably would not have mentioned Mr. Shea and Mr. Brown's names if they didn't lie about the female in the Victim Assistant Division. During Mr. Brown's phone call, he denied that there was such a person in the division. So, I had to be a liar and fabricated the story. Then who called the police? I didn't call and the Chicano woman was probably an undocumented alien; I doubt she dared to call police in order to break a lease. If she did, a police officer would not show up. If any police officer showed up, the officer would tell the caller that this was not a police matter and leave in no time. I did not mention my other encounters with personnel from DA's Office, they all tried to help their relatives or offspring. But Mr. Shea made illegal demands because he wanted to impress a housemaid or to show off how powerful he was to a housemaid. His action was less forgivable than the others'. How did I know Mr. Shea tried to show off how powerful he was? Actually, I didn't, but I did him a favor by presuming this was the case. He was the big boss and he could have only one housemaid at a time. So, there shouldn't be too many victims like me. If everyone in the DA's Office could do it, then there could be dozens of victims like me. Then the DA's office had a culture of corruption and would be out of control, the criminal court would have been doing nothing but persecuting innocent landlords.

On the one hand, the justice system prevailed for me. DA Shea probably hurt himself much more than he hurt me. I went before four different judges and every one of them treated me with dignity. There wasn't a minute I felt humiliated in the court. They all knew the DA should not have filed the charge against me and I was innocent until proven guilty. Mr. Shea's two immediate predecessors were appointed superior court judges upon retirement, but Mr. Shea just retired a few years ago. This made me a believer in the greatness and exceptionality of America.

On the other hand, my experience from this case let me understand some deficiencies in the local governments. At the local level, there is little separation of power, no checks or balances, and very little or no scrutinizing by the media. Judges Ream and Picquet were two of the most honorable judges in the last half century in San Luis Obispo. I appeared several times in their courtrooms during civil proceedings. I didn't always win my cases in their courtrooms. When I lost, I didn't always agree with their rulings. But I respected their reasoning and considered their justifications honorable. Unfortunately, I cannot say the same for some others. Almost all judges are at least basically fair, just as almost all commissioners are unfair. But in this case, they didn't perform their duties to dismiss the case outright. Mr. Shea misused his power and practiced racism and favoritism. He took an oath to uphold the law, yet he flagrantly disregarded it and acted as if he were above the law. But he got away with all the abuses. Every one of the four judges who handled the case had the power and the responsibility to dismiss the case, but none of them did. Yes! Usually a retired DA may become a judge, so none of the four judges wanted to offend their possible future colleague. It is just the typical political culture of "don't rock the boat!" At worst, a DA may take the law into his or her hands and abuse it, but, fortunately, the DA is not the legislator!

For housing development and land-use, local politicians are the legislators and the executives. The president of the US needs to answer to US senators and US House of Representatives, and a governor needs to answer to state senators and state representatives. But the mayor, city council members and county supervisors only answer to their own conscience. Federal courts rule against the president and the executive branch often. But locally, judges rarely go against local politicians. In a small community, the most powerful individuals almost always know each other and mingle socially. The saying: "You don't fight city hall!"

says it all. The only thing left is the local media. In this internet age, the traditional media struggles to survive. Since real estate interests and local politicians are usually the largest advertisers, local media is not strong enough to be the only checks and balance at the local level. So locally, politicians can do whatever they want. No wonder in many places in California the housing prices are out of control.

State Sen. Scott Wiener who represented a district in San Francisco, introduced SB827 in January 2018. It was a bill that would strip off a large part of local politicians' exclusive authority on zoning and land-use in California. The bill would have allowed the construction of apartment buildings up to five stories tall near every high-frequency mass transit stop in the state. Senator Wiener argued that taking zoning decisions away from local municipalities and forcing communities to build more densely near transit was the best way both to ease housing shortage in cities like San Francisco and help the state reach its ambitious environmental goals.

Sen. Wiener's bill was a big step in the right direction. We must admire his courage to take on the residents from wealthy and single-family home neighborhoods. They are the ones who got a windfall from rising house values and they wanted even more, at least they didn't want housing prices to crash. They used the NIMBY argument that the bill threatened neighborhood character and would lead to traffic and parking problems. The NIMBY side had some unexpected allies, among them the Sierra Club and advocates for "Public Housing in My Backyard," or PHIMBYs, who argued that the law would enrich developers and encourage gentrification in low-income minority neighborhoods. We know that local politicians and bureaucrats would not give up their domain without a fierce fight. We also know that many homeowners would not want to lose their profit on their houses. If there was suddenly plenty of affordable housing with convenient public transportation, their valuable investments in their over-sized houses would become a bunch of white elephants. So, these homeowners would not give up their gains or even their life saving without a fight. As expected, the bill died in committee by 7 to 4 votes. Sen. Wiener immediately reintroduced the measure as SB50 in 2019. As expected, local politicians fiercely resisted the bill and it was again shelved in committee. However, the support for the bill appeared to be growing after Sen. Wiener made a few concessions to Senators from rural areas.

Most state legislators, including the authors of AB302 and SB827, started their political careers from local offices and rose through the ranks. Sen. Wiener was a Supervisor in San Francisco before he was elected State Senator. So, state legislators know the importance of the authority on zoning and land-use to local politicians. Especially, politicians with ambitions for higher office would try to stay on good terms with all of them. If anyone has political ambition, the last thing the person wants to do is to offend all local politicians by taking away their ATMs for campaign funding.

To push any legislation to curtail local governments' land-use authority, the sponsors need to learn from their colleagues who successfully passed rent control legislation in California in 2019. Just about everyone in California knows that rent control laws cannot solve the high-rent problem. But California's legislators still pushed through a few rent-control bills and the new governor quickly signed them. This is a typical example of how politicians do their best at paying lip service. On October 8, 2019, newspaper headlines in California announced:

"Rent hikes will be capped at 5% each year plus inflation, bans no-cause evictions."

How would this law help any renters? If I am a renter, I don't think it would help me at all! We are in a low inflation time, inflation averaged about 2% in the last few years. If rent is high anywhere, one percentage point rent increase above inflation is one percent too much! Now California enacted a law that restricted rent increases to about three times of inflation. To call the law a rent control is laughable. We can look at an example to see why!

In 1977 I bought an apartment for about $30,000 a unit (2 bedroom and 1 bath apartment) and rented it for $300 a month. Forty years later, I sold it for $330,000 per unit in 2018 and the rent was $1800 a month. In 40 years, the property value increased about 1000% and the rent increased only 500%. The property changed hands on the open market. The rents were the fair market values. All these numbers are public records and one can easily verify. Any conclusions based on these numbers are true and correct! The rent increased 500% in 40 years, isn't this an average of over 10% a year? The answer is "No!" The increase is compounded yearly, the actual increase was far less than 10% a year. The actual increase was even less than 5% a year. If the rent had increased 10% a year since 1978, by 2018 the rent would have been over $11,000 per month! What if we capped the increase according to California's rent control law (AB 1428) of 2019? That was, the rate of increase was inflation plus 5% annually or 10%, whichever was lower? The rent would have been $6,940 in 2018. Thanks a lot! Governor Newsom and Assemblyman Chiu! The rent without rent control was only $1800! Or the annual increase was less than 1% plus inflation.

So what was the rent control for? I scratch my head to find an answer. Possibly, a lot of politicians just want to pay lip service to the problem of the housing shortage. California is now a one party state, Democrats control both houses of the legislature with a super majority and governor's mansion. Yet, they couldn't do a thing about high housing costs. Or more precisely and correctly, they don't want to do much about the high housing costs. So, they pass and enact rent control laws to show that they haven't forgotten about the renters' plight. Also, since the law was virtually useless, there was little or no resistance to it in the legislature. However, once it is in place, it might be easy to strengthen it further. Perhaps the limit of 5% above inflation can be reduced to 4%, 3%, 2% or even to 1%.

Senator Wiener's bill wanted to take land-use authority away from local politicians, but his bill died in committee twice in 2018 and 2019. If he used the same tactics his colleagues used to push through rent control, he might have better luck. His bill would allow the construction of apartment buildings up to five stories tall near every high-frequency mass transit stop in the state. Suppose in a rural county, there happens to be a high-frequency bus route. In this area there was no housing shortage at all, so there is no need for five story tall apartment buildings. One large apartment building may destroy the rural characteristic of the community and create a housing bubble. That was why, in 2019, he made concessions to some of his colleagues from rural areas to get their support for the bill. Instead of a one-size fits all measure, the bill could include various trigger mechanisms for the law to take effect. Many localities have no housing shortage or high housing cost problems, even if there are no five-story apartments or condominium. There is no need for the state to force local communities to allow multi-story apartment or condominium complexes everywhere in California.

Laws like SB827 should apply only to areas with severe housing shortages and high housing costs. There are numerous ways to measure housing shortages and high housing costs. For example, the ratio of the median housing price over median income in a location can be a good indicator of housing affordability.

Table 6: Housing Affordability in the US

Area of the US	Median House Price (MHP)	Median Family Income (MFI)	Housing Affordability (MHP/MFI)
Northwest	$303,300	89,766	3.38
Midwest	$221,800	78,045	2.84
South	$246,600	72,215	3.41
West	$419,900	84,914	4.95

In the Northwest, the ratio of a median house over median family income was 3.38. Or, in the Northwest, the median house price was 3.38 times the median family income in the region. A smaller the number implies higher affordability. In California, any place along the coast has a much higher ratio compared to the number above. For example, in San Jose in 2017, the ratio was 9.6 (= $1,000,000/$104,000). Senator Wiener's bill would likely get more support with a trigger point of 9, that is, in any city or county, as soon as the ratio is over 9, then five story tall housing developments shall be allowed.

The advantage of this trigger point is a warning to those counties and cities with the number slightly below 9. If those communities don't want to lose local control on land-use, they will need to increase housing supply to keep the ratio well below 9. To help the bill become law, the trigger point needs to be high. If it is set high enough, the law may be almost useless at first like the rent control law that Governor Newsom signed in 2019. If the bill doesn't apply to all local communities, it will not raise strong objections from most local communities and it will have a better chance of becoming law. Once the law is in place, adjustments can make it more effective. California AB1482 capping the annual rent increase at 5% plus the inflation rate may appear to be useless. But if the 5% is reduced to 1%, the bill may help some renters.

The SB827 (2018) and SB50 (2019) make perfect sense to increase housing density along the public transportation corridors. The measure can ease the housing shortage and also make public transportation more viable in California. Because of widespread single-family houses in the state, we can boldly conclude that almost no public transportation in California can operate without heavy subsidies. Even if SB827 or SB50 becomes law, it still cannot make any public transportation profitable or self-sufficient. But at least it can increase the number of users of public transportation, reduce subsides and cut down pollution.

One reason that SB827 (2018) or SB50 (2019) met fierce resistance from all local politicians was the one-size-fits-all rule. If the bill becomes law, it may disrupt the local housing market. We can look at an example.

Woodside is a small city in Silicon Valley, and housing prices are high in this city. Highway 84 or Woodside Road is a major corridor connecting US 101 and Interstate 280, two major highway arteries in Silicon Valley. Even though the City of Woodside is a small town, there could be high frequency bus lines along Woodside Road. There could be a couple of bus stops along the road inside the City of Woodside. According to the SB827 (2018) or SB50 (2019), high density housing structures of five stories high will be permitted around the bus stops. If a developer built a couple of five story high density apartments or condominiums, they may turn the local housing market upside down. The housing price crash could be worse than the sub-prime financial crisis of 2008. Those homeowners who are multi-billionaires may not care much. But those upper middle-class homeowners may lose their life savings. Here, a couple of landowners or developers get a windfall, while many homeowners may face financial ruins. So SB50 needs more refinement. What we need is a reasonable number of affordable housing everywhere, but not an excessive number that results in a housing bubble for the other residents.

It is reasonable to require each city to provide affordable housing for minimum wage workers. We need at least 10% of housing units in every city that minimum wage workers can afford. If we add this provision in the SB50, some small communities may not resist the bill. Once a community has 10% of their housing that minimum wage workers can afford, SB50 will no longer apply and there will be no housing bubble in the community.

5.5 Restore Free Market in Housing Development

The result of local control of land-use in California is plainly visible. Local control of land-use results in a mess much worse than the land-use problem in the lawless Wild West which had no general plan, no building codes or zoning ordinances.

Let us go back in time to the lawless Wild West. Suppose that a new railroad was completed and there was a stop along the way to get water and fuel for the steam engine. Then a town would spring up around the stop. Did it take a genius to figure out we needed a road? Perhaps perpendicular to the railroad. If there were more than a few persons who wanted to live and work around the stop, we needed another road, say, parallel to the railroad or even right next to the railroad. The cross or the middle of the "'I'" of the two roads should be close to the railroad station. All these basic "designs" didn't even need a college degree. Any illiterate person with a good common sense could devise the basic plan. Now, did it make sense to build a tiny single-family house at the large corner lot? Definitely not! What should be there? Perhaps a hotel or a general store.

What if the landowner just wanted to build a tiny house at the big corner lot, because the owner liked to watch the train going by every day? In a free society, the owner was free to do so. But most likely, the landowner was the railroad company and it would put up the lot for sale to the highest bidder. Who would offer a higher price for the land, the person who would build a tiny house or the person who would build a hotel? We all know that the future hotel owner would win. This was how the free market would dictate the land-use in the Wild West. It made little sense to build a single-family house or leave it to grow hay for horses. Only a senseless politician would zone a parcel at a busy intersection for agriculture.

But unfortunately, there is little or no free-market in land-use decisions today in the New California. What is the modern equivalent of a railroad stop? The closest thing is probably a freeway exit and entrance. Why does Silicon Valley have outrageously high housing prices? You only need to drive along Interstate 280 from Palo Alto to Burlingame in the north. You don't see high-rise hotels or apartments near freeway entrances and exits. You don't even see a single house around. Apparently, local communities don't want any development along that stretch of highway.

If local politicians make senseless decisions on land-use, then the state needs to take the decisions away from them. The advantages of high-density housing and commercial developments near freeway exits and entrances are obvious. Usually, if one has to go far to work or to shop, one uses the freeway as much as possible. For those who live in high-density housing near freeway entrances, they need not drive 10, 15 minutes or longer to get to the freeway. The round trip will save 20, 30 minutes or more driving time daily. For those who work in shops or offices near freeway exits, they don't even need to drive. They can just walk to their workplace. I own a condominium in a four-story complex near a freeway exit and entrance in Silicon Valley. There are shopping centers across the street within walking distance of my condo. Usually, I walk to buy groceries or to eat in one of those restaurants. In San Luis Obispo, I haven't done this for decades.

Figure 20: View from my condo. Behind the shopping center is the a high-density housing complex. I-280 is within one block of this shopping center behind trees.

Unfortunately, there are not enough similar developments in Silicon Valley. Even close to my condo, there are a lot of low-density housing units within walking distance to these shopping centers. Why not let more people enjoy the convenience of walking to a grocery store or restaurant?

SB827 or SB50 had proposed: To allow construction of apartment buildings up to five stories tall near every high-frequency mass transit stop in the state. We need a lot more similar rules that make sense. Every sensible rule that the state puts in place, there will be less chance for local politicians to make senseless and arbitrary land-use decisions. What are sensible rules we need in the State of California? One rule is that we reserve land within half a mile of a freeway exit or entrance for high density housing or commercial use.

Refer to Figure 20 above, it is an intersection of two 4-lane roads and one of the two roads has a direct access to a freeway. It is expensive to build a four-lane road, and it is even more expensive to build a freeway entrance or exit. It would be a monumental waste of resources for any local community to build a freeway entrance or exit and build a 4-lane road to access the freeway, then the corner lot with all these transportation infrastructures is zoned for agricultural use. It makes sense to zone the corner lots for high density housing or commercial use if the freeway is within a mile or two.

If we spend a little time to think about how to conserve energy by making good land use decisions, we always come up with the same ideas. I thought about this one for decades. Parcels next to 4-lane roads and within ½ mile from any college campuses should be for high density or commercial. I lived very close to the college campus where I taught about 50 years ago, so I often walked to the campus. Along the 4-lane road (Grand Avenue) to the campus, there was a public elementary school and a private school, the rest were nothing but single-family houses. Another street (Slack Street) right along the campus had only single-family houses along the street. While I walked to my office in the morning, I rarely saw any other pedestrians going the same direction. Yet there were always bumper to bumper cars rushed towards the campus. I wondered almost every day what a wasteful way of city planning! Why were these prime parcels zoned for single-family houses? Suppose these were high-density student housings and retail commercial buildings within half a mile from campus. How different would it be? How many more pedestrians would there be? How many fewer motor vehicles would there be?

Students living off campus but right next to the campus might not need to drive every day to class. I heard again and again from students who complained about the parking shortage on campus. They claimed that to buy a campus parking permit was just to buy a hunting license for a parking spot. You might not find one unless it was a half mile from your classroom. Those students who lived on campus also needed cars and parking lots, because there were no shops or restaurants within walking distance of campus.

From 1969 to 1979, Mr. Ken Schwartz was the Mayor of San Luis Obispo and one of the four Directors in the School of Architecture. He did a great deal of senseless things to push up the housing prices. Unfortunately, nobody ever blamed him for the high housing cost. Those who were not an insider of the housing industry usually didn't understand the cause of high housing prices. Those who knew the cause usually were the insiders but dared not offend local politicians and bureaucrats. So, the mayor wanted fewer but fancier housing developments. He got away with it easily. The immediate beneficiaries were architects. At first, local architects might not like the criticism from anyone to their designs. But the resistance was short lived. They couldn't do anything to resist the criticism so they learned quickly to live with it. They soon realized ARC was God sent to benefit them and gave them a chance to show off their talents to build fancy, complicated and pretty buildings. No wonder, Mr. Schwartz was elected a Fellow of the American Institute of Architects. The most efficient and practical design of affordable housing is well known and we don't even need an architect to design it. Any licensed contractor, I am one, can easily design one and a structural engineer can easily check it out if the building is sound. This was how it was done in the good old days; this was why housing used to be affordable. But Mr. Schwartz wanted to change it, he introduced Architectural Review Commission to stop anyone from build simple housing units again in the city. His students saw various honors piled on him. News media was full of tributes to his accomplishments, the beautiful downtown and Mission Plaza. The more honors heaped on him, the more his students would worship him as their role model. The less media held him responsible for the high housing prices, the more his students wanted to mimic his accomplishment. Few could repeat his feat, but all students could sell his tricks to other politicians in the state or beyond. This is at least one of the reasons if it was not the only reason why California has a runaway housing crisis.

A drug kingpin causes devastation for his drug trafficking and pushing, but he may be a generous benefactor to the folks in his hometown. Should we ignore his drug-pushing and only praise his generosity? I can make an argument to conclude what Mayor Schwartz did was far worse than a drug kingpin. People who don't touch illegal substances are beyond the reach of a drug kingpin. I can proudly proclaim that I never contributed a dime to any drug kingpin's fortune. But unfortunately, nobody could escape the deadly effects of Mayor Ken Schwartz's devastating policy. Yet, fortunate for the Mayor, many who reap a windfall from rising house values are still around San Luis Obispo to praise him for the beautiful downtown and Mission Plaza. Those who couldn't afford to live in town were long gone, they would never come back to bad-mouth about anyone. Hundreds of thousands of graduates from the local university may still be paying for student loans because of the high housing cost. Most of them have no idea who to blame.

I don't hold a personal grudge against Mayor Schwartz, but I want to expose him for what he did. When he was in power, nobody dared to offend him. His proteges continued his policy in town, they put a plaque to commemorate his accomplishment. If we let him get away with the devastation he did to this city, San Luis Obispo, this state and beyond, hundreds of local politicians will try to follow his footsteps to cause more destruction and undermine the foundation of this great country. We need to put a stop to the process and give a warning to thousands of local politicians that they can get away with what they do temporarily, but the damages that they do will come back to haunt them forever.

I have traveled a lot since I retired from teaching over 20 years ago. I have never seen another university campus with so many single-family houses right next to the campus. While I was teaching at the university, within about one-half mile of any entrance to the campus, there was not a single retail shop. Twenty years after I retired from teaching, there is a coffee outlet right next to the campus. Recently, I checked about the coffee outlet with someone who recently graduated from the university.

He told me that the coffee outlet was non-profit and sponsored by a church-affiliated organization. He actually worked there once as a volunteer to dispense free coffee to students. I wondered, since the land was not zoned for commercial, how could there be a coffee outlet for students. He solved the puzzle for me. The place doesn't sell anything, the coffee is free and it's a great study space with WiFi for students. We need more of it. It may take another twenty years to get a cafe next to the campus! Why can't the city rezone the R1 lots right next to campus to high density housing and commercial. Why was it so hard to do the right thing for the environment?

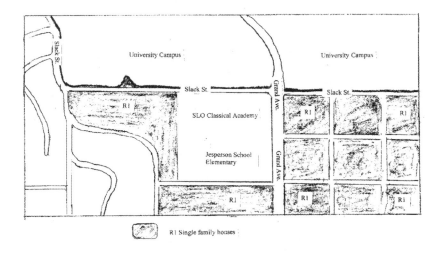

Figure 21: A simple sketch of the map of college campus, nearby schools and single-family detached houses. The blank area outside of school campuses are mostly single-family housings.

Figure 22: Houses right next to university campus in San Luis Obispo

In Figure 21, the California State University campus is at the top of the sketch. In the middle of the sketch is the campus of a private school and a public elementary school. There is no advantage for the three campuses next to each other. The private school could be anywhere else in the city, but it is right next to the university. The elementary school should be close to residential area for families with children. But the houses near the school are mostly occupied by college students now. A few college students can afford to pay more than an average family can. The location could have been high density student housing and retail shops and restaurants catering to students' needs. A tremendous amount of fossil fuel would have been saved.

Mr. Ken Schwartz could easily have done it. Instead of a few hundred houses and a private school within walking distance of the campus, there could have been a few thousands of apartment units and dozens of restaurants and shops catering to students' needs. Then thousands of students living on campus wouldn't need automobiles to get services in town and, thus, they wouldn't need parking on campus. Thousands of students who lived right next to campus could have walked to school and back. Again, thousands of parking spaces for students could have been eliminated.

Mr. Schwartz could have easily kept San Luis Obispo's housing affordable. The cumulative inflation from 1972 to 1978 was high, it was about 50%. But housing prices increased almost 300% or about 5 times faster than inflation. He could have made students housing affordable by changing the zoning of the parcels close to campus from low density housing to high density housing and reduce automobile traffic to and from campus a great deal, but he didn't.

Like many local politicians, Mr. Schwartz started his political career from the Planning Commission. He served on both Planning Commissions of San Luis Obispo City and County. So obviously, he understood the land-use process well, and it was fair to conclude that, during his watch, nothing about land-use in San Luis Obispo could happen by chance.

How could he push housing prices up? He didn't need to order a suspension of housing developments in the City, all he needed was to add a few red tapes to slow down the process. If the Planning Commission couldn't slow down the process enough, add one more Architectural Review Commission. For sure, bureaucrats knew the purpose of the commission was not to speed up housing developments or make housing affordable. To create red tapes, bureaucrats can excel. Many times, a staff in the Building Department told me he needed to know EXACTLY how I would do a job. This kind of requests always scared me. I understand that the Building Department may demand that the concrete for the driveway be at least four inches thick. But EXACTLY how to do it is none of any bureaucrat's business. If I needed to turn in a nailing specification about how to nail two pieces of wood together, that was easy for me to comply. But if I needed to explain how to put a nail into a piece of wood, it will not be easy. I could pound a three-inch nail into a piece of wood with two strikes of a 32-oz hammer in two seconds. But how could I describe EXACTLY, what needed to be done? I don't know if I need a one-page description or a ten-page description. I don't even know the name of the muscle on my wrist, so how could I explain EXACTLY what to do? I didn't know which muscle contracts which way when I lifted a hammer. Why did it matter? You cannot tell a bureaucrat: "It is none of your business!" Whatever I do, the person can always say "NO!" So usually, when I heard a city employee telling me anything like "Tell me EXACTLY how you will do!" I took it as a "NO!" to whatever I was applying to do. Apparently, there were enough red tapes in the housing development process, from

1973 to 1979 housing prices increased at least 20% a year. Also, it was clear whatever he did, it took 2 to 3 years for the effects to show up in the housing prices. I bought my first house from the developer for $23000. Minimum wage was $1.60, it took less than 15000 hours of minimum wages to buy the house. Now a similar house today is about $650,000. For a minimum wage earner to afford the house now, the minimum wage needs to be $45!

How could Mr. Schwartz keep the housing prices stable? That should be easy too. He could just tell the Planning Commission or ARC to speed up the approval processes and he could increase the density of housing developments. I bought my first house from a developer who built 50 houses on a track of 7 acres and 96 condominiums on 4 acres. My first house was 4-bedroom and 2 baths with a double garage on a 6000 square foot lot. The house with the garage only occupied 27% of the lot. The lot was big enough to have two houses, each being the same size. The two houses still only occupied 27% of the lot, provided that the two houses were two stories instead of one. San Luis Obispo is a small city. If the developer built 100 houses instead only 50 on the 7-acre track, the house prices probably would not have increased 20% to 30% in 1973. Or if the city allowed a few housing projects moving through the approval process faster, the housing prices would not increase as fast as they did year after year. After I lived in my new house, I noticed a few newer housing developments nearby. They were further away from the center of the city. There was a noticeable difference. The developer who sold me my first house built two high density units for each single-family house. But those new developments approved in later time were all single-family houses. Most of them were on much bigger lots.

So, it was easy for local politicians and bureaucrats to push housing prices up or down. Whatever happened to the City of San Luis Obispo would spread very quickly to the rest of the state. In the 70s, my advice to my friends and relatives in California was: "Buy any California real estate you can put your hands on!" A few of them did, and some of them still thank me for my good tip. When we look at a person's life-time accomplishments, we cannot just emphasize a few trivial ones. We need to start from the most important impact to the most people. Yes! Mr. Schwartz was friendly and likeable. He made the beautiful downtown San Luis Obispo even better than before. He also improved the San

Luis Obispo Mission Plaza considerably. He was an exceptional teacher and helped his students and his profession tremendously. If these were all he did, he had a full and enviable life worth of all the honors and praises bestowed to him. It would be a great honor for me to make his acquaintance. But how could we ignore the other things he did to the housing development process in the city? Instead of it being an honor for me to know him, I didn't want to touch him with a ten-foot pole.

Mr. Schwartz was in a unique position to set an example of superb city planning that could benefit hundred of millions of people in the US and beyond. But unfortunately, instead of a vision of a soaring eagle that could see the edge of earth, Mr. Schwartz had the vision of a stumbling chick seeing only inches around himself. Instead of benefiting hundreds of millions of people in the US and beyond, he chose to benefit only his re-elections, his own profession and his students in the School of Architecture, at the expense of the rest of the public. I wish I had the courage to criticize him and his policy when I was a penniless assistant professor. I saw what he was doing was terribly wrong and I knew the consequences of his misguided policy. I didn't speak out because I had my obligation to my wife and children. At the time, some of my best friends would not listen to my advice, I doubted if I could convince anyone else. Now the consequences of his misguided policy are plainly visible. Only as the damage is done, perhaps we have the wisdom to hold the responsible culprit accountable.

San Luis Obispo is not just the city with one of the least, if not the least, affordable housing in the US: it is also one of the most inconvenient cities in the country. Because of large number single-family detached houses on large lot and few high-density housing developments, public transportation is few and far in between both in time and in space. If people have ever travelled on US Highway 101, a freeway passing through the City, they have probably noticed there are 8 exits in the south bound and 10 in the north bound for a city with less than 50,000 people. There are bike lanes everywhere, but very few bikes. Travel from one end of the city to the other on bike takes about an hour. The City required an Environmental Impact Study for every large housing development in 1977 General Plan update. It was not really an environmental impact study, but an immediate neighborhood impact report. What the city wanted was good for the immediate neighborhood but may not be good for the city as a whole.

Most residents in town must have a car, so parking is a problem just about everywhere. While I was teaching at the university, there were no parking structures on campus. After I retired from teaching, I heard that there were new massive parking structures on campus. The City made an effort to make downtown cute and attractive, but the downtown needed more parking spaces. Three massive multi-level parking structures were built, so the small-town characteristic also disappeared. Why didn't the city build more multi-level housing and commercial structures instead? Those would encourage foot traffic and public transportation, and then parking structures on the university campus and city center might not be needed at all. That would have been a good impact on the environment.

Figure 23: A complicated roof in San Luis Obispo, Calif.

It was very clear that all those obstacles and hurdles local governments put up for housing developments did increase the costs of new developments but rarely increased the quality of the new development. For example, the simplest housing structure is a rectangular one with a gabled roof of two facets. But the ARC in San Luis Obispo, called it ugly card-board box structure. We could be sure that in the last one half of a century, the City did not approve a single new building like that. A lot of architects went out of their way to appease the ARC, so they designed more and more complicated structures with elaborated roofs to match. From my house, I see the roof of my neighbors' house across the road from mine, I can count 10 facets that do not include the ones I cannot see from where I am standing.

The following photo show how simple efficient and functional housing structures are common in rich European countries. In many ways Norway is richer than the US, unlike the US Federal Government, Norwegian Government is not in debt. Norwegian central government is in a net asset position, i.e. the government's total financial assets exceed the total debt. In the US, the gross federal debt amounted to around 69,060 U.S. dollars per capita at the end of year 2019. In

2020, NationMaster Website estimated GDP per capita at $99,557.73 for Norway and $51,748.56 for the US.

Figure 24: Vixna, Norway, February 2020

My own house in San Luis Obispo is not much better than my neighbor's. At one corner of the house is the nook in a pentagon shape with 6 ridges of roof on top. When the framer (the one who built the wood frame for the house) looked at the blue print before he gave me a bid, he said it was very complicated and it would be costly. During the construction, the framer built it and took it apart a couple times to make the roof work. I also noticed that he wasted a lot of lumber and plywood, because lumber and plywood were designed for rectangular structures. After these expenses, my house looks great, but it is not very functional. (Please see the photo on the back-cover.) I would rather have a rectangular nook so my furniture would fit in the room. Older and newer housing units function about the same, yet new units cost a lot more than old units. This is another reason why we need to restore free market function in housing developments. For those who pay a high price to buy a new housing unit, at least they deserve better and more functional units. At present, as California's housing prices go up and up, the extra cost mostly pays for local governments' meddling and manipulation and developers' cost to navigate through the maze of red tapes.

What we really need for good city and regional planning are clear rules in housing development. We need high-density housing near university campuses. This is a no brainer. Tens of thousands of students need to go to campus to attend classes or to meet teachers or to go to library. It doesn't make sense not to let them live right next to campus. Similarly, we need high-density housing and commercial developments near freeway entrances and exits, near major public transportation corridors, near the intersection of major roads, near hospitals, near downtown commercial centers or government centers etc. We need land for high-density housing to encourage foot traffic, to reduce the need to drive and to encourage the use of public transportation. This kind of city and regional planning can reduce the total carbon footprint of all residents. When a developer buys a piece of land, what the developer can do with the land should be clear to everyone. At present, land-use decision may be the most corrupt part of the political process. When there are no rules, no check or balance, no transparency, no scrutiny, the only things preventing local politicians from turning rotten are their own conscience.

College students used to work part time to finish a college education. Now, besides working part time, many still have to get a student loan. Graduation from college used to be an exciting new beginning. Now, most college graduates are deeply in debt and they worry about how they can pay off their loans. A full-time job in the US used to be a ticket to move up to middle class. Now, a full-time job cannot even guarantee the worker a room near where the job is. So high housing cost is not just an expensive living cost, to many, high housing cost is the stumbling block in the middle of the road of upward mobility. High housing cost is responsible to turn "America the land of opportunity" into "America the land of desperation".

Many think the housing crisis in California is the failure of the free market or capitalism. It is definitely a failure for the State. California is not like the kingdom of Monaco or the Territory of Hong Kong. Monaco and Hong Kong are tiny spots on the world map. There are many people living in these tiny spots, housing ought to be expensive at these places.

California is a big state, there are open spaces just about everywhere. If there is not enough affordable housing to go around, we need to blame someone. America is a free market economy; it should keep housing supply and demand in balance. Now, if house supply and demand are out of balance, shouldn't we try socialism? If we do, then we couldn't be more wrong. The housing crisis in California did not just happen, it took a lot of meddling and arbitrary restrictions to make it happen. It is not the failure of capitalism, but the lack of it. The housing market is not functional because local politicians choke it to death.

Silicon Valley represents the worst regional housing crisis in the US. We can easily solve the problem if we just enact two policies. First, every small city or town from Daly City to Cupertino would allow a few median-rise, five, six or seven story housing developments. Second, about 10% of the single-family dwellings in San Francisco and San Jose would be replaced with high density median-rise developments. Technically, we can easily do it. Economically, Silicon Valley's annual GDP may increase 400 billion to a trillion depending on which estimate we believe. Silicon Valley with reasonable housing prices will maintain its leadership in high-tech innovation for the foreseeable future. Politically, this will not happen, because local politicians will fight tooth and nail for their controls over housing developments. For most of them, housing developments are the ATMs of their campaign contributions. If we add the third prong for campaign reform, then the entire program should work. Who will have the rights to build the high-density housing developments? The answer: "The highest bidder!" We just auction off the rights to build high density housing units in every town. This way, every developer want-be can put in a bid. This has nothing to do with any connection to the elected officers a developer may have. It will be fair and square, and corruption in housing development will disappear. A developer has to pay into the public treasury for the right, so there is no windfall for any developer. Any windfall in housing development goes to the public coffer and part of the proceeds can be public finance of the local elections. When we cut the connection between housing development and campaign contribution, the local politicians don't like it at all. But there are no other ways to solve the housing crisis in California and beyond. We cannot count on local government to solve their problem. They created the problem, we, the people, must solve the problem for ourselves!

California SB35 was passed to streamline local housing approval processes. It also put some teeth into enforcement of state housing requirements. For parcels close to public transportation, SB35 would prohibit new single-family housing developments and would increase housing density. This bill gives us a ray of hope. If there is a severe shortage of housing, especially affordable housing, in California, we cannot solve the problem by building only single-family houses on spacious lots.

In Silicon Valley, there are enough open fields to build a lot of single-family houses to meet the housing demand. We should not just keep building single-family detached houses to provide affordable housing. Single-family houses contribute to energy waste, flood, loss of habitat for wild lives, global warming and other environment disasters. Even if single-family detached houses are environmentally sound, we still don't want to add a lot of single-family houses to bring down the housing price. In Silicon Valley, a modest 4-bedroom and 2-bath house can fetch three or four million dollars. If local governments in Silicon Valley were to allow a lot of new houses, the price may drop to one million only. Runaway inflation in housing prices is bad, but a sudden deflation in housing prices is also bad, if not worse. We only need to recall the burst of the housing bubble in the Subprime Mortgage Crisis of 2007-2010. This was a nationwide financial crisis, occurring between 2007 and 2010 and resulted in the U.S. recession. It started with a large drop in home prices after the burst of a housing bubble, leading to mortgage delinquencies, foreclosures, devaluation of housing prices and default in housing-related securities. Declines in housing sales lead to recession and were followed by delinquency of mortgage payments, reductions in household spending and then reductions in business investment. The financial meltdown required extensive government rescue and bailouts, including help for homeowners who lost equity in their houses. The total cost added to about two trillion dollars on the federal deficit.

If we compare California to Florida, population density is higher in Florida than in California. Florida's population density is 353.4 persons per square mile and California's number is only 251.3. Of course, California has large desert and mountain range that are not habitable, but Florida has an extensive area of wetland that is not habitable either. So, let us call it even, the population density on size of habitable land in the two states should be close. In Florida, one can buy an affordable single-family house just about everywhere, from Miami to Jacksonville, from San Augustine to Pensacola at one tenth of the price in Silicon Valley. Since there is enough land in California, why can't we just keep building single-family houses to bring down the price? You are right! We can build enough numbers of single-family houses to bring down the housing prices even in Silicon Valley, there is enough land. But do we want to solve California's housing crisis this way? Suppose that a family just bought a four-million-dollar house with a 3.5-million-dollar mortgage. Suddenly, a brand-new house of the same size is for sale nearby at five hundred thousand dollars. What should the family do? Buy the new house at no money down and abandon the old house. The new mortgage is only one seventh of the old mortgage, so is the monthly mortgage payment. The lender of the old mortgage will be in big trouble, it is the Subprime Mortgage Crisis all over again. Except it is few times worse. So we cannot solve one problem by creating a new problem!

The best way is to keep most of the open space in Silicon Valley and develop only a small portion of the space into high density housing units. Which landowner can build high density housing units and which landowner must leave the land as open space? Instead of letting local politicians arbitrarily pick and choose, let us auction off the right to build high-density housing units to the highest bidder. The right to build on a parcel of land is the square footage of living space instead of the number of units. This is drastically different from the current rules. The current zoning regulation mainly limits the number of units on a parcel of land. This is why we end up with rather large units. We see one-bedroom condos as large as one thousand square feet. What we need are small one-bedroom units with four or five hundred square feet per unit. Suppose that a landowner or a developer has won the right to build 40,000 square feet of living space on an acre of land. The developer could divide this living space into 40 two-bedroom units of 1000 square feet in each unit, or 80 one-bed room units with 500 square feet each, or 160 studio units or any combination of the three types. Even if the unit price stays at current level about $1000 per square foot of living space. A studio unit at $250,000 is fairly affordable by Silicon Valley standard. One person can live comfortably in a studio and a couple can get by for a few years. The beauty of this solution is to avoid the Subprime Mortgage Crisis all over again to solve the housing crisis. There are environmental benefits too. High density housing development on one parcel of land allows several other parcels of land to remain as open space. High density housing developments facilitate public transportation and foot traffic. In 2018, Sierra Club of California opposed Senator Wiener's Bill 827 to increase new high-density housing and recommended more funding for affordable housing in its Housing Policy: Meeting Our Housing Needs and Protecting the Environment. More funding is only a Band-Aid solution to California's housing problem. Many local governments have tried this solution for years, but the problem only gets worse. Based on my suggestion, there seems to be no need for government funding. Government will get more revenue from auctioning off building rights. Instead of funding for affordable housing, let us have more funding for infrastructures. To understand that we have too many single-family detached houses in the US, especially in California, we only need to look at the official residence, 10 Downing St., of the Prime Minister of the United Kingdom in London. It is a townhouse! Even at the pinnacle of the supremacy of the British Empire, those in power had the wisdom to put the prime minister's official resident in a townhouse instead of a manor with acres of garden. For sure, the Prime minister of the British Empire could afford one. Americans are slow to face the reality. While we can no longer afford to live in a lot of single-family detached houses, we don't seem able to wake up to face the reality and just turn our American Dream into an American Nightmare!

5.6 A Ladder Must Have All the Steps

When I was a little boy, I learned about the United States of America. The first thing I remembered was America, the land of opportunity. When I came to America in 1962, America was the land of opportunity to me. I started my life in the US from the lowest point in the lowest social and economic group. The minimum wage in the US was $1.15 an hour, I got only a dollar. I had no special talent or skill; I was not even physically strong. I have always been skinny. All I had was my willingness to work hard, and it was enough! I slowly climbed up the ladder. Now I am at least above the middle class in the US! If a person ever uses a ladder, the person knows a ladder is useless without all the steps.

In the ladder of upward social and economic mobility in the US, the first few steps are missing. The first step is the step for a minimum wage worker or a person making even less to move up. In San Francisco, the city leaders and most of its residents like to portray the city as a progressive city that welcomes even illegal immigrants. The city declared itself as a Sanctuary City. Thanks a lot! If I landed in San Francisco today as I did about 60 years ago, what does the city welcome me to do? If I could not even get a minimum wage job, where can I live? I guess anywhere on the street. Then I would be kicked around the rest of my life. What would be my chance of realizing my American dream? In early 2020, I pretended that I was making about $70,000 annually and was looking for a one-bedroom apartment online in San Francisco. The closest available unit was in Sausalito across the Bay. If housing costs become unaffordable, it is hard for many middle or low-wage workers in the US to climb up the social and economic ladder to realize their American dream.

We can also use Hong Kong as an example. The per-square-foot-of-live-space price in Hong Kong is around $2000, about twice the price in San Francisco. In Hong Kong, a typical one-bedroom flat is about 300 square feet. In San Francisco, a typical one-bedroom condominium is about 800 square feet. If one can find a 300 square foot one-bedroom condo, the price should be around 300,000 dollars. It is within the reach of even minimum wage workers in San Francisco. For a young couple, even if both of them work for minimum wages, their combined annual gross income of $60,000 makes the unit fairly affordable. They don't want to live there the rest of their lives. Once they are homeowners, they have a good chance to trade up. But good luck! I bet there is no such unit in San Francisco. Local politicians consider these kind of housing units substandard. It contributes to over-crowding and deterioration of the quality of lives for the occupants. To the local politicians, San Franciscans deserve better housing units than this. They don't allow this kind of choice for anyone. It is nothing but the best, too bad, if one cannot afford it. One can either become homeless or be a slave for life to the so-called "decent housing".

Minimum wage in Hong Kong was HK$ 37.5 in 2019, or less than US$5. Or, the minimum wage in Hong Kong was less than 1/3 of the minimum wage in San Francisco. Yet the cost of per square foot living space in Hong Kong was about twice as expensive as in San Francisco.

So a person who worked at a minimum wage job in San Francisco could not buy any housing units in San Francisco. Isn't it obvious that the person would be even less able to buy a housing unit in Hong Kong? Amazingly, the answer is a "No". US$15 an hour wage in Hong Kong was a rather decent hourly wage in Hong Kong, and a person who earned US$15 an hour was able to buy a dwelling. There are one-bed room flats with about 200 square feet of living space. Even at US$2000 per sq ft, the unit costs only $400,000. If a US$15-hourly wage full-time job is not enough to buy a brand-new small unit in Hong Kong, there are older small units and older units in out skirt region with lower price tags. The question now is why can't a minimum wage worker with an annual income of $30,000 to buy a dwelling in San Francisco where the per square foot price is only one half of the price in Hong Kong? There aren't any housing units for sale at $400,000 a piece in San Francisco! There aren't many housing units as small as 400 square foot living space in San Francisco! If we can find small units with only 200 square feet or 20 square meters of living space in Tokyo, Hong Kong, Berlin, Paris, London, etc, why can't we find similar units in San Francisco?

Please don't think Hong Kong is a model city with plenty of affordable housings. It doesn't have any affordable housing at all. Hong Kong was a British Colony prior to 1997 and the British milked Hong Kong like a cash cow for a long time. The Colonial Government didn't provide affordable housing to the masses. The government owned all land for housing development and it never released land for affordable housing. The land was always sold to the highest bidder, and it timed the sale to maximize revenue. But the Colonial Government didn't sell off all the land before it turned Hong Kong over to China. The current Hong Kong Government maintains the same practice on land sale for housing development. The result is that the per square foot of living space in a new housing unit is one of the highest unit prices in the world. Luckily, the Hong Kong Government does not use zoning regulation to limit the supply of small housing units or limit the number of individuals may occupy a unit. While Hong Kong's housing crisis should be SIX times worse than the housing crisis in San Francisco, it is no worse at all. This is possible because there are small housing units, such as a one-bedroom flat with three hundred square feet of living space or a studio flat with two hundred square feet of living space. The politicians in San Francisco should serve the voters who elected them, yet these politicians treat citizens worse than the colonial government treated British subjects!

Recently, a small city, Atascadero, along US Highway 101 almost exactly half way between Los Angeles and San Francisco approved a plan for micro-home housing on November 13, 2019. It is a development of 30 new affordable 500-to 900- square-foot houses on a 1.7-acre lot on El Camino Real, the main corridor of the city. This lot is only 5 blocks from a freeway exit and the El Camino Real in front of this lot is as wide as the Hwy 10l. On the back and on the north of this lot are single-family detached houses on very spacious lots about .4 of acre each. The city could have easily allowed only 4 houses on this lot and made the development comparable to the neighboring lots. Yet, the City Council unanimously approved the development of 30 small units of houses with a mix of 500 to 900 square foot living spaces. Suppose these 30 houses are all one story with an average size of 700 square feet, the total covered area is only 21,000 square feet, less than one third of the lot size. There is still plenty of room for a driveway, parking lots, playground, landscape and open space. No one would stop the City Council of Atascadero to approve twice the number of units for this project. All the developer needed to do was change the building from one story to two stories. It would not change the quality of life for the future occupants or the characters of this development. The only problem may be lack of parking spaces for the additional units. But El Camino Real is a major corridor of the city. There must be buses running along the road. To cut down the number of required parking spaces is a way to encourage the residents to use public transportation. The additional units would make the unit price more affordable. The saving in housing cost should allow residents to use Uber or Lyft to order rides once in a while.

The developer estimates the houses will cost $250,000 to $350,000, meaning mortgage payment would cost $1,400 to $1,800 per month. If there are 60 units in the project, the unit price should reduce by about $100,000 and the mortgage payment would be $900 to $1300 per month. In fact, Atascadero has an abundance of affordable housing priced $200,000 - $300,000 per unit. These units are conventional small single detached houses on large lots. Adding more small units will keep a lid on housing prices and make sure there will be affordable units available. Atascadero is not a city with high housing cost. Why did the City council approve the development for small housing units? This is the best way to prevent the housing crisis from happening. The City Council of Atascadero approved the right kind housing developments before it was needed, so there would never be a housing crisis in the city. We can also use it to demonstrate a few other aspects of California's housing crisis.

A lot of single-family detached houses alone do not create high house cost, even if a city allows only mostly single-family housing developments. The housing prices may not rise to the stratosphere, as long as there are enough houses. Atascadero has a lot of single-family houses, but there are still plenty of open fields within the city and it is easy to get building permits to build a house. So, there are still affordable conventional houses available in the city. Therefore, states like Nevada, Florida and Texas with high population growth, but still have affordable single-family houses.

Now let us look at San Francisco, it has about the highest housing prices anywhere in the US. Unfortunately, there aren't enough open fields to build more single-family houses in the City to bring down the housing prices. There are already plenty of high-rise housing developments. But there are still a lot of single-family detached houses in SF. If there isn't enough land for new housing developments, then we cannot afford to keep all those single-family houses. What we need are low-rise multi-level housing developments to replace some single-family houses. Also, we need entry level small units, so low-wage workers, including minimum wage workers, can afford to buy or to rent. All the city needs is just to allow developers to demolish single-family houses and to replace them with high-density low-rise small housing units. Housing is a low elastic commodity. This is the economic jargon to say that the demand for housing is not flexible. If there is a shortage in housing, price will increase a lot. Because everyone needs a roof overhead regardless how high the cost. By the same token, if there is plentiful supply, the housing price will drop a lot, especially in the rental market. If there is a vacant rental unit, the owner needs a renter to occupy the unit as soon as possible. The owner cannot save the vacancy for future use. A month of vacancy is a month of rent lost. But the expenses, such as mortgage interest, insurance premium, property tax, utility bill, upkeep are still due. A mom-and-pop owner cannot afford to let any rental be vacated for long. They will reduce the rent as much as necessary to get it rented, even at a loss. As soon as multilevel-housing with small units replace some single-family houses, the rental prices will come down fast. In the other words, the housing crisis in California is not that hard to solve.

The problem we have in California now is not too many small units or multi-story housing developments, but the lack of them. For example, look at the City of Pismo Beach, a beach town along the Pacific Coast about halfway between San Francisco and Los Angeles. There are plenty of multimillion dollars beach houses and new estates with an ocean view. There are also upscale hotels and restaurants catering to tourists. With a thriving tourism industry, there are a lot of low-wage workers in the city. Where do these low-wage workers live? Luckily, a city next door, Grover Beach, has a lot of low-cost housing. If one doesn't mind driving a little, one may save a lot to live in Santa Maria, a city in the northern Santa Barbara County about 20 miles from Pismo Beach. Also, there are many low-cost housing units within the city limit. On the south-eastern part of the city, there are acres and acres of mobile-home parks. Some double-wide mobile homes are very spacious with large yards and they are not cheap. But there are also a lot of inexpensive single-wide homes priced under $200,000 per unit. Mobile homes represent about 18% of the housing units in Pismo Beach. In late 2019, a quick search for available housing units on "zillow.com, Pismo Beach" resulted in the most expensive house of $4.5 million dollars to the least expensive mobile home of $125,000. It is a rather rare result in California that in a small city, there could be such wide range of housing prices. This demonstrates the fact that high priced housing and affordable units can co-exist. So, those who "invested" in expensive housing units should not be afraid of affordable housing units nearby. Not only can expensive housing co-exist with affordable ones in a small town like Pismo Beach, actually, they can exist side by side.

On one block in Pismo Beach, a new small two-bed condo valued above half million is right next door to a group of tiny cottages that are low cost rentals. Also, these housing units are in the same block with a house under 2000 square feet of living space but valued at over 2 million dollars. Many NIMBYs are afraid of any affordable housing developments nearby that may contaminate the neighborhood and devalue their investments. But based on the true situation in the City of Pismo Beach, this kind of comprehension may be unfounded.

Figure 25: Low rent housing and luxury condos side-by-side

Figure 26: Low cost housing and low rise condos side-by-side

In a rural area, opening-up a few mobile home parks may be a fast way to provide affordable housing units, but they are not the most efficient way to use limited land. Mobile homes are not much better than single-family detached houses. Like single-family houses, mobile homes are not very energy efficient. In areas with runaway housing prices, there is simply not enough vacant land for mobile home parks. In San Francisco, there are a few R-V parks. But there are few for mobile homes and there are very few places available to build one. There are just too many single-family detached houses. This is the problem and this is also the solution.

California already allows the addition of a granny unit in any single-family detached house. This is an excellent start, but local governments still impose restrictions on granny units. Same with tiny houses on wheels, some local governments allow them on the one hand, then impose a lot of rules to block them on the other hand. State needs to require city to relax not only the zoning requirements but also need to relax their building code except those necessary for health and safety.

We need to solve the problem of high housing costs, but we don't want to solve one problem by creating a different problem. Those who live in expensive houses didn't create the problem, so they should not be punished. These homeowners only play by the rules, they just want a place to settle down and raise their families. They are not responsible for the high housing costs; the local politicians are! So, while we need to provide affordable housing in Silicon Valley, we don't want those homeowners living there now and who paid high prices for their houses to lose their life savings. So here is a dilemma: A typical single detached house is three million dollars and a condominium is 1.5 million in Silicon Valley. A lot of people working in Silicon Valley cannot afford these housings. Of course, there is plenty of land available for new housing. If there are enough new houses, the price of a typical single-family house may drop to half a million and the price of a typical condo to about two hundred fifty thousand. Now the problem of housing shortage is solved, but a new problem rises. Those who bought housing before the drop face financial ruin.

We need to provide affordable housing, while preserving the value of existing housing. The best ways to solve the high housing cost is for local governments to loosen their grip on housing developments and gradually let the free market force to guide the future housing developments. If there is a severe housing shortage in an area, any kind of housing supply would help. But the free market will induce the developers to provide housing units to meet the greatest demand. In Silicon Valley, a developer can sell a three-million-dollar house with 3000 square feet of living space fast. However, if the developer builds 10 units of 500 square feet condominiums on the same lot, these small units will meet a demand that there is no supply for. These 10 units, at half a million a piece, will be sold much faster than the big house and also give the developer more profit. As far as quality of life is concerned, there is almost no difference between those living in the big house and those living in the small condo. The big house is eight times larger and 6 times more expensive, but those who live in the big house could not possibly 8 or even 6 times better off than those who live in the tiny condo. Assuming typical households of three or four residents occupy these units, almost all of the basic needs are comfortably fulfilled. They have rest room facilities for a human's urgent needs; they have comfortable beds to sleep on, they can take a shower or bath to get themselves ready to go to work or school, they have enough room to store food and to prepare meals, they have room to sit down and enjoy their meals, they have room to watch TV, to read, to study, to do home-work or to use computers. This is a win-win situation for everyone. If the free market demands more 300 square foot or even smaller units, so be it. The nice thing about this solution is that we don't need to destroy the value of the big conventional houses to provide affordable housing. When there is a supply of affordable small units, we can solve the housing shortage fast. In the meantime, the value of big houses will not crash, but owners of big houses will not get a big windfall either.

Of course, a big house still has its advantages, every household can always use an extra room. Those who live in the big house can entertain a large number of guests or can throw big parties, while the occupants in the tiny condo cannot. The question is how often does a household need to entertain a lot of guests or to throw a big party. If the need is very often or daily, the big house may be necessary. While the housing cost, both financial or environmental, is fairly proportional to its size, the usefulness of a house is not. As the size of a house increases, the usefulness of the extra space becomes less and less crucial, or less useful to the household. Comparing a house with 4000 square feet of living space to a house with 200 additional living space, the difference is almost negligible. But to a homeless person, the difference between homeless and a proper shelter of 200 square feet of living space is almost night and day.

If extra large houses are not extremely useful to most residents, why are there so many of them? Part of the answer was discussed in Chapter 4 of this book, that was, a lot of homeowners consider their houses not just a roof over their heads or just a necessity of life, but an important investment. I believe I am one of them. As my children were growing up and my mother-in-law was living with us, we needed a big house to be comfortable. But the house had more than 3000 square feet of living space, it was more than enough for comfortable living. Instead of just a place to raise my family and providing a secure and cozy retirement for mother-in-law, it was a great investment. I bought the housing in 1978 for $100,000 and sold it in 2003 for $540,000. My house value increased 440% over about 25 years while the cumulative inflation was only 172%. I never liked this type of investment and I knew this kind of trend, housing values appreciating far above inflation rate was detrimental to the economy and to the country. But I believe that I did it with cynical attitude: "Cannot beat them, join them!"

I sold my house not because I down-sized. I moved into an even bigger house than the one I sold. For only two of us, my wife and I, we absolutely didn't need it. Of course, it was an investment! I earned a little respect too because I could afford to live in a big house. It was more of a trophy than a necessity to me.

But this time, the investment is not nearly as profitable as my last two houses. Over the last 15 years, my new house did increase in value but it has barely kept pace with the inflation. The cumulative inflation rate over the last 15 years was about 40%. I bought a condo in the Bay Area in 2010, and in less than 10 years, it has doubled in value. Not because Bay Area housing values increased faster than those in my area; instead, a condo is in great demand just about everywhere in California while an extra large house or the high end housing is not in great demand in my area.

I could have made a better investment building moderate priced condominiums than building a huge single-family detached house. The problem was not my lack of 20-20 foresight, but a lack of land zoned for the condominium. There is plenty of land available in

California, but zoning regulations prevent enough affordable housing from being built.

Do we need the state government to raise money for affordable housing like California's bond sale in 2019? Do we need the state government to provide billions in the budget for affordable housing like in 2019-2020? Do we need a hundred million dollars to help renters pay for deposit like the California State Budgeted in 2019? Do we need rent control to help renter get affordable housing? The answers to these questions are "NO!" California's housing crisis did not originate from lack of investment in housing constructions, especially not because of lack of investment in affordable housing. When there was a demand, the free-market would find a way to meet the demand provided that the free-market was allowed to function.

As for the rental market, there are plenty of competitions, if there are plenty of supplies. In most area in California, anyone with a $100,000 investment (down payment) can buy a house or condo and put it for rent. If there are no takers, the rent for the house or the condo has to come down. A small investor cannot afford to let a house or a condo vacated for long. If the rental market is fully competitive and the rent is too high, then artificial rent control cannot solve the problem. The problem is lack of supply. Large rental housing owners or small mom & pop owners don't control the supply, local politicians do. When politicians advocate rent control or enact rent control, they are totally irresponsible. They create a problem, and they try to fool renters to blame landlords for the problem. Not only are the local politicians irresponsible, but also counter productive. Rent increases because of lack of supply. Instead of increase in supply, rent control discourages investment in rental housing and allows the lucky few to pay below market rent. The lucky few who enjoy below market rent, they tend to live in bigger rental units that they don't need. So rent control actually reduces rental supply for the majority of the renters. Politicians are smart people, they understand this better than everyone else, they just hope the rest of us are too dumb to understand.

About 30 years ago, Japan had a big real estate bubble. The land value of the Imperial Palace in Tokyo was worth more than the land value of the State of California. At the time, if California were an independent country, it would have been the world's 5th largest economy according to its GDP. Whenever there is a runaway housing price there are a lot of homeless people. So, Tokyo had a lot of homeless people at the height of real estate bubble. After the Japanese bubble burst in early 90s, Japan's economy went into deep recession. Japanese public debt has been one of highest among the rich countries if not the highest. According to the International Monetary Fund report on May 14, 2018, Japan's government debt to GDP ratio sat at 236% in 2017, more than double that of the U.S., which stood at 108%. Since 1996, Bank of Japan cut interest rate to below 1%. As Japan had neither fiscal tools (government spending to revive the economy) nor financial tools (lower interest rate to encourage spending for consumption and investment) to combat the recession, the government could not just throw money on the problem of homelessness. The City of Tokyo used the best solution to solve the problem, and it cost the city practically nothing to reduce homeless people in the city by 80% in the last 20 years. The City just relaxed their zoning regulations. This was reported in Economist, a British news magazine, in the last issue of year 2019. The magazine didn't elaborate on the details of the policy. But a search on the internet for the least expensive rental in the city resulted a listing for a studio unit at $600 a month rent. The size of the unit had only 100 square feet of living space. As per square foot rent, this unit is not cheap. But in San Francisco the least expensive rental unit was about $2350 for a studio apartment with 400 square feet living space around the same time. The per square foot rent was almost exactly the same in the two cities in 2019. But the problem with San Francisco was that the 400 square foot studio was absolutely the smallest unit available and there were few of them. In Tokyo, one could easily find a studio with a 100 – 200 square feet of living space and thus the least expensive housing units were 200% to 400% more affordable in Tokyo than in San Francisco. Apparently, these affordable small units are the reasons why the number of homeless in Tokyo reduced by 80% in the last 20 years. But Tokyo is by no means an exception, one can find small housing units around the globe where housing prices are high. The smallest I have ever seen is the one in London 10'4" x 8'4 priced at $260,000, CNN reported on October 5, 2012. The per square foot price was high even by London's standard. The reasons were understandable; the location was great and people were willing to pay a premium for the bare essentials.

San Francisco should follow Tokyo's and other big cities' example around the world and just relax the zoning requirements. Suppose the homeless population in San Francisco didn't increase in the last 20 years and instead decreased by 80%, then the number of homeless in San Francisco should be less than 800 instead of more than 8000. Wouldn't that be great? It would be idealistic to think we can solve the homeless problem completely; it would be naïve to think we can solve the homeless problem by just curing the symptoms of homeless. The City of San Francisco spends a quarter billion dollars for rent subsidizing and to help homeless. Since the City didn't even try to investigate the causes of high rent or homelessness, no ends to these problems were in sight.

As of 2014, San Francisco was believed to have approximately 7,000 homeless residents. As of 2015, approximately 71% of the city's homeless had housing in the city before becoming homeless, while the remaining 29% came from outside of San Francisco. Who are those 71%? One report showed a full-time college instructor who was making about $60,000 a year. She paid about $2,500 a month for a one-bedroom apartment and had troubles to pay off her $4,000 credit card debt. Her boyfriend asked her to join him to live in his tent for a few months. After a few months, she paid off her debt and the two of them saved enough to start their new lives.

But sixty-thousand-dollar-annual-income is twice the current San Francisco minimum wage. How can a minimum wage worker live in San Francisco? What are these people supposed to do? The City of San Francisco budgets about a quarter of a billion a year for the housing subsidy and sheltering for the homeless. According to city's Dept. of Homelessness and Supportive Housing, a bed to house a homeless person for a night cost the city $100 in 2019. A budget of $250,000,000 would be barely enough to house 7000 of them, but, of course, the city employees would take a chunk of the budget for administrative expenses. So the city cannot possibly house 7000 with a budget of a quarter of a billion dollars. Would the city ever have a viable program to house all homeless people as well as those who worked there but can't afford to live there? Even for a rich city like San Francisco, the city could never budget enough to help them all. In 2014, 29% of homeless in San Francisco came from outside. If word gets out that there is free housing in San Francisco, the city will be a magnet for homeless and there will be no end to the problem.

Throwing money at the problem of homeless can never solve the problem. The only sensible solution for the housing crisis is to provide more housing units, especially small housing units, in California. So, every one working on a minimum wage job can afford to live near the job. It is not necessary for the state to have a big budget to provide affordable housing, if only the state can make sure the local communities relax their control over land-use and let the free-market work its wonder. If we cannot get local communities to relax their stringent control on housing development, there is no hope to solve the housing crisis anywhere by any other means. California could spend the whole state budget on housing assistance and sheltering homeless, and it would still not be enough. If we get local communities to relax their zoning requirements, then the state doesn't need to spend a dime and the housing crisis will dissipate by itself.

In January 2020, California Governor Newsom proposed a $222 billions state budget for the coming fiscal year. The Budget projected a surplus of $5.6 billions. On May 7, Newsom disclosed a memo ahead of releasing his revised budget. The sudden recession brought by the new Coronavirus was expected to drive the state into a $54.3 billion deficit. Instead of budget surplus, the state asked for Federal bailout. His original budget had proposed funding for the homeless. Now, this program is just a pie in the sky. The high housing cost is a self-inflicted crisis. The way to solve the problem is to get to the root of the problem. If the problem started from local politicians' meddling of land-use, the only way to solve the problem is to stop such meddling.

Last but not least, for local politician to agree to relax zoning requirements and control on land-use, we have to reform local campaign financing. It would take only part of the state budget for housing assistant or for sheltering homeless to finance local campaigns. If public finance of local campaigns is established, then anyone with a vested interest in local land-use may not make any campaign donation to a candidate who has control over local land-use. Then, we can be sure that the housing crisis will disappear!

Throughout human history, during peacetime in a rich country, there have never been a large group of diligent, willing and able workers who have had to struggle to survive. That is until now in the US, or in California particularly. California was not like this a little over a generation ago. I know it firsthand. I was able, but not very strong. I had a college degree, BA, Bachelor of Art, from a foreign country, but no one would hire me based on the degree. To be honest, I didn't study very hard for the degree, so I didn't blame anyone for my hardship. I started my new life by working for $1 an hour while the minimum was $1.15. But I was diligent, willing and able to put in hard work. I had no trouble to save almost $2000 in a little over a year's time, and then went to graduate school. The reason that I could save a large portion of my take home pay was that I paid cheap rent for a room. From this humble beginning, I made my way into the middle class and realized American dream for my family.

I worked hard enough to guarantee that my wife and I could enjoy a comfortable retirement with financial security. In addition, I guarantee my children and their families and their children worry-free lives provided they are diligent, willing and able to work. But I also like to see everyone else, who is diligent, willing and able to work to be able to do the same. Yet this may be wishful thinking now! If I landed in the US today instead of in 1962, I don't think I can accomplish the same feat. I might do it in another state, but I couldn't do it in California. Why not?

Try to tell a person who works for minimum wage now to save about $16,000 in 16 months. $16,000 is the inflation-adjusted amount in year 2020 for $2000 in 1962. Sixteen months was how long it took me to save about $2000. Obviously, no one could do it in San Francisco, probably not in Los Angeles either. America's low-wage workers have struggled harder than those in any other rich country. If I tried to do this in San Francisco, I would be homeless for sure. Even if I could get my graduate degree and get my teaching job now, I could not save fast enough to realize my American dream in my lifetime at today's high housing price in California.

Tens of millions of American workers get up early in the morning and put in an honest day's work to earn a living. They do it day after day, month after month and year after year. We cannot expect them to do much more. We expect them to enjoy their lives in comfort, to have their own families, raise their own children and fulfill their American Dreams. Not everyone, but the vast majority of their children should be able to have a better life than their parents. I came to the US in 1962, and I was very grateful to be allowed to come to this country. I was even more grateful to be accepted and become a US Citizen and to realize my American Dream, and now I have a better family than I ever wished I could have. But in less than 50 years, the country that allowed me to realize my American dream has changed for the worse.

Many low-wage workers cannot make ends meet, so they cannot save for rainy days and, thus they don't have a bright future that they can look forward to. So, what is wrong? I was not a very smart person when I came to the US, that was why I got paid only a dollar an hour while minimum wage was $1.15 an hour. But I rented a room for only $17 a month. So, I could save the majority of my take home pay and I had hope for a better future. For today's low-wage workers, because there is no room anywhere in the state of California that costs only about $200 a month rent, they are in big trouble. California's minimum wage in 2020 was $12, 12 x 17 = $204. San Francisco's minimum wage in year 2020 was $16.07, tried to rent a room for $273.19, that is, 17 hours' minimum wage, a month. We have two new terms; "working poor" and "affordable housing". They have jobs and they are contributing to the society, but pillars of the society or the elected officials don't even allow them to live where they work. We call them the "working poor" and some of them become homeless. No wonder San Francisco has a lot of homeless people. When I was working for less than the minimum wage, I could save most of my income and did not feel being poor. Housing prices have increased, many workers cannot live near where they work, so we desperately need "affordable housing". If a person works, the person should not be poor. Most housing should be affordable just like most food should be affordable. We don't hear or use the term "affordable food," because most food is affordable. It has never happened in human history that workers anywhere have to spend one half of their income for a roof overhead, until now in the US. This is what has happened in the last fifty years.

As I mentioned before, in 1972, I bought my first house, a new track 4-bedroom house, for $23,000. My assistant professor's annul gross salary was about $16,000 and the national median house price was about $27,500, 20% more than I paid for my house. In 2018, the same house at almost fifty years old was valued around $650,000. An assistant professor's annual gross salary in 2018 was about $80,000 and national median price of a house was about $259,000. The value of the fifty-year old house is now 250% of the national median house value. This shows the extreme increase in housing price in California compared to the national median, and how hard it is now to buy a house on a typical middle-class salary. [National median house prices, based on https:// dqydj.com/historical-home-prices]

America is supposed to be the land of opportunity. There are hundreds of thousands of researchers, innovators, entrepreneurs and small businessmen who work hard and take risks to improve the lives of everyone in the country. But all their efforts are in vain. Not because they didn't accomplish anything; they accomplished a lot. The issue is that, at most, a few hundred local politicians have managed to push up the housing prices. The ill effect of the rising housing prices wipes out the gain the rest of us work so hard to acquire. Housing is not the only sector of the US economy that the price increase far exceeded inflation in the last few decades; medical expenses and college tuition cost increases also exceed inflation. But, to enter the field of medical and college teaching professions requires the highest academic training and degree. In housing construction, a high school dropout can do most of the work without any formal training. It makes the housing price increase unreasonable and absurd.

It is time we all wake up to the reality, stop pretending everything is fine. We all want to live; we have to let our fellow countryman live. Why can't a worker with a full-time job live close to their job? When we look at the morning rush hour traffic jam on California's freeways, this is a human tragedy and an environmental disaster. We need to hold those responsible for high housing prices accountable and demand change!

INDEX

Printed in the United States
By Bookmasters